Praxis II
Physical Education: Content and Design (5095) Exam

SECRETS

Study Guide
Your Key to Exam Success

Praxis II Test Review for the
Praxis II: Subject Assessments

Dear Future Exam Success Story:

First of all, **THANK YOU** for purchasing Mometrix study materials!

Second, congratulations! You are one of the few determined test-takers who are committed to doing whatever it takes to excel on your exam. **You have come to the right place.** We developed these study materials with one goal in mind: to deliver you the information you need in a format that's concise and easy to use.

In addition to optimizing your guide for the content of the test, we've outlined our recommended steps for breaking down the preparation process into small, attainable goals so you can make sure you stay on track.

We've also analyzed the entire test-taking process, identifying the most common pitfalls and showing how you can overcome them and be ready for any curveball the test throws you.

Standardized testing is one of the biggest obstacles on your road to success, which only increases the importance of doing well in the high-pressure, high-stakes environment of test day. Your results on this test could have a significant impact on your future, and this guide provides the information and practical advice to help you achieve your full potential on test day.

Your success is our success

We would love to hear from you! If you would like to share the story of your exam success or if you have any questions or comments in regard to our products, please contact us at **800-673-8175** or **support@mometrix.com**.

Thanks again for your business and we wish you continued success!

Sincerely,
The Mometrix Test Preparation Team

Need more help? Check out our flashcards at: http://MometrixFlashcards.com/PraxisII

TABLE OF CONTENTS

Introduction

Thank you for purchasing this resource! You have made the choice to prepare yourself for a test that could have a huge impact on your future, and this guide is designed to help you be fully ready for test day. Obviously, it's important to have a solid understanding of the test material, but you also need to be prepared for the unique environment and stressors of the test, so that you can perform to the best of your abilities.

For this purpose, the first section that appears in this guide is the **Secret Keys**. We've devoted countless hours to meticulously researching what works and what doesn't, and we've boiled down our findings to the five most impactful steps you can take to improve your performance on the test. We start at the beginning with study planning and move through the preparation process, all the way to the testing strategies that will help you get the most out of what you know when you're finally sitting in front of the test.

We recommend that you start preparing for your test as far in advance as possible. However, if you've bought this guide as a last-minute study resource and only have a few days before your test, we recommend that you skip over the first two Secret Keys since they address a long-term study plan.

If you struggle with **test anxiety**, we strongly encourage you to check out our recommendations for how you can overcome it. Test anxiety is a formidable foe, but it can be beaten, and we want to make sure you have the tools you need to defeat it.

Secret Key #1 – Plan Big, Study Small

There's a lot riding on your performance. If you want to ace this test, you're going to need to keep your skills sharp and the material fresh in your mind. You need a plan that lets you review everything you need to know while still fitting in your schedule. We'll break this strategy down into three categories.

Information Organization

Start with the information you already have: the official test outline. From this, you can make a complete list of all the concepts you need to cover before the test. Organize these concepts into groups that can be studied together, and create a list of any related vocabulary you need to learn so you can brush up on any difficult terms. You'll want to keep this vocabulary list handy once you actually start studying since you may need to add to it along the way.

Time Management

Once you have your set of study concepts, decide how to spread them out over the time you have left before the test. Break your study plan into small, clear goals so you have a manageable task for each day and know exactly what you're doing. Then just focus on one small step at a time. When you manage your time this way, you don't need to spend hours at a time studying. Studying a small block of content for a short period each day helps you retain information better and avoid stressing over how much you have left to do. You can relax knowing that you have a plan to cover everything in time. In order for this strategy to be effective though, you have to start studying early and stick to your schedule. Avoid the exhaustion and futility that comes from last-minute cramming!

Study Environment

The environment you study in has a big impact on your learning. Studying in a coffee shop, while probably more enjoyable, is not likely to be as fruitful as studying in a quiet room. It's important to keep distractions to a minimum. You're only planning to study for a short block of time, so make the most of it. Don't pause to check your phone or get up to find a snack. It's also important to **avoid multitasking**. Research has consistently shown that multitasking will make your studying dramatically less effective. Your study area should also be comfortable and well-lit so you don't have the distraction of straining your eyes or sitting on an uncomfortable chair.

The time of day you study is also important. You want to be rested and alert. Don't wait until just before bedtime. Study when you'll be most likely to comprehend and remember. Even better, if you know what time of day your test will be, set that time aside for study. That way your brain will be used to working on that subject at that specific time and you'll have a better chance of recalling information.

Finally, it can be helpful to team up with others who are studying for the same test. Your actual studying should be done in as isolated an environment as possible, but the work of organizing the information and setting up the study plan can be divided up. In between study sessions, you can discuss with your teammates the concepts that you're all studying and quiz each other on the details. Just be sure that your teammates are as serious about the test as you are. If you find that your study time is being replaced with social time, you might need to find a new team.

Secret Key #2 – Make Your Studying Count

You're devoting a lot of time and effort to preparing for this test, so you want to be absolutely certain it will pay off. This means doing more than just reading the content and hoping you can remember it on test day. It's important to make every minute of study count. There are two main areas you can focus on to make your studying count:

Retention

It doesn't matter how much time you study if you can't remember the material. You need to make sure you are retaining the concepts. To check your retention of the information you're learning, try recalling it at later times with minimal prompting. Try carrying around flashcards and glance at one or two from time to time or ask a friend who's also studying for the test to quiz you.

To enhance your retention, look for ways to put the information into practice so that you can apply it rather than simply recalling it. If you're using the information in practical ways, it will be much easier to remember. Similarly, it helps to solidify a concept in your mind if you're not only reading it to yourself but also explaining it to someone else. Ask a friend to let you teach them about a concept you're a little shaky on (or speak aloud to an imaginary audience if necessary). As you try to summarize, define, give examples, and answer your friend's questions, you'll understand the concepts better and they will stay with you longer. Finally, step back for a big picture view and ask yourself how each piece of information fits with the whole subject. When you link the different concepts together and see them working together as a whole, it's easier to remember the individual components.

Finally, practice showing your work on any multi-step problems, even if you're just studying. Writing out each step you take to solve a problem will help solidify the process in your mind, and you'll be more likely to remember it during the test.

Modality

Modality simply refers to the means or method by which you study. Choosing a study modality that fits your own individual learning style is crucial. No two people learn best in exactly the same way, so it's important to know your strengths and use them to your advantage.

For example, if you learn best by visualization, focus on visualizing a concept in your mind and draw an image or a diagram. Try color-coding your notes, illustrating them, or creating symbols that will trigger your mind to recall a learned concept. If you learn best by hearing or discussing information, find a study partner who learns the same way or read aloud to yourself. Think about how to put the information in your own words. Imagine that you are giving a lecture on the topic and record yourself so you can listen to it later.

For any learning style, flashcards can be helpful. Organize the information so you can take advantage of spare moments to review. Underline key words or phrases. Use different colors for different categories. Mnemonic devices (such as creating a short list in which every item starts with the same letter) can also help with retention. Find what works best for you and use it to store the information in your mind most effectively and easily.

Secret Key #3 – Practice the Right Way

Your success on test day depends not only on how many hours you put into preparing, but also on whether you prepared the right way. It's good to check along the way to see if your studying is paying off. One of the most effective ways to do this is by taking practice tests to evaluate your progress. Practice tests are useful because they show exactly where you need to improve. Every time you take a practice test, pay special attention to these three groups of questions:

- The questions you got wrong
- The questions you had to guess on, even if you guessed right
- The questions you found difficult or slow to work through

This will show you exactly what your weak areas are, and where you need to devote more study time. Ask yourself why each of these questions gave you trouble. Was it because you didn't understand the material? Was it because you didn't remember the vocabulary? Do you need more repetitions on this type of question to build speed and confidence? Dig into those questions and figure out how you can strengthen your weak areas as you go back to review the material.

Additionally, many practice tests have a section explaining the answer choices. It can be tempting to read the explanation and think that you now have a good understanding of the concept. However, an explanation likely only covers part of the question's broader context. Even if the explanation makes sense, **go back and investigate** every concept related to the question until you're positive you have a thorough understanding.

As you go along, keep in mind that the practice test is just that: practice. Memorizing these questions and answers will not be very helpful on the actual test because it is unlikely to have any of the same exact questions. If you only know the right answers to the sample questions, you won't be prepared for the real thing. **Study the concepts** until you understand them fully, and then you'll be able to answer any question that shows up on the test.

It's important to wait on the practice tests until you're ready. If you take a test on your first day of study, you may be overwhelmed by the amount of material covered and how much you need to learn. Work up to it gradually.

On test day, you'll need to be prepared for answering questions, managing your time, and using the test-taking strategies you've learned. It's a lot to balance, like a mental marathon that will have a big impact on your future. Like training for a marathon, you'll need to start slowly and work your way up. When test day arrives, you'll be ready.

Start with the strategies you've read in the first two Secret Keys—plan your course and study in the way that works best for you. If you have time, consider using multiple study resources to get different approaches to the same concepts. It can be helpful to see difficult concepts from more than one angle. Then find a good source for practice tests. Many times, the test website will suggest potential study resources or provide sample tests.

Practice Test Strategy

When you're ready to start taking practice tests, follow this strategy:

Untimed and Open-Book Practice

Take the first test with no time constraints and with your notes and study guide handy. Take your time and focus on applying the strategies you've learned.

Timed and Open-Book Practice

Take the second practice test open-book as well, but set a timer and practice pacing yourself to finish in time.

Timed and Closed-Book Practice

Take any other practice tests as if it were test day. Set a timer and put away your study materials. Sit at a table or desk in a quiet room, imagine yourself at the testing center, and answer questions as quickly and accurately as possible.

Keep repeating timed and closed-book tests on a regular basis until you run out of practice tests or it's time for the actual test. Your mind will be ready for the schedule and stress of test day, and you'll be able to focus on recalling the material you've learned.

Secret Key #4 – Pace Yourself

Once you're fully prepared for the material on the test, your biggest challenge on test day will be managing your time. Just knowing that the clock is ticking can make you panic even if you have plenty of time left. Work on pacing yourself so you can build confidence against the time constraints of the exam. Pacing is a difficult skill to master, especially in a high-pressure environment, so **practice is vital**.

Set time expectations for your pace based on how much time is available. For example, if a section has 60 questions and the time limit is 30 minutes, you know you have to average 30 seconds or less per question in order to answer them all. Although 30 seconds is the hard limit, set 25 seconds per question as your goal, so you reserve extra time to spend on harder questions. When you budget extra time for the harder questions, you no longer have any reason to stress when those questions take longer to answer.

Don't let this time expectation distract you from working through the test at a calm, steady pace, but keep it in mind so you don't spend too much time on any one question. Recognize that taking extra time on one question you don't understand may keep you from answering two that you do understand later in the test. If your time limit for a question is up and you're still not sure of the answer, mark it and move on, and come back to it later if the time and the test format allow. If the testing format doesn't allow you to return to earlier questions, just make an educated guess; then put it out of your mind and move on.

On the easier questions, be careful not to rush. It may seem wise to hurry through them so you have more time for the challenging ones, but it's not worth missing one if you know the concept and just didn't take the time to read the question fully. Work efficiently but make sure you understand the question and have looked at all of the answer choices, since more than one may seem right at first.

Even if you're paying attention to the time, you may find yourself a little behind at some point. You should speed up to get back on track, but do so wisely. Don't panic; just take a few seconds less on each question until you're caught up. Don't guess without thinking, but do look through the answer choices and eliminate any you know are wrong. If you can get down to two choices, it is often worthwhile to guess from those. Once you've chosen an answer, move on and don't dwell on any that you skipped or had to hurry through. If a question was taking too long, chances are it was one of the harder ones, so you weren't as likely to get it right anyway.

On the other hand, if you find yourself getting ahead of schedule, it may be beneficial to slow down a little. The more quickly you work, the more likely you are to make a careless mistake that will affect your score. You've budgeted time for each question, so don't be afraid to spend that time. Practice an efficient but careful pace to get the most out of the time you have.

Secret Key #5 – Have a Plan for Guessing

When you're taking the test, you may find yourself stuck on a question. Some of the answer choices seem better than others, but you don't see the one answer choice that is obviously correct. What do you do?

The scenario described above is very common, yet most test takers have not effectively prepared for it. Developing and practicing a plan for guessing may be one of the single most effective uses of your time as you get ready for the exam.

In developing your plan for guessing, there are three questions to address:

- When should you start the guessing process?
- How should you narrow down the choices?
- Which answer should you choose?

When to Start the Guessing Process

Unless your plan for guessing is to select C every time (which, despite its merits, is not what we recommend), you need to leave yourself enough time to apply your answer elimination strategies. Since you have a limited amount of time for each question, that means that if you're going to give yourself the best shot at guessing correctly, you have to decide quickly whether or not you will guess.

Of course, the best-case scenario is that you don't have to guess at all, so first, see if you can answer the question based on your knowledge of the subject and basic reasoning skills. Focus on the key words in the question and try to jog your memory of related topics. Give yourself a chance to bring the knowledge to mind, but once you realize that you don't have (or you can't access) the knowledge you need to answer the question, it's time to start the guessing process.

It's almost always better to start the guessing process too early than too late. It only takes a few seconds to remember something and answer the question from knowledge. Carefully eliminating wrong answer choices takes longer. Plus, going through the process of eliminating answer choices can actually help jog your memory.

Summary: Start the guessing process as soon as you decide that you can't answer the question based on your knowledge.

How to Narrow Down the Choices

The next chapter in this book (**Test-Taking Strategies**) includes a wide range of strategies for how to approach questions and how to look for answer choices to eliminate. You will definitely want to read those carefully, practice them, and figure out which ones work best for you. Here though, we're going to address a mindset rather than a particular strategy.

Your chances of guessing an answer correctly depend on how many options you are choosing from.

How many choices you have	How likely you are to guess correctly
5	20%
4	25%
3	33%
2	50%
1	100%

You can see from this chart just how valuable it is to be able to eliminate incorrect answers and make an educated guess, but there are two things that many test takers do that cause them to miss out on the benefits of guessing:

- Accidentally eliminating the correct answer
- Selecting an answer based on an impression

We'll look at the first one here, and the second one in the next section.

To avoid accidentally eliminating the correct answer, we recommend a thought exercise called **the $5 challenge**. In this challenge, you only eliminate an answer choice from contention if you are willing to bet $5 on it being wrong. Why $5? Five dollars is a small but not insignificant amount of money. It's an amount you could afford to lose but wouldn't want to throw away. And while losing $5 once might not hurt too much, doing it twenty times will set you back $100. In the same way, each small decision you make—eliminating a choice here, guessing on a question there—won't by itself impact your score very much, but when you put them all together, they can make a big difference. By holding each answer choice elimination decision to a higher standard, you can reduce the risk of accidentally eliminating the correct answer.

The $5 challenge can also be applied in a positive sense: If you are willing to bet $5 that an answer choice *is* correct, go ahead and mark it as correct.

Summary: Only eliminate an answer choice if you are willing to bet $5 that it is wrong.

Which Answer to Choose

You're taking the test. You've run into a hard question and decided you'll have to guess. You've eliminated all the answer choices you're willing to bet $5 on. Now you have to pick an answer. Why do we even need to talk about this? Why can't you just pick whichever one you feel like when the time comes?

The answer to these questions is that if you don't come into the test with a plan, you'll rely on your impression to select an answer choice, and if you do that, you risk falling into a trap. The test writers know that everyone who takes their test will be guessing on some of the questions, so they intentionally write wrong answer choices to seem plausible. You still have to pick an answer though, and if the wrong answer choices are designed to look right, how can you ever be sure that you're not falling for their trap? The best solution we've found to this dilemma is to take the decision out of your hands entirely. Here is the process we recommend:

Once you've eliminated any choices that you are confident (willing to bet $5) are wrong, select the first remaining choice as your answer.

Whether you choose to select the first remaining choice, the second, or the last, the important thing is that you use some preselected standard. Using this approach guarantees that you will not be enticed into selecting an answer choice that looks right, because you are not basing your decision on how the answer choices look.

This is not meant to make you question your knowledge. Instead, it is to help you recognize the difference between your knowledge and your impressions. There's a huge difference between thinking an answer is right because of what you know, and thinking an answer is right because it looks or sounds like it should be right.

Summary: To ensure that your selection is appropriately random, make a predetermined selection from among all answer choices you have not eliminated.

Test-Taking Strategies

This section contains a list of test-taking strategies that you may find helpful as you work through the test. By taking what you know and applying logical thought, you can maximize your chances of answering any question correctly!

It is very important to realize that every question is different and every person is different: no single strategy will work on every question, and no single strategy will work for every person. That's why we've included all of them here, so you can try them out and determine which ones work best for different types of questions and which ones work best for you.

Question Strategies

Read Carefully

Read the question and answer choices carefully. Don't miss the question because you misread the terms. You have plenty of time to read each question thoroughly and make sure you understand what is being asked. Yet a happy medium must be attained, so don't waste too much time. You must read carefully, but efficiently.

Contextual Clues

Look for contextual clues. If the question includes a word you are not familiar with, look at the immediate context for some indication of what the word might mean. Contextual clues can often give you all the information you need to decipher the meaning of an unfamiliar word. Even if you can't determine the meaning, you may be able to narrow down the possibilities enough to make a solid guess at the answer to the question.

Prefixes

If you're having trouble with a word in the question or answer choices, try dissecting it. Take advantage of every clue that the word might include. Prefixes and suffixes can be a huge help. Usually they allow you to determine a basic meaning. Pre- means before, post- means after, pro - is positive, de- is negative. From prefixes and suffixes, you can get an idea of the general meaning of the word and try to put it into context.

Hedge Words

Watch out for critical hedge words, such as *likely, may, can, sometimes, often, almost, mostly, usually, generally, rarely,* and *sometimes*. Question writers insert these hedge phrases to cover every possibility. Often an answer choice will be wrong simply because it leaves no room for exception. Be on guard for answer choices that have definitive words such as *exactly* and *always*.

Switchback Words

Stay alert for *switchbacks*. These are the words and phrases frequently used to alert you to shifts in thought. The most common switchback words are *but, although,* and *however*. Others include *nevertheless, on the other hand, even though, while, in spite of, despite, regardless of.* Switchback words are important to catch because they can change the direction of the question or an answer choice.

Face Value

When in doubt, use common sense. Accept the situation in the problem at face value. Don't read too much into it. These problems will not require you to make wild assumptions. If you have to go beyond creativity and warp time or space in order to have an answer choice fit the question, then you should move on and consider the other answer choices. These are normal problems rooted in reality. The applicable relationship or explanation may not be readily apparent, but it is there for you to figure out. Use your common sense to interpret anything that isn't clear.

Answer Choice Strategies

Answer Selection

The most thorough way to pick an answer choice is to identify and eliminate wrong answers until only one is left, then confirm it is the correct answer. Sometimes an answer choice may immediately seem right, but be careful. The test writers will usually put more than one reasonable answer choice on each question, so take a second to read all of them and make sure that the other choices are not equally obvious. As long as you have time left, it is better to read every answer choice than to pick the first one that looks right without checking the others.

Answer Choice Families

An answer choice family consists of two (in rare cases, three) answer choices that are very similar in construction and cannot all be true at the same time. If you see two answer choices that are direct opposites or parallels, one of them is usually the correct answer. For instance, if one answer choice says that quantity x increases and another either says that quantity x decreases (opposite) or says that quantity y increases (parallel), then those answer choices would fall into the same family. An answer choice that doesn't match the construction of the answer choice family is more likely to be incorrect. Most questions will not have answer choice families, but when they do appear, you should be prepared to recognize them.

Eliminate Answers

Eliminate answer choices as soon as you realize they are wrong, but make sure you consider all possibilities. If you are eliminating answer choices and realize that the last one you are left with is also wrong, don't panic. Start over and consider each choice again. There may be something you missed the first time that you will realize on the second pass.

Avoid Fact Traps

Don't be distracted by an answer choice that is factually true but doesn't answer the question. You are looking for the choice that answers the question. Stay focused on what the question is asking for so you don't accidentally pick an answer that is true but incorrect. Always go back to the question and make sure the answer choice you've selected actually answers the question and is not merely a true statement.

Extreme Statements

In general, you should avoid answers that put forth extreme actions as standard practice or proclaim controversial ideas as established fact. An answer choice that states the "process should be used in certain situations, if..." is much more likely to be correct than one that states the "process should be discontinued completely." The first is a calm rational statement and doesn't even make a definitive, uncompromising

- 11 -

stance, using a hedge word *if* to provide wiggle room, whereas the second choice is a radical idea and far more extreme.

Benchmark

As you read through the answer choices and you come across one that seems to answer the question well, mentally select that answer choice. This is not your final answer, but it's the one that will help you evaluate the other answer choices. The one that you selected is your benchmark or standard for judging each of the other answer choices. Every other answer choice must be compared to your benchmark. That choice is correct until proven otherwise by another answer choice beating it. If you find a better answer, then that one becomes your new benchmark. Once you've decided that no other choice answers the question as well as your benchmark, you have your final answer.

Predict the Answer

Before you even start looking at the answer choices, it is often best to try to predict the answer. When you come up with the answer on your own, it is easier to avoid distractions and traps because you will know exactly what to look for. The right answer choice is unlikely to be word-for-word what you came up with, but it should be a close match. Even if you are confident that you have the right answer, you should still take the time to read each option before moving on.

General Strategies

Tough Questions

If you are stumped on a problem or it appears too hard or too difficult, don't waste time. Move on! Remember though, if you can quickly check for obviously incorrect answer choices, your chances of guessing correctly are greatly improved. Before you completely give up, at least try to knock out a couple of possible answers. Eliminate what you can and then guess at the remaining answer choices before moving on.

Check Your Work

Since you will probably not know every term listed and the answer to every question, it is important that you get credit for the ones that you do know. Don't miss any questions through careless mistakes. If at all possible, try to take a second to look back over your answer selection and make sure you've selected the correct answer choice and haven't made a costly careless mistake (such as marking an answer choice that you didn't mean to mark). This quick double check should more than pay for itself in caught mistakes for the time it costs.

Pace Yourself

It's easy to be overwhelmed when you're looking at a page full of questions; your mind is confused and full of random thoughts, and the clock is ticking down faster than you would like. Calm down and maintain the pace that you have set for yourself. Especially as you get down to the last few minutes of the test, don't let the small numbers on the clock make you panic. As long as you are on track by monitoring your pace, you are guaranteed to have time for each question.

Don't Rush

It is very easy to make errors when you are in a hurry. Maintaining a fast pace in answering questions is pointless if it makes you miss questions that you would have gotten right otherwise. Test writers like to include distracting information and wrong answers that seem right. Taking a little extra time to avoid careless mistakes can make all the difference in your test score. Find a pace that allows you to be confident in the answers that you select.

Keep Moving

Panicking will not help you pass the test, so do your best to stay calm and keep moving. Taking deep breaths and going through the answer elimination steps you practiced can help to break through a stress barrier and keep your pace.

Final Notes

The combination of a solid foundation of content knowledge and the confidence that comes from practicing your plan for applying that knowledge is the key to maximizing your performance on test day. As your foundation of content knowledge is built up and strengthened, you'll find that the strategies included in this chapter become more and more effective in helping you quickly sift through the distractions and traps of the test to isolate the correct answer.

Now it's time to move on to the test content chapters of this book, but be sure to keep your goal in mind. As you read, think about how you will be able to apply this information on the test. If you've already seen sample questions for the test and you have an idea of the question format and style, try to come up with questions of your own that you can answer based on what you're reading. This will give you valuable practice applying your knowledge in the same ways you can expect to on test day.

Good luck and good studying!

Content Knowledge and Student Growth and Development

Stages of Life

- The **eight stages of life** are infancy, early childhood, middle childhood, late childhood, adolescence, early adulthood, **middle** adulthood, and late adulthood or old age. In physical development,
- **infancy** (birth to 1~1.5 years) involves the most rapid growth in size, weight, and brain development; and the first rudimentary form of voluntary movement.
- **Early childhood** (1.5 to 3~4 years) involves the development of fundamental movements.
- During **middle childhood** (3~4 to 5~6 years), children further develop these fundamental movements and extend them to sport skills.
- In **later childhood** (6-12 years), children develop their sport skills further.
- In **adolescence** (puberty to 18-20 years), teens develop secondary sex characteristics and undergo sexual and physical maturation during and after puberty. They learn to accept their physiques and use them effectively.
- **Young adults** (c. 18-30s) achieve their peak physical abilities and performance.
- **Middle adults** (c. 30s-50s~60 years) make transitional adjustments as physical energy, strength, and endurance decline somewhat.
- This decline becomes more pronounced in **later adulthood or old age** (60s to death).

Piaget's Stages of Cognitive Development

Jean Piaget described infants as being in the **sensorimotor stage** of cognitive development, perceiving the world through received sensory stimuli and responding and interacting through motor activities. They learn to repeat chance actions to reproduce their results, eventually developing intentional activities. They develop object permanence (the understanding that unseen objects still exist) and form schemata or mental concepts about the environment. In Piaget's **preoperational stage**, toddlers and preschoolers think intuitively, not logically, with animistic (ascribing human qualities to inanimate objects) and magical (believing their own thoughts and words affect external events) thinking. They are egocentric, unable to see things from another's perspective, both literally/physically and figuratively/mentally. They concentrate on one aspect of a situation at a time and cannot reverse operations or conserve quantities. The shape, arrangement, or context of a quantity influences their perception of its amount. In the concrete operations stage, middle children develop the ability to perform logical mental operations, but only with concrete objects or events. They can reverse operations, categorize items, and conserve **quantities of liquids, solids, and numbers, regardless of context. In the formal operations stage**, pre-adolescents, adolescents, and adults can perform mental operations with abstract concepts; without concrete objects or events; understand intangible ideas like liberty; and accept multiple alternatives, possibilities, consequences, and ambiguities.

Erikson's Stages of Psychosocial Development

Erik Erikson described infancy with the central conflict of **trust vs. mistrust**. Infants whose needs are met fully and consistently develop trust in the world; if not, they develop mistrust. The positive outcome from resolving this conflict is **hope**. Toddlers face auto**nomy vs. shame and doubt**. Those developing self-control feel security and confidence, those who do not develop inadequacy and self-doubt instead. The positive outcome is **will**. Preschoolers encounter **initiative vs. guilt**. Successfully exerting power over the environment develops capability and leadership; destructiveness and/or experiencing disapproval causes guilt and lack of initiative. The positive outcome is **purpose**. School-age children confront **industry vs. inferiority**. Successful social interactions and academic efforts with positive

- 14 -

feedback develop belief in their abilities, while failure causes inferiority and inadequacy. The positive outcome is **competence**. Adolescents confront **identity vs. role confusion**. Success develops independence and sense of self; failure, confusion and insecurity. The positive outcome is **fidelity**. Young adults address **intimacy vs. isolation**. Success develops relationships; failure, loneliness. **Love** is the positive outcome. Middle age involves **generativity vs. stagnation**. Success brings feelings of contribution and involvement; failure, feeling unproductive and uninvolved. The positive virtue is **care**. Old age involves **integrity vs. despair**. Success brings satisfaction and peace; failure, bitterness and regret. The positive virtue is **wisdom**.

Physical Growth and Development

Genetically inherited traits can influence physical development for better or worse. For example, some children inherit natural strength, speed, agility or a relative lack thereof, and earlier or later maturation; others can inherit chromosomal syndromes which cause physical abnormalities and intellectual, emotional, and/or learning disabilities. **Good nutrition** enhances physical development. **Malnutrition** causes delayed physical, cognitive, and behavioral development; stunted growth; or obesity and diabetes. **Exercise** not only promotes physical development, but also cognitive development. Many research studies demonstrate a strong connection between physical fitness and mental fitness. **Environmental factors** like lack of sensory and intellectual stimulation, social isolation, and poor sanitation can hamper children's health, growth, and social and cognitive development. Exposure to **hazardous substances** and **unsafe conditions** in their play areas can jeopardize children's safety, well-being, and development. Parents who prevent environmental threats and provide healthy environments for children contribute to their thriving and strong development.

Cognitive Development

Factors that **influence cognitive development** can be divided into two main categories: biological and environmental. Among **biological factors**, the sense organs influence cognitive development by receiving environmental stimuli. Developed correctly, the sense organs receive stimuli correctly, enabling children to form the correct sensory concepts. If defective, sense organs will gather defective stimuli, causing incorrect concept formation and imperfect cognitive development. Intelligence is another biological factor, directly affecting the rate and extent of cognitive development. Heredity from parents influences cognitive development. Motor and mental maturation also facilitate children's interaction with the environment, influencing cognitive development. **Environmental factors** include learning opportunities, whose quality influences cognitive development. Economic status, when higher, provides more learning opportunities and better instruction; lower status allows fewer opportunities and poorer training. Play is another environmental factor enabling interaction with and response to environmental stimuli, enabling knowledge acquisition; pretend play develops symbolism and imagination; various activities help form imagery and connections, contributing to cognitive development. Family and society are environmental influences providing intellectual stimulation, examples, and interactions, also developing cognition.

Emotional and Social Development

Some factors affecting children's **emotional and social development** are **intrinsic factors** within the individual child. For example, a difficult temperament is observed in some children during infancy and early childhood. Some babies are fussier, harder to calm or soothe, and less inclined to happy dispositions; others are naturally easygoing, contented, and equable. Some children experience serious health problems. Some have developmental delays or disorders. Another category of factors influencing child emotional and social development is **family**. Some families contain risk factors. For example, the mother may suffer from depression during pregnancy, postpartum, and/or during the child's subsequent life. Substance abuse within the family is another risk factor. Violence within the family affects children's

- 15 -

emotional and social development. Family poverty is another risk factor for how children develop emotionally and socially. A third category of factors is **environmental**. Children who live in communities that are not safe, lacking in resources, and/or deficient in policies to support families and children are at higher risk of developmental problems with acquiring emotional competencies and/or social skills. Moreover, all of these factors interact in children's emotional and social development.

Growth Spurts

Individual differences in **pubertal growth spurts** among American adolescents vary widely. Therefore, normal adolescent growth and development include a broad range of physiological differences. Among major influences on adolescent growth, two significant factors are individual exercise training and **individual nutritional conditions**. In the United States, some teens independently restrict their dietary intake, which causes them to suffer from nutritional deficiencies. At the same time, some of these teens also train to compete in sports, expending a great deal of energy. When these two factors interact, and are additionally influenced by the interaction of the adolescents' individual body types, some teenaged athletes—for example, students who participate seriously in such activities as wrestling, dance, or gymnastics—grow more slowly than the average for their peers. Because of the complexity of these interactions, it is hard for researchers who measure teen growth rates to determine which individual variables contribute more or less to slower growth.

Typical Growth Patterns

Just before puberty, boys and girls both typically experience a "**preadolescent dip**" in growth, when previous growth slows to all-time lows. Thereafter, they experience sudden, often dramatic **adolescent growth spurts** during middle stages of puberty. Girls typically have growth spurts about two years earlier than boys. However, female growth spurts do not last as long as male growth spurts, and girls typically do not gain as much total height as boys. While boys begin growth spurts later than girls, they grow for longer durations, gaining more total height, which accounts for average greater heights of males than females. Height growth becomes slower in later stages of puberty. Once girls are about 15 and boys about 17, their skeletons undergo epiphyseal fusion, which all but stops height growth. Adolescents also gain significant weight, attaining about 50 percent of their adult body weights. While boys tend to reach their fastest rates of gaining height and weight around the same age, girls tend to gain weight fastest about six months later on average than when they gain height fastest. Both boys and girls undergo slowing of weight gain similarly to reductions in height growth rates during the later stages of puberty.

Health Risks in Athletes

Researchers have found American boys **wrestling** competitively have used diet, exercise, dehydration, and other means to lose weight to qualify in lower weight classes, often beginning by 8 years old. The American Medical Association and American College of Sports Medicine have issued position statements that student wrestlers should be discouraged from such practices. Studies have found adolescent wrestlers gained less weight, fat, and muscle mass during sport season despite heavy training, and more afterward. Girls have had menarche delayed longer when training intensively in **gymnastics** than in swimming, tennis, or speed skating. Dancing and running had similar but smaller effects compared to gymnastics, which is the only sport associated with significant delays. While female gymnasts are smaller in size than peers, often from childhood, researchers have identified selection bias as affecting both delayed menarche and body size: both favor selection for and continuing participation in gymnastics, particularly at elite levels. More than 90 percent of adult bone mass is formed during puberty; female gymnasts and runners risk **lifelong deficiencies** in bone mineral density from interactions of sexual steroid hormones, calcium intake, and other nutritional deficits, despite sufficient weight-bearing exercise. Low bone mineral development has been implicated in gymnasts' skeletal injuries.

Culture and Media Influence

In our culture, the **media** have profound effects on individual and group perceptions and behaviors. The following are just a few examples.

Unrealistic body images: Many celebrities, a minority of the population, have physical attributes everyday people cannot attain. They often have taller heights, lower weights, larger chest and smaller waist and hip measurements, and greater muscular development than average individuals. Children, teens, and adults can be overly influenced by such role models, causing them low self-esteem, negative body images, and unhealthy behaviors in futile attempts to attain similar attributes. Irresponsible marketing: Manufacturers and sellers of consumer products bombard children and adolescents having undeveloped or underdeveloped critical thinking skills with advertising for unhealthy junk foods containing excessive refined sugar and flour, trans fats and saturated fats, and artificial additives without any beneficial fibers, phytonutrients, healthy unsaturated fat, lean protein, or naturally occurring vitamins and minerals. Unrealistic physical activity models: In our culture and media, professional athletes are aggrandized and paid enormous salaries. Impressionable youth aspire to this status, unaware of the odds against it. They may train excessively when moderate physical activity would promote better health with average physical attributes, and/or unrealistically neglect academics.

The **media** have great power to influence people's thoughts, beliefs, and attitudes; hence they are often wielded as effective **tools** for marketing, public interest, or other purposes. An additional consideration is that different individuals have different reactions to the same imagery presented in the media. Some people have lower self-esteem than others. Those who do are more vulnerable to make unfavorable comparisons between themselves and images they see in the media. This only exacerbates their low self-images. Standards of beauty promoted in media imagery are air-brushed and otherwise manipulated, and thus unrealistic. People who already do not feel good about themselves are more susceptible to feeling worse if they do not realize this and find they do not measure up to these standards. Another effect of media on our bodies is the way TV advertising contributes to our obesity epidemic. Children are targeted by junk food advertising. Unable to judge advertising critically yet or even realize TV is marketing to them, younger children believe marketing messages about unhealthy foods—often associated with toys— and believe they should eat these foods. Watching TV itself also supports sedentary and inactive lifestyles.

In our society, **BMI (body mass index)** is a popular tool. While it is often useful to indicate whether a person is underweight, overweight, obese, or a healthy weight, it can also be overemphasized and not always interpreted correctly. For example, two men can be the same height and weight, yet one has a much greater proportion of lean muscle mass vs. fat, while the other has much more fatty tissue and less muscle. Although the more muscular man is undoubtedly in better condition, having identical height and weight, both have exactly the same BMI, which is calculated as a ratio of weight to height. Experts remind us BMI is only one facet of one's **health profile**. We should discuss other measurements and risk factors like waist size, physical activity, dietary/nutritional content, smoking, drinking, etc. Also, the concept of fitness derives from the athletic model. Presidential fitness testing, weight-lifting standards, and other performance-based models assess fitness levels, not health. Recommended exercise amounts range from 30 minutes most days to 60 minutes daily. Experts advise 20 minutes several days weekly confers equal health benefits as 60 minutes daily.

Growth Milestones

Birth to 3 Months

From birth to 3 months, most infants use **rooting and sucking reflexes** to nurse, and **grasping reflexes** to hold things in their hands. They begin to raise their heads slightly when lying on their stomachs. Given support, they begin to hold up their heads a few seconds at a time. They start forming their hands into

- 17 -

Rollover
+ pull up body

fists. They pull and tug at their own hands. They begin repeating body movements they have made before. From 3-6 months, babies develop more **strength and agility**. They start to roll over, pull their bodies forward using arms and hands, grasp edges of cribs and furniture to pull themselves up, reach for objects and grasp them, bring objects to their mouths with their hands, and shake and otherwise play with objects they hold. From 6-9 months, their **mobility** expands. They start to crawl, grasp objects and pull them toward their bodies, and transfer toys and objects between hands. Parents can support babies in attaining physical development milestones by providing ample space for rolling, crawling, and playing; and many objects they can safely grasp, shake, and put into their mouths.

9 to 12 Months

From the ages of 9-12 months, most babies demonstrate the major milestones of **sitting up** without support, **standing up** without help, and **walking** without assistance. In addition to these gross motor skills developments, they also demonstrate advances in **fine motor skills development**. They begin to pick up objects and throw them. They demonstrate the ability to roll a ball. Their ability to pick up small objects between their thumb and one finger also typically develops during this period. Between the ages of 1 and 2 years, children develop more **independence**. Their motor skills start to emerge for performing tasks that require body balance and hand-eye coordination. Most children in this developmental stage can walk backwards, walk up and down stairs without help, pick up objects while standing (without squatting or sitting), sway and otherwise move along with music, use their whole arm to paint or color, scribble using crayons or markers, and turn handles and knobs.

2 to 3 Years

Most children aged 2-3 years build on skills developed earlier, gaining skill for activities needing **speed and coordination**. They become able to jump in place, balance on one foot, run forward, kick a ball, turn book pages, hold a crayon between thumb and fingers, and draw a circle. From ages 3-4 years, most children learn to walk in a straight line, throw and catch a ball, slide down a slide unassisted, ride a tricycle, pull and steer toys, build tall block towers, and shape clay. From ages 4-5 years, children typically gain more **confidence** in their abilities. Most children these ages start to be able to walk backwards; jump on one foot; perform somersaults; cut paper using child-safe scissors; print some of the letters of the alphabet; and copy crosses, squares, and other simple shapes. Parents can support children's achievement of major milestones in physical and motor development by providing environments encouraging them to explore safely; space, resources, and time to balance, jump, run, roll balls, and play; draw, assemble puzzles, string beads, etc.; and practice their emerging skills.

Changes in Ability by Age

Throughout life, as we grow and age, we experience both gains and losses in various **physiological abilities**. While these changes depend on age, the relative rates at which they occur throughout life depend on individual lifestyle, physical activity, and exercise. Also, at every age physically trained vs. untrained individuals exhibit major physiological differences. Some key areas of physiology that change across the lifespan include strength, flexibility, body composition, and body weight; the skeletal system; the cardiovascular system; and the pulmonary system. For example, heart rate is 120-140 beats per minute (bpm) at birth; 80-100 bpm by 1 year old; 57-60 bpm for male, 62-63 for female adolescents; 75-80 for adults; and slightly lower after age 60, with maximum heart rate declining by 0.8 bpm per year. When crying, newborns can reach 170 bpm. Children have 30-40 bpm faster heart rates than adults at the same workload levels. Cardiac output, or CO (amount of blood the heart pumps out in one minute), is the main factor limiting endurance exercise in older adults. Maximum CO depends on age and physical condition. CO is higher in adults than children. CO declines up to 58 percent from age 25-85, by 1 percent each year.

Strength

While little research exists on young (under 6 years) children's strength, by puberty girls usually have **strength spurts** the same year as growth spurts; boys' strength spurts are a year or more behind height spurts until puberty. In puberty, boys gain **muscle mass**, while girls gain **fatty tissue**. Muscle develops to around 40 percent of boys' total body weight during puberty. Adult women have around 63.5 percent the absolute body strength of adult men. Between 25-50 years old, muscle mass starts decreasing. This decrease escalates after age 50. By age 80, people have lost half their muscle mass. While pediatric experts say bodybuilding and powerlifting are unsafe for prepubescent children (**weight training** is safe and can enhance sport performance and motor fitness skills) Adolescence is the critical period when muscle mass increases most, and resistance training improves strength and endurance. Strength declines with age regardless, but training slows the rates. Strength directly affects independent mobility. Even the elderly can improve their strength. **Resistance training** also manages fat-to-muscle ratios. Aging causes loss of both type I/slow-twitch and type II/fast-twitch muscle fibers, but more so of fast-twitch fibers, slowing muscular contraction speed.

Flexibility and Body Composition

Flexibility appears to peak in the late teens/early 20s. Anatomically, females are more flexible than males. Aging-related structural joint changes reduce flexibility as tendons lose elasticity, ligaments fray, synovial fluid loses viscosity, and cartilage cracks. However, according to research studies, people can maintain or increase their flexibility just by being active. At birth, average **body composition** is 11 percent fat in boys and 14 percent in girls. The size and number of fat cells grow to 26 percent in boys, 28 percent in girls, during their first year of life. During puberty, girls experience greater increases in size and number of fat cells than boys. The only time fatty tissue decreases in early life is when babies begin walking. Adult norms are 10-25 percent body fat for men, 18-30 percent for women. Fourteen to 17 percent body fat in men and 21-24 percent in women are associated with fitness. Obesity standards are at more than 25 percent fat in men and 32 percent in women. Increased or excess fat around the organs is highly correlated with heart disease. While some adults lose fat with aging, others gain fat with slowing metabolisms and muscle loss. Physical activity and exercise cannot stop, but can help manage age-related fat, weight gain, and muscle loss.

Diet and Exercise

Diet and exercise are **interdependent**. For example, it can be difficult to achieve optimal energy, effort, or results from exercising after eating nothing but junk food. Alternatively, people who do eat healthy diets but never exercise may find it hard to maintain optimal weights. According to the American Council on Exercise, only about 5 percent of people losing weight exclusively through diet maintain the loss. Weight loss requires a negative balance of calories, attained by either burning more calories from exercising, eating fewer calories, or a combination of the two. The individuals most successful in losing weight and maintaining weight loss exercise more and eat fewer calories than people who cannot lose weight or lose it and then regain it. Snacks containing complex carbohydrates and some protein afford energy before exercising. Afterward, water, milk, and juice rehydrate; carbohydrates replenish energy; and protein supports muscle repair and growth. Nutritional experts recommend eating 15 percent of calories from protein, 55 percent from carbohydrates, and 30 percent from fat for optimal exercising.

Reactions to Stress

Stress is inevitable; however, effective **stress management skills and techniques** enable healthy coping. According to the Mayo Clinic, individuals begin stress management by understanding how they currently react to stress, and then adopting new stress management techniques or modifying existing ones to keep life stressors from leading to health issues. There are several unhealthy but common reactions to stress.

- **Pain**: internalized or unresolved stress can trigger headaches, backaches, upset stomachs, shortness of breath, insomnia, and muscular pain from unconsciously tensing the shoulders and neck and/or clenching jaws or fists.
- **Eating and/or activity**: some people skip eating from stress, thereby losing weight; others overeat or eat when not hungry and/or skip exercise, gaining weight.
- **Anger**: some people lose their tempers more easily over minor or unrelated things when stressed.
- **Crying**: some people cry over minor or unrelated things when stressed; experience unexpected, prolonged crying; and/or feel isolated and lonely.
- **Depression and anxiety**: stress can contribute to depressive and anxiety disorders, including problem avoidance, calling in sick, feeling hopeless, or giving up.
- **Negativity**: individuals not coping effectively with stress may exaggerate the negative qualities of undesired circumstances and/or always expect the worst.
- **Smoking and/or substance use**: people may escalate current smoking, drinking, or drug use under stress; those who had previously quit may relapse.

Stress Management Techniques

- **Cut back**: when overextended, examine duties and delegate, eliminate, or limit some.
- **Prepare**: set realistic goals for major and minor tasks; improve scheduling; allow time for unexpected events like traffic jams, car trouble, minor medical emergencies, extra work, etc. to prevent stress from accumulating.
- **Reach out**: revisit lapsed relationships; form new ones; volunteer. Surrounding oneself with supportive friends, relatives, colleagues, and spiritual leaders enhances psychological well-being, boosting capacity for coping with stress.
- **Hobbies**: enjoyable activities that do not stimulate competitiveness or anxiety are soothing. These vary individually. Some choices include crafts, music, reading, dance classes, gardening, woodworking and carpentry, electronics, fishing, sailing, etc.
- **Relaxation techniques**: these include meditation, yoga, massage therapy, physical activities, etc. The technique selected is less important than increasing body awareness and refocusing attention onto calmness.
- **Adequate sleep**: lack of sleep exacerbates stress. Insufficient sleep impairs judgment and the immune system. Sleep-deprived individuals are more prone to overreacting to minor irritants. Most of us require eight hours of sleep nightly. Interrupted or irregular sleep impedes REM sleep, dreaming, and deep sleep-enabling physical and neurological repairs.
- **Professional help**: if stress management techniques are insufficient, see a physician before uncontrolled, ongoing stress causes health problems.

Approaches to Stress Management

Four major life skills that people can apply to cope with common life stressors are values clarification, decision-making, communication skills, and coping skills. The following are typical life stressors in early childhood, adolescence, middle adulthood, and later adulthood; and coping mechanisms they can apply from the life skill perspective of **values clarification**.

- Early childhood: a pet's death – according to values clarification, reviewing the pet's **positive qualities** (similarly to adults' celebrating the life of the deceased) and considering getting another pet can address stressors.

- Adolescence: unwanted pregnancy – discussing **feasible alternatives** and their ramifications for the teen, unborn baby, family, and society is not only required to make decisions, but also provides positive coping.
- Middle adulthood: divorce – evaluating its **impact** on the couple and their relatives and friends; and the roles played by marital status, social expectations outside home, and religion inform values clarification coping mechanisms.
- Later adulthood: retirement – when people retiring from careers or employment view retirement in terms of their **values**, this can facilitate their ability to choose feasible options for post-retirement living.

Life Stressors – Decision Making

Among life skills that enable coping with the stress of common life events are values clarification, decision-making, communication skills, and coping skills. Common stressors in four life stages follow, accompanied by coping mechanisms utilizing the **decision-making** life skill.

- Early childhood: a pet's death – helping the child discuss the **pros and cons** of each alternative for disposing of the pet's remains is a decision-making-oriented way to cope with the loss.
- Adolescence: unwanted pregnancy – careful consideration and evaluation of such **alternatives** as abortion; carrying the baby to term and surrendering it for adoption (and open or closed, public or private adoption, etc.); carrying to term and keeping the baby, etc. are necessary decisions to make and cope proactively with stressors. Decisions about future birth-control methods are also indicated.
- Middle adulthood: divorce – from the decision-making perspective, considering alternatives, risks, and consequences and making **choices** among career options, life roles, and future social relationships have major impacts on post-divorce living.
- Later adulthood: retirement – the decision-making life skill enables the retiree to consider **alternatives** and their advantages and disadvantages, e.g., not retiring, pursuing leisure activities, embarking on a second career, volunteering, realizing a long-deferred dream, etc.

Life Stressors – Communication Skills

Four major life skills are values clarification, decision-making, communication skills, and coping skills. Examples of common stressors in each life stage, plus ways to cope using **communication skills**, follow.

- Early childhood: a pet's death – when a child feels sadness and anxiety over the loss, encouraging the child to **communicate** his or her feelings and thoughts can mediate psychic distress.
- Adolescence: unwanted pregnancy – teenage mothers need support from various sources including family, friends, counselors, educators, and health professionals. Effectively utilizing communication skills enables them to know how, where, and from whom to **solicit help and advice** to cope with their situation.
- Middle adulthood: divorce – adults undergoing divorces often have to assume various new life roles, including some that their former spouses may always have addressed. As a part of the process of divorce, adults need to apply communication skills to seek out **supportive friends, relatives, and professionals** as they establish and adjust to these new roles and experiences.
- Later adulthood: retirement – when older adults retire, they may lose some of their autonomy. Using communication skills assertively can help them maintain their **independence**.

- 21 -

Life Stressors – Coping Skills

- Four life skills for coping with stressors are values clarification, decision-making, communication skills, and coping skills. Following are stressors common in each of four life stages, and corresponding coping methods associated with the **coping skills** portion of stress management.
- Early childhood: a pet's death – children can emerge from early loss experiences to discover personal abilities and strengths. From the coping skills perspective, they can prevent normal grief becoming depression through **developing aptitudes and interests**.
- Adolescence: unwanted pregnancy – before and after processes of values clarification and decision-making, teen mothers should examine their personal response to pregnancy for its **significance** in the context of their life.
- Middle adulthood: divorce – it is not unusual for adults to experience lowered self-concept and self-esteem during and after divorce. From the coping skills perspective, the individual can cope better with the stressor of divorce through engaging in behaviors that **enhance self-esteem and self-concept**. Personal and/or professional activities that affirm or reaffirm one's skills, talents, abilities, accomplishments, and sense of self facilitate coping.
- Later adulthood: retirement – retirees often encounter changing responsibilities and roles. Physical activity and exercise, hobbies, social activities, traveling, etc. are **positive coping behaviors** to enhance post-retirement life.

Recognition and Regulation

EQ includes self-awareness, self-regulation (self-management), social awareness, and relationship management. EQ affects physical health, mental health, school and work performance, and relationships. Five **skills to develop EQ** are:

- ability to reduce stress quickly in various contexts;
- ability to recognize our emotions and prevent their overwhelming us;
- ability to relate to others emotionally through nonverbal communication;
- ability to maintain connections during challenging circumstances through playfulness and humor; and
- ability for confident, positive conflict resolution.

To function well under stress, identify your **physiological responses to stress** (e.g., shallow/rapid breathing, tight stomach, muscle tension/pain, clenched hands). Recognition enables **regulation**. Identify your individual stress response: those who become agitated or angry can relieve stress with calming, quieting activities. Those who become withdrawn or depressed can relieve stress through stimulating activities. Those who slow down in some ways and speed up in others, causing paralysis, need activities combining stimulation and comfort. Sensory engagement rapidly decreases stress. Individuals should discover which sense(s) (vision, hearing, touch, smell, taste) and technique(s) are most energizing and/or soothing personally.

Reconnection

Five **skills to develop EQ** are:

- relieving stress rapidly in different situations,
- identifying one's feelings and keep from being overwhelmed by them,
- using nonverbal communication to make emotional connections with others,
- sustaining interactions under stress via humor and play, and (5)
- resolving conflicts positively and confidently.

To recognize your emotions and stay focused and calm during stressful interactions, ask yourself about the quality of your **relationship with your emotions**. Do your emotions flow from one to another along with your changing momentary experiences? Do you feel physical sensations in your body associated with your emotions? Do you feel distinct emotions, e.g., joy, sadness, anger, and fear; and do your subtle facial expressions show each of these? Are you able to feel intense emotions, strong enough to capture both your and others' attention? Do you attend to your emotions? Do they affect your decision-making? If any of these are unfamiliar, you may have shut your emotions off. Many people do this in reaction to negative childhood experiences. Reconnecting with, becoming comfortable with, and accessing **core emotions** are necessary to emotional intelligence and health. Mindful meditation can facilitate these.

Non-Verbal Communication

EQ skills include:

- quick stress control,
- emotion recognition and management,
- nonverbal communication for relating to others,
- using play and humor to preserve relationships under stress, and
- confidence and positivity in resolving conflicts.

To interact well with others, **nonverbal signals** can be more important than words—i.e., how you say things more than what you say. This includes body posture, muscle tension, physical gestures, facial expressions, eye contact, vocal tone, etc. Nonverbal cues convey interest or disinterest, trust or mistrust, excitement or apathy, confidence or fear, clarity or confusion, and connection or disconnection. Nonverbal communication requires both conveying what you intend, and reading others' subtle nonverbal signals. To improve it, attend to others rather than planning what to say next, thinking about other things, or daydreaming so as not to miss cues. Make eye contact to gauge others' responses, maintain conversational flow, and convey interest. Attend to nonverbal signals you are sending and receiving—not only face, body, touch, and tone of voice, but also the pace, timing and rhythm of conversation. If what you say does not reflect what you feel, your body will contradict your words.

Playful Communication

Five **EQ skills** are

- rapid stress reduction during interactions;
- knowing and regulating your feelings;
- interacting with others through nonverbal communication;
- managing stressed interactions through humor and play; and
- confident, positive conflict resolution.

Being able to **laugh** and make others laugh can relieve stress, improve moods, rebalance nervous systems, lighten mental loads, place things in perspective, and increase EQ. Laughing and playing enable us to take setbacks and difficulties in stride. Gentle humor enables communicating messages that could otherwise offend, anger, or provoke defensiveness in others. Humor also soothes **interpersonal differences**. Communicating playfully both energizes and relaxes, simultaneously alleviating fatigue and dissipating physical tension. It moreover loosens rigid thinking, enabling creativity and new perspectives. To develop playful communication, experts recommend practicing by interacting often with outgoing, playful people;

- 23 -

playing with young children, babies, and animals; discovering activities you enjoy that access your playful qualities and loosen you up; and setting aside time regularly for quality playing, joking, and laughing.

Conflict Resolution

EQ consists of these skills:

- quickly decreasing stress,
- identifying and managing our feelings,
- effective nonverbal communication,
- using playfulness and humor to dissipate stress in interactions, and
- resolving conflicts positively and confidently.

Conflict is inevitable, but when constructively managed, it can promote relationship safety, trust, freedom, and creativity. When interpersonal conflicts are not viewed as punitive or threatening but managed positively to build trust, they can strengthen relationships. This skill is informed by the previous four: stress management, emotional awareness, nonverbal communication, and playfulness and humor facilitate skillful handling and defusing of emotionally charged interactions. To develop positive, trust-building **conflict-resolution skills**, focus on the present and acknowledge current reality as an opportunity to resolve old reactions to conflicts, rather than clinging to old resentments and wounds. Regarding arguments, pick your battles: arguing, particularly toward positive resolutions, uses energy and time. Decide whether an issue is worth or not worth arguing over. Forgiveness is also necessary: we must let go of desires for revenge or punishment for others' past hurtful actions to resolve conflicts. Even when a conflict cannot be resolved, continuing it takes two people; although disagreeing, you can end the conflict by disengaging from it.

Emotional Health

Mental or emotional health describes an individual's overall **psychological well-being**. This incorporates a person's self-esteem, i.e., the way s/he feels about herself/himself, a person's ability to manage her/his emotions and ability to cope with stress and problems in life, and the quality of an individual's relationships. Mental and emotional health are analogous to physical health in the sense that, just as we must make conscious efforts to maintain or build up our physical health, we must equally make conscious efforts to sustain or establish our mental and emotional health. Good mental and emotional health is not simply an absence of anxiety, depression, or other mental health problems. It is moreover the presence of positive attributes. It is not merely the absence of feeling bad, but the presence of feeling good. Some people may not experience any overtly negative feelings, yet it is still necessary for them to do things that afford them positive feelings to attain emotional and mental health.

Positive Personal Characteristics

When people are **healthy**, both emotionally and mentally, they feel and demonstrate **positive personal characteristics**, enabling them to engage in meaningful, productive activities and relationships that promote full participation in life. These include: high self-esteem, i.e., they feel good about themselves. They feel and demonstrate self-confidence in themselves and their abilities. They are able to have fun and laugh, and they experience and display a zest for life. They are able to cope with stress and can bounce back from the impacts of any adverse events they encounter. They feel a sense of contentment. They demonstrate flexibility for adapting to changes and learning new things. They are able to develop and sustain satisfying relationships. In both their relationships and their activities, they experience senses of purpose and meaning. In living their lives from day to day, they achieve a balance between opposites like activity and rest, work and play, waking and sleeping, exercising and eating, physical and mental activity, etc.

Resilience

It is a normal part of life to experience **changes**; disappointments; losses; difficult times; and emotional problems that can provoke anxiety, sadness, and stress. While all people encounter these, some cope better than others. Some people experience a very traumatic event and never recover from it. Some suffer permanent damage, significantly impairing their ability to live normal lives. Others carry on, but with major impingements on their ability to participate in and enjoy life fully. **Resilience** is the ability to bounce back from stress, trauma, and other adverse experiences. People with good emotional and mental health have resilience. One component of resilience is having **personal tools** to keep a positive perspective and cope with difficulties. While some people begin developing these early in life, those who did not can still acquire them later with effort and help. Resilient individuals maintain focus, flexibility, and creativity through good and bad times. Additional components of resilience are stress management and emotional self-regulation skills. Being able to recognize our feelings and appropriately express them prevents becoming lodged in negative emotional states like anxiety or depression. Another component of resilience is a strong **network** of supportive people.

Supportive Physical Health

The body and mind are interdependent and constantly interact. Better **physical health** automatically confers better **mental and emotional health**. For instance, when we exercise, we not only make our hearts and lungs stronger, but the activity also releases endorphins, i.e., neurotransmitters in the brain that relieve pain, elevate mood, energize, and promote euphoria or feelings of well-being. Physical health practices supporting mental and emotional health include adequate **sleep**, about 7-8 hours for most individuals. Learning about and practicing good **nutrition** is also important; it is complex and sometimes not simple to implement, but the more we learn about how what we eat affects mood as well as energy, strength, endurance, etc., the easier it can become to eat for physical and psychological health. **Exercise** not only promotes physical fitness; it powerfully relieves anxiety, depression, and stress. Restricting it to going to a gym is unnecessary: regularly incorporating physical activity into daily life, e.g., taking the stairs, walking more, etc. has enormous benefits. Ten to 15 minutes of sunshine daily improves mood (longer durations require sunscreen to prevent skin damage and cancer). Alcohol, tobacco, and other drugs may produce short-term good feelings, but long-term they impair mood and both mental and emotional health, and so should be avoided.

Living Strategies

Attending to our own emotions and needs is necessary to mental and emotional health by preventing buildup of negative feelings and stress. Striking a balance between duties and enjoyable pursuits is important. **Self-care** enables better coping when encountering challenges. **Endorphins** (brain chemicals promoting well-being) are released not only by physical exercise and activity, but also by the following: helping or positively affecting others, which also enhances self-esteem; practicing self-control and discipline, which counters negative ideas, helplessness, and despair and promotes hope; discovering and learning new things—taking classes, learning languages, attending museums, traveling ("mind candy"); enjoying nature, e.g., walking paths through woods or gardens, sitting by a lake or on a beach, hiking, etc., which research proves not only releases endorphins but also lowers blood pressure and dissipates stress; enjoying art, e.g., art galleries, architecture, etc., which have the same effects; managing stress levels; and consciously avoiding absorption in mental habits like excessive worrying or negative thoughts about the world and/or oneself.

Promote Good Mental Health

The following practices are strategies recommended to care for ourselves that promote good **mental and emotional health**: do things appealing to the senses, like listening to mood-elevating music; looking at beautiful scenes of nature, art and craft objects, and animals; looking at and smelling flowers; savoring the flavors and temperatures of foods and beverages; massaging one's hands and feet, or giving and receiving these to and from partners; scented baths; petting animals, etc. Adopt a pet. Though they incur responsibilities, caring for pets makes us feel loved and needed; pets give unconditional love, and some promote going outside, exercising, and finding new places and people. Do creative, meaningful work, for pay or not. Building things, playing musical instruments, composing music, drawing, painting, sculpture, pottery, writing, gardening, etc. stimulate creativity, engender feelings of productivity, and result in products we can feel proud of, enjoy, and share. Prioritizing leisure time is not self-indulgent; playing and doing enjoyable things for their own sake, e.g., reading, watching movies, visiting or talking with friends, or enjoying nature are necessary to mental and emotional health. Meditating, praying, reviewing reasons for gratitude, watching sunrises and sunsets, etc. are ways to take time to contemplate and appreciate life.

Supportive Social Interactions

Humans are naturally **social**, with emotional needs for connections and relationships with others. Improving mental and emotional health includes social as well as private activities. **Social interactions** provide companionship, intellectual stimulation and exchanges, intimacy, humor and laughter; talking to others about problems and feelings can decrease stress. People who are supportive and listen well without criticizing or judging benefit our psychological health; reciprocally, so do listening well to and supporting others. Some ways to engage in social interactions include: periodically walking away from the screens of our computers, tablets, smartphones, and TV sets for the real world to engage in face-to-face, direct interaction that includes nonverbal communication. Another strategy is to make it a priority to spend face-to-face time with friends, co-workers, neighbors, relatives, and other people that we like and enjoy, and who have positive attitudes and interest in us. When we meet people we like, we can make it a point to ask about them. Volunteering benefits both recipients and ourselves, expanding and enriching our lives. Many organizations rely on volunteers to function. Another way to meet potential friends is joining groups that share our interests and meet regularly.

Risk Factors

Experiences in life, particularly in early childhood, influence mental and emotional health. While genetic and biological influences are involved, these interact with and are affected by **environmental experiences**. Some **risk factors** that can threaten mental and emotional health include: inadequate attachment to one's parent or primary caregiver in infancy or early childhood; feeling unsafe, isolated, lonely, confused, or abused early in life; serious traumas or losses, e.g., parent death, hospitalization, or war, particularly in early childhood; negative experiences whereby an individual develops learned helplessness, i.e., the belief that one has little or no control over the circumstances of one's life; serious illness, particularly disabling illness, chronic illness, or illness that isolates the individual from other people; medication side-effects, which can often become hazardous for older people taking multiple medications that interact unfavorably; and substance abuse. Abusing alcohol and/or other drugs can both exacerbate pre-existing mental health disorders, and cause new mental health or emotional problems.

Warning Signals

Some behaviors, feelings, or thoughts to pay attention to as signals to seek **professional help** for emotional or mental health problems include: you are unable to sleep, not just for one night but recurrently. You feel discouraged, sad, helpless, or hopeless a majority of the time. You have trouble

- 26 -

concentrating, such that it interferes with work and/or life at home. You are using food, tobacco, alcohol, or other drugs to cope with problematic emotions. You are having negative or self-destructive thoughts or fears you cannot control. You think more often than normal about death and dying. You have thoughts about suicide. Even if you think these are only speculative and you would never act on them, any thoughts of suicide are serious warning signs. If you have consistently worked to improve your mental and emotional health without success, this is reason to pursue professional help. Our natural **human social orientation** makes us amenable to input from caring, knowledgeable professionals. Their knowledge, training, experience, expertise, perspective, techniques, advice, and counsel can help us do things we could not do on our own to help ourselves.

Stress Process Theory

Conservation of resources (COR) theory (Hobfoll, 1988, 1989, 1998, 2001) views the main element in stress as **resource loss**. People lose resource and also use additional resources during stress. Hence throughout the process, they accumulate greater susceptibility to **negative stress impacts**. While many theorists view stress as either environmental/external or psychological/internal, COR is an integrative theory equally incorporating both orientations. Its essential premise is that people endeavor to get, keep, cultivate, and protect things they value. To combat perceived environmental threat, they need a combination of cultural belonging, social attachments, and personal strengths. These attributes are **resources**: energy, condition, personal characteristic, and object resources. They are both cultural products and cross-cultural in nature. When individuals lose resources, resource loss is threatened, or individuals invest significant resources without gaining resources, stress ensues. COR theory principles are:

- resource loss is disproportionately more impactful than resource gain.
- To prevent resource loss, recover from loss, and gain resources, people must invest resources.

Proactive coping and positive stress outcomes are also aspects considered in COR theory.

Conservation of Resources Theory

Two **conservation of resources (COR) theory principles** are: losing resources has disproportionately more impact than gaining resources; and people have to invest resources to prevent losing them, recover from losing them, and acquire additional resources. There are also four corollaries to these principles.

- **Corollary 1**: those with more resources are more able to gain and less vulnerable to lose resources; conversely, those with fewer resources are less able to gain and more likely to lose resources.
- **Corollary 2**: initial loss causes future loss.
- **Corollary 3**: initial gain causes additional gain.
- **Corollary 4**: lacking resources engenders defensive responses of conserving what resources one does possess.

One example of a **loss spiral** is in research (Lane & Hobfoll, 1992) with people suffering chronic obstructive pulmonary disease (COPD). They experienced a series of increasing resource losses. The more resources they lost, the angrier they became. The angrier they became, the more they alienated possible support givers, increasing their resource loss vulnerability. Another study (Rini et al, 1999) reported lower self-esteem, mastery, and optimism—i.e., personal resources—in lower-income, less-educated Hispanic mothers-to-be, causing greater stress, which caused major infant risk factors of shorter gestation and low birth weights—predicting greater ongoing resource demands and stress.

Rules For K-12 PE Classes

Some recommended **rules for K-12 students** when attending PE classes include the following. Students should be prepared for PE class. This includes wearing only athletic shoes, not wearing dresses, and tying back long hair. Students should pay attention. This includes treating their classmates, PE teacher, and equipment the same way they want to be treated themselves, and not eating or bringing food to PE class or chewing gum during class. Students should be safe and respectful. This includes following directions, staying on task, and cooperating with others. Some PE teachers also inform students of consequences for violating rules during PE classes. One method has three steps:

- The PE teacher gives an oral, verbal warning that the student(s) is/are disobeying class rules.
- If the student(s) do/es not comply, the PE teacher gives the student(s) a time-out, i.e., brief individual separation from the class to take time and refocus their attention.
- After this initial time-out, if the student(s) is/are still not following the rules, the PE teacher assigns an additional time-out during which the student(s) must write a response, e.g., identifying which rule(s) he or she broke and what he or she will do to follow the rule(s).

PE Rules Across the Country

A Maryland teacher uses "Freeze Up": stop, look at the teacher with eyes and ears open and mouth closed; "Move Under Control": avoiding running into persons or objects; "Get Equipment": politely (teacher demonstrates and explains this), carefully, one at a time; and "Reminder for Any Cue": the teacher asks, "What am I looking for?" This teacher also advises consistently praising good work when assisting students at school year's start and periodically after holidays and other school breaks during "refresher courses." An Oregon teacher tells students to "be nice" to one another and try their hardest; he comments that in 23 years of teaching elementary-grade PE, "I have found...pretty much everything can be handled within these two rules." An Illinois teacher adds the rule "Hands Off." He reviews rules often, asking students to identify and explain them; tests fifth through eighth graders on rules; and assigns papers for rule violation to fourth through eighth graders. Another uses the mnemonic acronym **RESPECT**: Right to learn; Effort; Safety; Purpose; Enthusiasm; Challenge; Trust/Team building. She engages students in "meaningful discussion" of these concepts in school's first week and includes the acronym in home letters and newsletters.

PE Classroom Management Methods

Two Texas elementary teachers, male and female, use the acronym "**PEACE**" for their PE class rules: "Protect PE equipment; Enter and Exit quietly; Attention – follow directions the first time; Cooperation – work well with others; Esteem – respect others." These teachers issue "behavior tickets" to students breaking rules; tickets count against student conduct grades. A Wisconsin teacher writes rules on a stairway drawing for middle school, and posts them on a totem pole made by an art teacher for elementary grades. The stairway basement/pole bottom = "below-the-line" behavior. Step 1/second pole face = self-control. Step 2/third pole face = participation. Step 3/fourth pole face = self-directed learning. Step 4/fifth pole face = "kind and caring." She starts classes discussing these levels for the first two school weeks. She also has students self-assess their behavior quarterly, sending self-assessments to parents. A Pennsylvania elementary teacher uses these rules: "EYES watching, EARS listening, MOUTH quiet, HANDS to yourself, BRAIN thinking, RESPECT others, USE equipment correctly, and SAFETY – Stop, look, and listen." Two New Jersey teachers add "Win without boasting, lose without blaming," and high-fives before leaving to respect self, others, and the environment.

PE Class Rules

One elementary school in Ohio has four rules: "Safety; Use good manners; Respect self, others and equipment; Have fun and enjoy PE class." They report students created these rules and follow them well. Teachers say that despite being broad, these rules "...for the most part, cover all that can happen in a [PE] class." A Connecticut teacher tells students to "Stop, look, and listen when [the] whistle blows"; "Demonstrate good sportsmanship"; and "Be responsible for gym equipment." His rewards are "1. Praise"; "2. Recreation day"; and "3. Awards." His consequences are "1. Time out"; "2. 'F' for the day"; "3. Letter home"; and "4. Referral to administrator." Another teacher instructs students to find a place in the gym and prepare for the activities; show kindness to others; "know when to talk"; follow all instructions; and participate for the whole activity. Another teacher at a Maryland elementary school instructs students, "Always try your best. If someone in class is having trouble, HELP instead of laughing. The equipment belongs to all of us – let's take care of it! Keep hands, feet, and objects to yourself. When the teacher or your classmates are talking, you are not."

Classroom Management Practices

A Wisconsin elementary PE teacher sends lists of expectations and rules to students' parents at the beginning of every school year. She issues students rules to enter the gym, sit on their numbers, and listen for directions; show courtesy and kindness to opponents and teammates; discuss any disputes using words, involving the teacher for unresolved disputes; stop any activity upon a signal; and leave the gym from their numbers, preparing for resuming classroom activities. For each class period, she first gives an "S" warning for violations; second violations get an "I", third violations a "T" = "**SIT**" = students sit out for specified durations until they can verbalize how they will return "ready to learn." This starts over with each class. Violations repeating across class periods incur parent letters. Parents must review the rules with their children and sign the letters for students to be permitted to return to PE class. An Alaska elementary teacher uses "**ABCD**": Act safely; Be prepared and be positive; Cooperate; Do your best"; and the motto "Have Fun – Work Hard – Learn." He comments, "For 18 years...these ABCD guidelines and...motto have served me well."

Class Management

An elementary PE teacher in Washington state states three rules, all beginning with "**RESPECT**:" "Yourself (by working hard and safely every day to improve your fitness level); Others (always encourage, never put down); Equipment (by using it for intended purposes)." This teacher comments, "These are my posted rules. I haven't found anything I couldn't somehow relate to these rules." Another teacher in Illinois comments, "We believe in using a few simple rules that can cover any situation. These rules are sent to all parents at the beginning of the school year." These rules are: "Follow directions; Actively listen when a teacher is talking; Respect others; "Keep your hands and feet to yourself." An elementary teacher in New York state comments, "I explain each rule in some detail; the older the students, the more detail they get. For example, being a good listener means: eyes on the speaker, hands quiet, voices quiet, and raise your hand to speak." His rules for students are: "Be a good listener; Always follow directions; Treat others with respect; Use equipment correctly; Always try your best."

Psychological Factors That Affect Learning

Factors that influence learning include readiness, i.e., physiological and psychological variables that affect individual ability and interest for learning; motivation, i.e., intrinsic conditions of needs and drives required for individuals to initiate goal-directed activities; reinforcement, i.e., actions, behaviors, and events, positive or negative, augmenting the probability that an individual will repeat the same response to a stimulus; and individual differences, i.e., student abilities, backgrounds, intelligence, personalities, and learning styles. In the cognitive stage of motor learning, learners understand the goal and nature of the activity, and make first attempts, including major errors. In the associative stage, learners practice to master skill timing; errors are more consistent and less numerous. In the autonomous stage, learner movements seem effortless and are well coordinated; errors are minimal; and performance automaticity enables learners to redirect attention to other skill aspects. Peak athletic performance is enabled by optimal individual arousal levels. Attention ranges from narrow to wide, and internal to external. Attentional flexibility is capacity for shifting voluntarily and quickly among different attentional styles according to task demands. Anxiety affects performance by narrowing and internalizing attentional focus. Physical activity reduces general or non-competition anxiety; pre-competition warmups reduce performance anxiety, as well as prevent injuries and enhance movement.

Five Conditions for Cooperative Learning

Merely grouping students does not achieve cooperative learning, which requires a common group goal whose achievement the group is rewarded. Conditions required for **cooperative learning** include these five basic elements:

- The students have positive interdependence and clearly perceive this.
- The students engage in substantial amounts of face-to-face, promotive interaction.
- The students are personally and individually accountable and responsible for achieving the goals of the group, and they clearly perceive they are.
- The students often make use of the small-group and interpersonal skills that are pertinent to their cooperative learning activity.
- The students regularly and frequently engage in group processing of their current group functioning to improve the effectiveness of the group in the future.

All effective cooperative relationships, including work groups, partner learning, peer tutoring, peer mediation, families, etc., always incorporate these five fundamental conditions or elements. Cooperative relationships do not necessarily occur naturally through simply grouping students; teachers need to structure and manage them for students.

Patterns of Group Learning

Students in **cooperative groups** first learn skills, procedures, knowledge, and strategies together. Then they apply this learning individually to show they have mastered it personally. Teachers must evaluate each individual student's contribution to group work; give individual students and groups constructive feedback; help groups eliminate work redundancy by multiple members; and assure all members' responsibility for their final results. Six ways to structure **individual accountability** in cooperative student groups are:

- Keep group size small to increase individual accountability.
- Give each individual student a test.
- Randomly call on individual students to present group work to the teacher or class for oral examinations.
- Observe each student group and record how often each member contributes to the group.
- In each group, assign one student to the function of checker. This student asks other members of his or her group to explain rationales and reasoning behind the group answers they formulate.
- Have individual students teach what they have learned to another. "Simultaneous explaining" is when all students participate in this activity.

Positive Interdependence

In the shared responsibility termed **positive interdependence**, students perceive they cannot succeed unless their group mates do, and vice versa, and they must coordinate their work with other members' work to accomplish any task. Students perceive that reciprocally, their group mates' work benefits them and their work benefits their group mates. Students maximize the learning of all small-group members when they collaborate by giving each other mutual encouragement and support, sharing resources, and celebrating their group success. When students clearly comprehend positive interdependence, they realize no member of their group gets a free ride: every member's work is indispensable and necessary for the group to succeed. They also understand that every member of the group has unique roles, responsibilities, and resources; therefore, every member makes a unique contribution to the collective endeavor. In **cooperative learning groups**, all students are responsible for learning the assigned content, and for assuring every member of their group also learns it.

Structuring Positive Interdependence

- **"Positive Goal Interdependence"**: Students understand that the only way to accomplish their learning goals is if all group members also achieve their learning goals. A shared goal unites the group, giving them a concrete reason for the group's existence. Students must care about how much every other group member learns, and must perceive that they "sink or swim together." To establish this perception, teachers must structure a clear mutual or group goal, incorporated in every lesson. For example, the teacher might assign the goal that each student learns the assigned information, and also makes sure all members of his or her group learn it.
- **"Positive Reward – Celebrate Interdependence"**: The teacher gives every group member the same reward for accomplishing group goals. Teachers may also include joint rewards adding to goal interdependence; for example, each student gets five extra credit points if all group members score 90 percent or higher on the test. Teachers may give students individual test grades, group grades for overall results, and extra credit for all members' meeting test criteria. Experts find cooperation quality enhanced through regularly celebrating group success and effort.

Organizing Positive Interdependence

- **"Positive Resource Interdependence"**: Every group member only has part of the information, materials, or resources needed to complete a task; therefore, members must combine resources to attain group goals. To accentuate cooperative group relationships, teachers may give students limited resources that they have to share, e.g., one copy of the task or problem for each group; or they can use the "jigsaw procedure," only giving one piece or part of the necessary resources to each group member, and they then must fit their pieces together to make a whole.
- **"Positive Role Interdependence"**: Each group member is assigned a role, specifying responsibilities needed for the group to complete a joint task. Each role is interconnected and complementary with the others. For example, roles include reader, recorder, participation encourager, understanding checker, and knowledge elaborator. Numerous well-controlled, high-quality research studies show checking for understanding correlates significantly with higher student learning and achievement levels.

External Variables Affecting Performance

External factors are things outside ourselves, over which we usually have little or no control but which still have impacts on our physical performance. Weather in outdoor environments can have helpful or detrimental impacts on physical performance, depending on the activity. For example, a strong wind blowing steadily can interfere with performance when playing tennis, but will aid performance when

- 31 -

sailing a boat. Equipment is another external variable. Although individual or team performance is aided by better equipment, there is also always a chance of equipment malfunction or failure. Technology is an external variable gaining importance as it develops and advances. Video and computer technology enable more precise and sophisticated analysis of sports and movement techniques. Computer technology also enhances equipment capabilities and use. In sports, other players constitute an external variable. Performance is affected by both teammates and opponents. Poor teammate performance can interfere; good teammate performance can inspire. Poor or good opponent performance can make competing easier and less challenging, or harder and more challenging. Decisions made by referees, umpires, and other officials are external factors that can increase or destroy motivation.

Relative Availability of Resources

According to research findings, **smaller** PE class sizes and student-teacher ratios improve student safety, activity levels, and learning as well as how much time students participate in PE, whereas **larger** class sizes and student-teacher ratios correlate with decreased physical activity by students] Also, in schools with enough teachers teaching only PE and no other subjects, students receive more PE weekly. Student activity levels and physical fitness knowledge correlate positively with numbers of available, qualified PE teachers. Teachers having to teach both PE and other subjects give shorter lessons, with less student physical activity. Similarly to human resources, material and curricular **resources** affect student physical activity during PE classes, directly influencing how much of class includes student engagement in moderate-to-vigorous physical activity (MVPA). Educational researchers are reaching increasing consensus that standards-based PE curricula augment students' physical activity. Access to safe, appropriate, well-maintained, aesthetically appealing facilities and environments also enhance physical activity. Another resource contributing to greater opportunities for physical activity during PE classes is having enough exercise and sports equipment, suitable for students' sizes and in good condition.

Amounts of Physically Active Time

Researchers find that one mechanism whereby students are physically active during less of their PE classes is the proportion of time PE teachers must devote to **administrative tasks**. For example, studies have revealed PE teachers may take up to 21 percent of their class time on class management and administrative duties. This can be decreased by providing sufficient resources: high student-teacher ratio and large classes entail more time taking attendance and making transitions between activities. Similarly, equipment selection and transitions among spaces take more time when access to suitable equipment and facilities is inadequate. A positive influence increasing student PE class time spent in physical activity is access to curriculum resources aligned with best PE practices, particularly when physical educators use these resources in focused, organized lesson planning. In some studies, investigators have found that the minority of schools studied offered PE every day, averaging fewer than three days weekly; average lessons lasted less than 47 minutes; and students were very active only during one-fourth of class time, spending over 20 percent of the time walking, over 20 percent sitting, over one-third of the time standing, and lying down a small amount of time.

Allocation, Organization, Management of Resources

Some studies have revealed that an average of over 23 percent of time in PE classes was used for **class management**. Students were found to be engaging in moderate to vigorous physical activity (MVPA) during 45.3 percent of the time during PE classes, which averaged 21.2 minutes per class and equated to only 10.4 minutes per school day, because most schools studied only offered PE classes 2.47 days per week. Researchers found that of the schools they examined, only 17.4 percent offered PE five days of the week. Elementary school PE teachers were found to spend a significantly larger amount of class time than middle school teachers on class management; hence middle school students received more minutes per

- 32 -

day of PE. Students were exposed to more PE daily when schools had more teachers dedicated to teaching only health and PE. Students engaged in MVPA during more of PE class, and teachers used less class time on management, when student-teacher ratios were lower. Higher student MVPA and lower management time were also associated with better access to adequate physical activity facilities and exercise and sports equipment.

Recommendations vs Actual Activity

The Institute of Medicine has recommended (2005) that children engage in **moderate to vigorous physical activity (MVPA)** for 60 minutes per day. However, researchers found that in the actual schools they used for their study samples, children had approximately 23 minutes of PE class per day, and were engaged in MVPA for less than half of that time, i.e., around 10 minutes a day. This equates to about one-sixth of the national recommendation. The researchers acknowledge that, obviously, children must be active outside of PE classes to attain the recommended levels of physical activity; but they also advise that to support children in doing so, schools must nevertheless increase the proportions of PE class time when children are active physically. They conclude that a low ratio of students per full-time equivalent (FTE) PE teacher affords significant gains in both PE class duration and proportions of student physical activity during those classes. They find school district allocation of enough resources for hiring and retaining PE teachers with superior skills will enable longer PE classes and student activity.

Quality of PE Instruction

Although enough exposure to PE of high enough intensity is proven to contribute effectively to healthy lifestyles among children and adults, research finds that many PE programs do not meet national recommendations for either **duration of class time** or **physical activity intensity**. Some researchers (cf. Bevans et al., 2010) differentiate between structural and process factors for predicting levels of student physical activity. For example, among resources that promote student physical activity, adequate facilities, equipment, and quantity and quality of PE teachers are defined as structural factors. Instructional practices by PE teachers are defined as **process factors**. Even though both structural and process factors predict student activity levels, and thus comprehensive approaches for enhancing children's health and well-being through more effective PE must address both of these, the researchers also note the importance of differentiating them for the purposes of differentiating approaches for improving each. Federal, state, and district policies that require allocating sufficient funding for procuring and maintaining facilities and equipment, and for hiring and retaining enough PE teachers for ideal teacher-student ratios, will improve structural factors. PE teacher professional development in techniques for decreasing class management time will improve process factors.

Individual and Situational Interest

Individual interest describes the relatively lasting psychological preference or predisposition of an individual to repeatedly engage with certain categories of events, ideas, or objects over time. It is specific to the content involved, develops gradually and slowly, and is comparatively stable. Individual interest also evolves in relation to the individual's values and knowledge. As such, individual interest figures significantly in students' preferences for engaging in certain activities or tasks over time, and is predictive of their future motivation. In contrast, situational interest describes the momentary affective responses generated by environmental stimuli. The effects of this may be short term, and its influence on individual values and knowledge may be marginal. Appealing or specific environmental features usually stimulate **situational interest**, which can also potentially lead to true interest. Both individual and situational interest influence learning. Although the former proceeds from internal psychological characteristics and the latter from external environmental stimuli, they do not exist separately: they interact and influence each other's development. Situational interest can help long-term individual interest to develop, and

- 33 -

strong individual interest can enable an individual to respond differently to stimulating environmental situations than others lacking such interest.

Increasing Internal Motivation

Research finds that despite ongoing concern and priority for enhancing all Americans' physical activity for its physical and mental health benefits, daily PE for high school students has **decreased**; worse, fewer high school students elect to take available PE courses. Thus, effective PE teachers and programs have critical roles for giving children positive experiences with physical activity early in life. These are accompanied by the necessity of creating environments structured for motivating students to engage in healthy lifestyles with ongoing physical activity. One strategy to increase internal motivation is giving students freedom to choose. Example practices are giving students choices of two or more activities, and involving them in decision-making processes whenever possible. Another strategy is modifying activities and skills, and letting students do so. Example practices are changing the rules, space, or equipment to facilitate student success, and giving students flexibility to be creative in modifying activities to fit their individual needs and interests. A third strategy is giving every student ideal challenges. Practice examples are matching activities to students, and offering students choices among different task difficulty levels, e.g., letting students select among differently shaped balls or scarves in juggling lessons.

Perceived Physical Competence

According to research into students' reasons for engaging in physical activity, their main **motives** are to enjoy it for its fun, and for how enhancing skills and learning enable a sense of accomplishment. Students' perception of their physical abilities—**perceived physical competence**—frequently determines willingness to try new activities and keep participating. To develop perceived physical competence, students must have chances to learn and practice, without which they can develop negative attitudes regarding physical activity, decreasing its future probability. Teaching frequently requires specific numbers of trials within a time limit, counterproductively inducing students to sacrifice quality of movement for completing required quantities. Giving students certain durations for practice without specifying trial numbers enables focus on correct form. Moreover, practice durations long enough to develop skill, yet short enough to sustain concentrated attention, preserve enthusiasm and motivation. Teachers should let students experiment while learning and perfect processes, and give them positive feedback describing what they did right technically, instead of stressing products—e.g., emphasizing correct basketball-throwing technique rather than making the basket—to enhance motivation to practice.

Enhancing Perceived Physical Competence

- **Give students enough time to practice**. As an example, teachers can specify a certain length of time to work on skills, but not require them to complete a certain number of trials during that time. This will allow them to concentrate on performing the skills correctly rather than focusing on performing actions enough times without perfecting their technique. Teachers can reduce off-task student behavior by changing or varying the activities assigned.
- **Give students positive, specific instructional feedback**. Teachers can make it easier for students to take on challenges and risks of errors or failing by communicating relevant, meaningful, task-specific and technique-specific instructional feedback to students. For example, when a PE teacher tells a student the way he or she held his or her elbows in or bent his or her arms when throwing or catching was admirable and to keep it up, the student will experience approval, appreciation, and encouragement of his or her efforts and be more motivated to continue practicing and participating.

- 34 -

Improve Perceived Physical Competence

- Stress personal improvement. PE teachers can instruct students to determine their fitness or activity baselines, e.g., by counting the number of times they can make a chest pass or bounce pass against the wall, and encourage them to establish personal goals, repeating these actions to match or exceed baseline numbers.
- Group students rapidly. If PE teachers quickly group students, they prevent students from comparing peers to choose teams. Teachers can instruct students to move through the space randomly, and upon hearing a specified number of teacher whistle-blows, move into groups with other students in nearest proximity to them. This avoids comparing some students unfavorably to others, which impedes their developing perceived physical competence.
- Ask students their permission in advance to demonstrate skills. When a PE teacher observes a student performing a technique correctly, he or she should ask the student first whether he or she is willing to demonstrate for the class instead of unexpectedly telling the student to demonstrate. Putting a student on the spot is more stressful; offering the student choice and preparation better enables developing perceived physical competence.

Peer Comparisons Negative Affect

Younger elementary school students, e.g., first and second graders, frequently assume they are competent in all physical activities they perform. However, in third and fourth grades they typically begin noticing some of their peers perform certain skills better than others. Consequently, they start judging their own **physical competence** by comparing it to that of other students. This negative outcome is reinforced by separating individual students or groups by focusing everybody's attention on them, encouraging their perception that their abilities are being judged by others. PE teachers can use a strategy of having students practice in scattered formations, not in a circle where they tend to perceive everybody is watching them, and of not waiting in line to take turns, also exposing each student to an audience, which both make students feel uncomfortable that others are judging them. Even with positive teacher feedback, students become embarrassed over performing unsuccessfully in front of peers, damaging their perceived physical competence. Another strategy is to ask individual students or groups in advance if they are comfortable demonstrating a skill, rather than surprising them.

TARGET (T, A, and R)

TARGET stands for Task, Authority, Recognition, Grouping, Evaluation, and Timing. For **Task**, strategies include giving several activities with varying difficulty levels, and adjusting skills and activities to be developmentally appropriate. For example, PE teachers can instruct first graders to try catching beanbags with their preferred hand, their non-dominant hand, or both hands. For **Authority**, a strategy is to allow students to have some of the responsibility for their choices of activities. For example, PE teachers can tell each student to select his or her favorite among upper-body exercises, and perform their selected exercises while music is playing. For **Recognition**, strategies include recognizing the process rather than the product, focusing on self-improvement rather than outcomes, and helping students focus on self-improvement by establishing an environment that eliminates or reduces peer performance comparisons and by delivering positive feedback. For example, the PE teacher can praise a student in a voice just above a whisper, commenting that he or she can tell the student is working hard because the student is using the other foot or hand, thus complimenting the student's efforts.

TARGET (G, E, and T)

The **TARGET** acronym represents Task, Authority, Recognition, Grouping, Evaluation, and Timing. For **Grouping**, teaching strategies include using "toe to toe" and other techniques to form groups quickly, avoiding peer comparisons, and augmenting the aspect of social interactions in the PE environment by encouraging students to partner with different classmates often. For example, teachers can instruct students to seat themselves in groups of four following the class rule of one girl and one boy to each group; inform them they will stay in the group for a few minutes and then switch; and thank them for quickly forming groups. For **Evaluation**, strategies include engaging students in self-evaluations targeting self-improvement, and involving students in evaluation processes, ensuring each student's evaluation is private, meaningful, and specific. For example, the teacher tells a student, "Awesome pass! I like how you're making a table and moving your feet, remembering the cues. Excellent work!" For **Timing**, strategies include maximizing learning and practice time, and not introducing competitive play too soon; helping students make time outside class to practice and be physically active; and individualizing teaching and practices so all students have time and motivation for practice. Examples include specific fielding instructions, and suggesting additional practice at home later.

Responsible Behaviors

Pre-K/K students may be expected to show consideration of and cooperation with others, like taking turns and sharing, to maximize activity times. **Grades 1-2** may be expected to show good fitness partnership behaviors, e.g., cooperation, willingness to work with any partner, and giving encouragement. **Grades 3-5** may be expected to show respect by avoiding "put-downs," encouraging peers, communicating respectfully with students having similar and different fitness or skill levels, and to identify and experience diverse cultures' physical habits and activities. **Grades 6-8** may be expected to demonstrate sensitivity and respect for others' feelings when they participate in fitness activities with students having different cultures, skills, abilities, and genders, and to analyze how health behavior is both challenged and enriched by cultural diversity. **Grades 9-12** may be expected to participate with and invite others to physical activities irrespective of different cultural backgrounds, abilities, skills, and limitations, and analyze how developing appreciation of physical, gender, ethnic, and cultural diversity is influenced by sport participation. Higher education students may be expected to invite their family members and friends to participate in physical activities.

Positive Relationships

Some researchers have found that middle school students perceive close friendships more highly through **positive affect related to physical activity**, and that those perceiving peer acceptance more highly experienced higher **physical self-worth**, which in turn predicts more positive affect. Positive affect also promotes physical activity and challenge preference. Studies have shown that psychosocial outcomes are enhanced through independent contributions from both peer acceptance and friendship. Quality experiences in physical activity have been observed to benefit from the motivation supplied by positive affect, self-perceptions, and relationships with significant others. Multiple studies have found peers critical to such quality experiences with physical activity. Areas of research interest have included how peers influence affect in the physical domain, shape self-perceptions, affect moral attitudes and behaviors, and affect motivation for making choices of physical activity, seeking challenges, and sustaining long-term commitment to physical activity. Studies have found peer relationships and health behavior reciprocally influence each other. Research into sports implies that individuals identifying exclusively as athletes risk more adjustment problems when undergoing injuries or leaving the sport; some researchers suggest peer relationships may influence identity formation.

Appropriate Vs. Inappropriate PE Practices

To establish a **productive learning environment**, PE teachers systematically plan, develop, and sustain atmospheres of teacher and peer respect and support, emphasizing participation and learning. Sarcasm or insults are unsafe and unsupportive, causing student discomfort, embarrassment, or humiliation.

Productive environments support all students' development of positive self-concept, enabling them to try, fail, and try again without fear, teacher or peer criticism, or harassment. Inappropriate environments view more physically fit and skilled students as successful, ignoring or overlooking those who are less fit or skilled. Intrinsic, not extrinsic motivations are stressed, guiding student responsibility for learning and behavior, not fear of punishment. Teachers use and promote exercise for fun, skill development, and health benefits, not punishment. **Classroom management practices** are consistent and fair, not using inconsistent, unclear rules. Teachers immediately address bullying, taunting, and inappropriate student behaviors and comments firmly, not ignoring or overlooking them. They actively teach safety and post and practice emergency plans, not ignoring or permitting unsafe student practices (pushing, shoving, tackling; swinging bats close to others, etc.). They match activities to ability levels, not permitting dodge ball or drills enabling aggressive behaviors. Updated CPR and AED certifications and regular facility and equipment safety inspections are imperative.

Promoting Productive Learning Environments

PE teachers should purposefully design situations and activities that teach and help students develop social skills for **cooperation**, **collaboration**, **competition**, and **sportsmanship** rather than leaving these only for "teachable moments" or assuming they are learned incidentally. They must take advantage of strategies including peer teaching, group work, letting students choose equipment, and involving students in making rules. PE class sizes should be similar to other subject classes: teachers should not regularly combine classes with one supervising a doubled class while the other does something else. Teachers must closely monitor students for safety rather than leave classes unsupervised periodically or position themselves without views of all students. They should create environments including and supporting all children regardless of diverse abilities and characteristics, not preferential to skilled athletes. Teachers should include culturally diverse activities, not exclusively teach American team sports, and challenge students of all developmental and ability levels including those with disabilities appropriately, not allowing highly skilled students to dominate. Socialization, support, and encouragement should be equal between genders, without identifying certain activities (e.g., football or dance) with boys or girls; teachers should use gender-neutral language.

Planning Effective Class Behavior Management

Experienced experts advise PE teachers to get to know every single student as soon as they possibly can as a means of developing **rapport** with students and classes. Teachers should learn some unique fact about each student. Greeting each student by name as he or she arrives to class daily will demonstrate teacher recognition and interest for every individual. Teachers should establish all class routines and procedures, such as for using and returning equipment, bathroom breaks, etc., to be consistent from class to class day to day. PE teachers are advised to develop a set of their written expectations. These should not exceed five in number, as students will not be able to remember or keep track of more. Teachers should enforce these expectations consistently. Expectations should not focus on the negative, i.e., what teachers want students not to do, but on the positive, i.e., what teachers want students to do. They should post copies of these expectations in the locker room or on the bulletin board in their classrooms.

Effective Behavior Management Techniques

PE teachers should make sure that they prepare gym equipment in **advance**, before classes begin. They should not set up the equipment in the presence of their students. However, they can enlist willing students to help them set up equipment in the mornings before school starts. Another practice for PE teachers to support effective behavior management is putting their agendas on paper and **posting** them on a bulletin board before class. They should hold students accountable for checking the day's agenda and initiating assigned learning experiences. PE teachers should train students always to look at the bulletin

- 37 -

board before asking what they are doing that day. Another recommended technique is to use "**high activity roll call taking strategies**" rather than letting students remain inactive while taking attendance. Inactivity encourages misbehavior, and allows students to forget the point of PE class—physical activity. Another technique is to make use of transitions by assigning **time limits**, e.g., giving 10 seconds to get to the basketball court, 30 seconds to get from the gym to the outdoor playing field, etc.

Keeping Classes Running Smoothly

One component for PE teachers to include in an effective behavior management plan involves how to give students **directions**: teachers should make sure that before telling students *what* to do, they tell them *when* to do it. For example, do not simply say "Each team, pick up a soccer ball" first, or students will stop listening to follow that direction. Instead, say, "When I say 'go,' each team pick up a soccer ball." That way, they will keep students' attention as they will not act until they hear the identified prompt. To keep instructional cues concise, teachers can use the "**rule of threes**" (SPARK PE website), e.g., three players, three passes, three feet, three minutes, three seconds, etc. Also from the SPARK PE website, teachers can use the "**80/20 rule**": teach the class a concept until 80 percent of the students understand it; during the subsequent learning experience, the other 20 percent will figure it out through doing it. Another piece of expert advice for PE teachers is not to talk too much when teaching. PE teachers should use **pair-and-share strategies** and **questioning techniques** to give their students opportunities to talk with one another.

Expert Recommendations

To **engage** students in their own learning, PE teachers should use approaches like **cooperative learning methods** and **peer assessment** instead of direct instruction. Some experts advise that the teachers should not have to work harder than their students. Another way to prevent behavior problems and delegate effort while teaching responsibility to students is to assign **management and leadership roles** for capable students to perform, such as team captains, referees, equipment managers, squad leaders, warmup leaders, and new student buddies. An additional behavior management method that is effective is to hold students **accountable** for their own behavior through a combination of positive reinforcement for desired behaviors and consequences for undesired ones. In addition to regularly giving ample informal, verbal positive reinforcement for desirable behaviors, the PE teacher should define formal rewards and consequences for students in advance, and enforce them consistently. Experts also advise that when PE teachers discipline students, they should talk to them as if their parents are standing directly behind them.

Plans for Class Behavior Management

In effective **behavior management plans**, PE teachers should privately and quietly discipline individual students when needed. They should never hold disciplinary talks in front of the other students. When disputes between or among students develop during classes, one strategy that PE teachers can use is to settle them using the "rock, paper, scissors" method. This ensures randomness for objectivity instead of subjective or preferential decisions. When assigning students to groups, PE teachers should consider their individual differences and needs, such as disabilities or special needs, skill levels, English language proficiency, race, gender, etc. To balance groups evenly, teachers should divide their classes into high, middle, and low achievers and then place one from each level into each group. English language learners and special-needs students should be paired with supportive buddies or partners. PE teachers are advised to respect students. Teachers should begin and end class on time, teaching from "bell to bell."

- 38 -

Applying Effective Behavior Management Plans

To **prevent behavior problems** and **motivate students**, PE teachers should play school-appropriate, current, student-friendly music. Students comply more with clearer expectations. PE teachers should model everything they expect; for example, on rainy days, not running but walking from the gym to the auditorium. To call on students in an equitable manner, PE teachers should set up a tracking system. They should try to alternate calling on female and male students. Over a day or week, depending on student learning experience and class size, PE teachers should ensure each student has a chance to respond. Experts advise PE teachers to enlist students' parents as their allies. They can do this by calling them early in the school year and staying in frequent communication; being sure to talk about students' positive behaviors; using very specific terms and objective descriptions to communicate concerns; focusing not on the student but the behavior; and always allowing time to calm down before contacting parents regarding undesirable behaviors. According to experts, the best behavior management plan is a strong instructional plan. Thus PE teachers should prepare for each lesson. The more students are engaged in learning activities, the less they will demonstrate maladaptive behaviors.

Major Human Body Systems

The **skeletal system** provides the body's structural framework of bones to support it, protects the soft vital organs from harm, collaborates with muscles to produce body movement, stores calcium in the bones, and produces red blood cells in the bone marrow. The **integumentary system** includes the hair, nails, and especially skin, which is the body's largest sensory organ. It provides tactile sensation, including pain, heat, cold, pressure, and pleasure; regulates loss of blood and other fluids; synthesizes vitamin D; and protects deeper tissues. The **muscular system** maintains body posture, creates body movements with the support of the bones, generates heat, and consumes energy. The **immune system** is composed of parts of many other systems, including parts of the lymphatic system, the cardiovascular system, the respiratory system, the gastrointestinal system, etc. It works to protect and defend the body against disease organisms and other foreign elements.

Major Human Body Systems Functions

The **lymphatic system** retrieves fluids that leak from the capillaries (small blood vessels) and contains the white blood cells, hence supporting parts of the immune system. The **cardiovascular system** transports nutrients containing oxygen and other necessities throughout the bloodstream, transports gaseous wastes for elimination, and supports immune functions. The **urinary system** regulates balances of fluids, electrolytes, and pH; and removes nitrogenous wastes from the blood. The **digestive system** breaks foods down into proteins, sugars, amino acids, and other building blocks for the body's metabolic processes, growth, replenishment, and repair. The **respiratory system** performs gas exchanges by taking in, warming, and moistening environmental air, delivering oxygen, and expelling carbon dioxide. The **nervous system** provides sensory input, interprets the sensory information, evokes and signals responses, and coordinates muscle functions. The **endocrine system** secretes hormones that regulate the body's growth, metabolism, and general functionality. The **reproductive system** produces hormones enabling reproduction and creates, nurtures, and delivers offspring.

Muscular System

Among cardiac, smooth, and skeletal muscles, **skeletal muscles** are used in voluntary body movement. They are wrapped in several layers of connective tissue, which join to form tendons attaching to bones. **Tendons** extend connective tissue around muscles, giving individual muscle fibers support and stability. **Ligaments** connect bones at joints, and exercise is thought to strengthen ligaments. Tendons and ligaments, combined with muscle and skin elasticity and joint structure, determine flexibility, which can

- 39 -

be enhanced through stretching exercises. **Type I/red/slow-twitch muscle fibers** are needed for endurance activities like long-distance running and cycling, and need more aerobic energy. **Type II/white/fast-twitch muscle fibers** need less oxygen and are used in short-term, maximum-force exertion like sprinting, jumping, and weight-lifting. Both types are activated in activities needing maximal force production. Lesser force requirements activate slow-twitch fibers first, then fast-twitch if needed. Muscle fibers are always activated in groups called motor units, which include motor neurons. Dumbbell curls use more motor units than picking up a pencil, for example. Resistance and weight training increases muscle fiber size, and strengthens and thickens connective tissues, resulting in larger muscles and greater muscular strength and endurance.

The Cardiopulmonary System in Exercise

The heart's right side receives blood from the veins. When the heart muscle contracts, it pumps blood from its **right ventricle**, through the **pulmonary arteries**, to the **lungs**. This blood acquires fresh oxygen in the lungs from atmospheric air the individual has inhaled, and releases carbon dioxide into **pulmonary capillaries**. Exhaling expels this CO_2. The freshly oxygenated blood travels through the pulmonary veins, to the heart's left atrium, to the left ventricle. When the left ventricle contracts, it pumps blood through the **aorta**, the largest artery, to the entire body. The left and right ventricles contract simultaneously, so the cardiopulmonary system functions in a perpetual cycle. Oxygen consumption directly affects cardiorespiratory fitness: heart and lung function determine oxygen transportation to body tissues. The volume of air inhaled and exhaled each minute is pulmonary ventilation, which typically increases when exercising. The differential between oxygen inhaled and exhaled is the measure of oxygen consumption. Its maximum, **VO_2max**, equals maximal aerobic capacity, frequently regarded as indicating cardiorespiratory fitness. It defines the cardiovascular system's greatest ability to deliver oxygenated blood to working muscles, and how quickly the body can produce adenosine triphosphate (ATP) to supply energy to muscles.

Hierarchy of Neural Systems

Many areas of the brain, including parts involving motivation, emotions, and memory, are included in the **highest level** of the **motor control hierarchy**. In this level, command neurons formulate the intention to move the body and its parts. This message is sent to the hierarchy's **middle level** in the cerebral cortex's sensorimotor cortex, subcortical nuclei's basal ganglia, cerebellum, and brainstem. The highly interconnected structures in this level determine postures and movements needed to perform an action. Midlevel neurons additionally receive input from receptors in the eyes, vestibular system, skin, joints, and muscles regarding current surroundings and body posture. The middle level uses this complex of data to produce a motor program, which defines the information necessary for performing the activity. It sends this program information along descending pathways, originating in the sensorimotor cortex and brainstem, to the **lowest hierarchy level**, the motor neurons and interneurons. These determine joint angles and degrees of muscle tension. Continuous monitoring and updating of movements allow for unexpected events. Initial motor programs generate rapid, crude execution of movements. Repeating a movement allows the middle level to supply more accurate information, requiring fewer corrections and enabling learning.

Fundamental Processes of Life

- **Organization**: Labor is divided at every level of life, each part cooperatively performing its function. Loss of organization, i.e., integrity, causes death, even to a single cell.
- **Metabolism**: All the chemical reactions in the body, e.g., breaking substances down to simpler components and releasing energy.

- **Responsiveness**: Also known as irritability, detecting changes in external and internal environments and reacting to them—sensing and responding to stimuli.
- **Movement**: At the cellular level, molecules move among locations. Blood moves among body parts in the circulatory system. As we breathe, our diaphragms move. Our muscles produce movement through contractility, i.e., ability to shorten.
- **Reproduction**: Specifically, transmitting life across generations by creating new organisms. Generally, cellular reproduction means new cell formation to repair or replace old cells and affect growth.
- **Differentiation**: How unspecialized cells developmentally become specialized, with distinct structures and functions, e.g., into tissues and organs.
- **Respiration**: How oxygen and carbon dioxide are exchanged between cells and the environment, including ventilation, diffusion, and transportation in blood.
- **Digestion**: Breaking down foods into simple molecules for absorption and use.
- **Excretion**: Removal from the body of digestive and metabolic waste products.

Major Body Systems

The **nervous system** includes the brain, nerves, and spinal cord. It interprets sensory input, enables thought and emotion, and sends messages to the rest of the body. The **circulatory system** includes the heart and blood vessels. It delivers blood to and from the lungs and the rest of the body to supply oxygen and remove carbon dioxide. The **respiratory system** includes the lungs, bronchi, diaphragm, trachea, larynx, and pharynx. It enables us to breathe. The **skeletal system** includes the bones, cartilage, tendons, and ligaments. It protects the organs, structurally supports the body, and collaborates with the muscles in body movement. The **digestive system** includes the salivary glands, esophagus, stomach, intestines, liver, gall bladder, pancreas, rectum, and anus. It breaks down and processes food we eat; extracts nutrients to build tissues and supply energy; stores fats, amino acids, etc. for future use; and eliminates waste products. The **lymphatic system** includes the lymph nodes and vessels. It produces white blood cells for the immune system and transports lymph between the tissues and the bloodstream.

Major Body Systems Identification

The **immune system** includes the white blood cells (leukocytes), tonsils, adenoids, thymus, and spleen. It protects the body against organisms and other agents that cause diseases and infections. The **muscular system** includes all of the many muscles in the body. It enables the body to move with support and cooperation from the skeletal system (bones). In addition to the head, neck, chest, back, arm, hand, leg, and foot muscles, the heart is also a muscle, which pumps blood to and from the lungs and the rest of the body to supply oxygen and remove carbon dioxide. The **integumentary system** includes the skin, nails, and hair. The skin protects the tissues from injury and fluid loss, provides sensation, and synthesizes vitamin D. The nails protect the fingertips and toes. The hair protects the skin, particularly on the scalp. The **reproductive system** includes the ovaries, fallopian tubes, uterus, vagina, and mammary glands in females; and testes, vas deferens, seminal vesicles, prostate, and penis in males. It enables reproduction via the conception, gestation, and delivery of babies. The **endocrine system** includes the hypothalamus; pituitary, pineal, thyroid, parathyroid, and adrenal glands; and pancreas. It secretes hormones regulating various body functions.

Food Calorie

A **food calorie**, also called a dietary calorie, nutritional calorie, kilogram calorie, or large calorie, equals the approximate amount of energy required to increase the temperature of one kilogram of water by one degree Celsius. (Another calorie term, the gram calorie or small calorie, refers to the approximate amount of energy required to increase the temperature of one gram of water by one degree Celsius. The food calorie/large calorie/kilogram calorie equals 1,000 small calories, or one kilocalorie [Kcal].) Because energy produces heat, we describe "burning" calories. Foods have calories, i.e., potential energy. When we digest food, build and repair body cells, engage in physical activity, and use our brains, we expend energy, or "burn" calories. When people or animals ingest more calories than they expend, surplus calories not used get stored as **body fat**. Hence overeating results in extra fatty tissue and weight gain. When one expends more calories than one eats, initially the body burns fat for fuel, resulting in **weight loss**. When no extra fat exists, the body metabolizes muscle for protein and energy, causing muscle wasting. Additional energy expense without sufficient food causes weight loss, emaciation, and ultimately starvation.

Movement During Physical Activity

The **skeletal system** gives our bodies their structural framework. The bones interact with the muscles to allow our body parts to move when the muscles contract. The skull is a bone that protects the brain, which regulates all body functions including movement. The vertebrae protect the spinal cord in general, including during movement. The joints where bones meet contain sensory receptors that send information about the body's position to the brain. The brain controls the contractions of the muscles to regulate the positions of the bones. The brain interacts with the cardiovascular system to regulate the heart rate and blood pressure, increasing these during physical activity. Baroreceptors in the cardiovascular system send the brain blood pressure information. Receptors in the muscles send the brain body position and movement information. The brain interacts with the **respiratory system**, controlling breathing rates and monitoring respiratory volume and blood gas levels. The respiratory system provides oxygen to and removes carbon dioxide from blood during breathing, whose rate increases during exercise. The integumentary system's skin receptors send temperature and other sensation information to the brain. The **autonomic nervous system** controls sweat gland secretions and peripheral blood flow during exercise.

Energy for Muscular Contraction

Adenosine triphosphate (ATP) is a molecule with an adenosine nucleotide attached to three phosphate groups, providing energy for muscular contractions, converted via cellular respiration from food energy. Its energy store is released for muscles to access when the bond is broken between its second and third phosphate groups. When this bond is broken, the third phosphate group is released by itself, reducing the ATP molecule to **adenosine diphosphate (ADP)** with two phosphate groups. Replacing the third phosphate group, i.e., rephosphorylization, restores ADP into ATP again. The process of cellular respiration that converts food energy to ATP depends largely upon how much oxygen is available. Exercise intensity and duration affect the amounts of oxygen the muscle cells demand and the oxygen supply available to them. Depending on the amount of oxygen available, any one of three exercise energy systems can be accessed selectively: the alactic anaerobic energy system, the lactic anaerobic energy system, or the aerobic energy system.

Energy to Muscles: When and How

Short-term (10 seconds or less), high-intensity, explosive exercise recruits the **alactic (not producing lactic acid) anaerobic (not using oxygen) energy system**, e.g., a 100-meter sprint or one weightlifting set. Also called the **ATP-PCr (adenosine triphosphate-phosphocreatine) or phosphagen energy system**, this is the first accessed for exercise. It uses ATP stored in muscles and then rephosphorylizes the resulting ADP via phosphocreatine. It stops supplying energy when PCr is depleted until muscles have rested and regenerated PCr. High-intensity exercise for up to 90 seconds, e.g., one ice hockey shift or an 800 meter sprint, uses the lactic anaerobic energy system. It functions when the alactic anaerobic system is depleted and the aerobic system cannot handle the exercise intensity's demands. It produces lactic acid

- 42 -

as a byproduct in the muscles but does not use oxygen. It directly accesses cellular respiration to convert food energy to supply ATP. Continuous/long-term (beyond 2-5 minutes), lower-intensity aerobic exercise, e.g., running marathons, accesses the aerobic energy system, which depends upon how efficiently oxygen can be sent to and processed by the muscles. It also recruits cellular respiration to get ATP from food energy; however, oxygen is available to the muscles, so no lactic acid is produced.

Principle of Specificity

The **principle of specificity** in exercise science means one must exercise the specific body part, muscle(s), or sport movements and techniques that one wants to improve. To strengthen the upper body, one must do exercises targeting the upper body, and the same for the lower body; one will not help the other. Someone who wants to play football must practice the skills specific to this sport; general body conditioning, while it might be a prerequisite, will not improve specific football skills. While core and cardio workouts are necessary to conditioning for improving overall endurance and strength, and the principle of specificity dictates that attaining one's specific goals requires tailoring one's exercise regimen, neither one of these cancels out the other. The principle of adaptation means the body adapts to exercise, so that with regular practice, certain activities become easier. To continue improving, one must vary one's workouts with different training and/or routines. The body adjusts to demands made of it. **Adaptation** also means the body adapts to the processes of executing specific tasks.

Principles of Overload and Individual Differences

The **principle of overload** means the body only responds beyond its normal level if new stimuli or additional pressures are introduced. Stopping within comfort zones maintains current skill levels, but brings no improvement. This is true for gaining strength, improving athletic ability, or losing weight. To increase what muscles can do, we must require them to function in unaccustomed ways. This is one reason exercise science professionals are helpful: they can push and motivate clients to work past their comfort zones. The principle of individual differences means not everybody will attain the same results from the same training programs and levels. Every individual has different body chemistry: some must work harder than others for the same results. Another aspect of this principle is that some people are more predisposed to succeed in certain sports or workouts than others, who in turn are more predisposed to other activities. The **principle of individual differences** indicates the importance of personal training: individuals must tailor their exercise programs for meeting goals at their own paces. Even individuals with stronger talents or skills in a certain activity or sport need to practice it to enable their bodies to adapt.

Principles of Progression and Exercise Science

The **progression principle** means, one must progress at a certain, individual rate to get results. While people must push past their comfort zones to improve, pressing oneself overly hard negates natural progression and can cause injury. An appropriate exercise routine is a science. While there is no "one-size-fits-all" formula, there is a formula determining how one should push oneself. The principles of progression and **overload** balance delicately: progression indicates specific times of being unready for overload, or benefiting from it. The **principle of use/disuse** means one must use muscles to sustain muscular strength—the proverbial "use it or lose it." When we do not practice a sport we want to improve in or use muscles we want to develop, we lose our skills and strength. Anytime we stop exercising or exercise less and notice we are no longer seeing results, this is evidence of the use/disuse principle. With disuse, muscles lose definition; the body compensates for the lack of practice. This is also called the **reversibility principle.** At times disuse can be valuable: muscle overuse requires healing. Otherwise, moderately high year-round fitness levels are better than seasonal detraining or retraining.

- 43 -

Physical Training and Health

Motivation to follow and continue physical fitness routines can be supported by both the **short-term** and **long-term effects of exercise** on the body, including the brain. For example, training energetically accesses the body's glycogen stores to supply energy. Glycogen depletion then triggers the release of endorphins, hormones that bring feelings of well-being and euphoria (the word endorphin comes from Greek root words meaning "morphine within") in the short term. Additionally, in the long term, exercising regularly can both prevent and relieve depression. Some research studies comparing exercise to antidepressant medications have found exercise equally effective. In addition to the brain, exercise improves cardiovascular health. Physical activity requires the heart rate to increase to deliver oxygenated blood to the muscles. People new to exercising may initially feel dizzy and winded. However, in the short term, exercise increases blood circulation. In the longer term, exercising for a few months can lower one's blood pressure and pulse. Exercising regularly significantly predicts heart health. People who perform cardiovascular (aerobic) exercise consistently lower their long-term risks of heart attacks, strokes, and other cardiovascular disorders.

Individual Differences on Learning

Research has shown that **situational interest** can help motivate students to become engaged in the process of learning. Studies find that teachers can change and arrange task presentation, the structuring of learning experiences, and instructional strategies to enhance student situational interest. Although most research into motivation in physical education is related to theories of achievement goals, these reportedly are not very predictive of motivation or performance. However, researchers find **student interest** to have greater influence on student learning behavior, as well as on student intentions for future participation. Despite educator recognition of the importance of interest to learning, researchers find teachers still lack clarity in understanding the roles they can play in helping to stimulate and develop students' interest. When individuals interact with the environment, two kinds of interest emerge: situational and individual. Both kinds have two phases. Situational interest has a phase when interest is **activated**, and an ensuing phase when interest is **sustained**. Individual interest has a phase when interest emerges, and an ensuing phase when interest is defined.

Performance in Physical Education Activities

One element of individual differences is **age**. Some activities are not appropriate for students who have not attained physical maturity. Students also need to understand what their bodies can and cannot do as they pass through different developmental stages and periods. Students of very different ages should not be expected to compete against one another. Age affects strength, aerobic capacity, reaction time, flexibility, and experience. Humans do not attain full strength until about age 20. Humans are most flexible in their teens. Experience, which increases with age, is a crucial element in sports. Another individual difference is **somatotype**, i.e., body shape. This informs appropriate sport choices. There are three basic somatotypes.

- **Ectomorph**: a long, narrow, thin shape with minimal muscle or fat. Good sports for ectomorphs include long-distance running and the high jump.
- **Endomorph**: fat, and often pear-shaped, with narrow shoulders and wide hips, with small ankles and wrists but more fat on the torso, arms, and legs. Good sports for endomorphs include shot-putting and wrestling.
- **Mesomorph**: muscular, often wedge-shaped, with wide shoulders and narrow hips, strong limbs, and little body fat. Good sports for mesomorphs include gymnastics and swimming.

Physical Education Performance

Individual differences include biological, physiological, and environmental factors affecting performance. For example, muscular tissue composition will influence individual strength, flexibility, and endurance. Individual deficits in rod and cone development in the eyes would inhibit perceptual-motor ability, which could alter reaction times. Children participating more in formal schooling will develop their verbal and reasoning skills further, while children participating more in physical education and/or sports will develop their motor skills further. Development rates across and within individuals vary by maturation and growth differences. **Perceptual-motor abilities** affecting individual skill performance include: control precision, e.g., hockey-puck handling; rate control, like racecar driving; aiming, e.g., texting; response orientation and choice reaction time, e.g., football quarterbacking; reaction time, e.g., sprinting; manual dexterity, e.g., basketball-dribbling; finger dexterity, e.g., typing; arm-hand steadiness, e.g., performing surgery; and wrist and finger speed, e.g., speed-stacking. Physical proficiencies affecting performance include: explosive strength, e.g., standing long jumps; static strength, e.g., weight-lifting; trunk strength, e.g., pole-vaulting; extent flexibility, e.g., yoga; dynamic flexibility, e.g., squat-thrusts; limb movement speed, e.g., javelin-throwing; static balance; dynamic balance, e.g., gymnastics; object-balancing; multi-limb coordination, e.g., stick-shift driving; gross body coordination, e.g., hurdling; stamina, e.g., marathons; and dynamic strength, e.g.

Positive Effective Physical Education

In the **psychomotor domain**, effective PE enhances student movement skills for participating in sports and other physical activities, and for being a spectator as well. It affords skills for applying cultural and intellectual pursuits to use leisure time, and skills for preserving the natural environment. In the **cognitive domain**, effective PE supports higher-order thinking processes through motor activity, enhances academic performance, provides understanding of the human body and knowledge of health and illness and of exercise, enhances understanding of the roles of sports and physical activity in American culture, and supports knowledgeable consumerism with goods and services. In the **affective domain**, effective PE supports a healthy response to physical activity. It adds to student aesthetic appreciation of beauty. It contributes to student self-esteem and facilitates self-actualization. It helps students direct their lives for setting worthwhile goals. PE reinforces humanistic values. It enables students to use the medium of play for enjoying rich social experiences. PE also informs cooperative play and social interactions. It teaches students fair play, good sportsmanship, and courtesy. Moreover, it supports humanitarian ideals and behaviors.

Risks Associated with Physical Inactivity

According to Johns Hopkins medical experts, research has definitively proven that a **lack of physical activity** is a risk factor for cardiovascular disease and other health conditions. People who are less physically fit and less physically active are at higher risk of developing hypertension (high blood pressure). Research shows that even after eliminating the factors of smoking tobacco, drinking alcohol, and eating an unhealthy diet, people who are physically active are still less likely to develop coronary heart disease than people who are physically inactive. Moreover, depression and anxiety can be caused or exacerbated by lack of physical activity. Additionally, scientists think physical inactivity may raise risks for certain cancers. Studies have found obese or overweight people decreased their risks of disease significantly through physical activity. Scientists say lack of physical activity causes many thousands of deaths annually. People tend to become less active as they age. Women are more likely to live sedentary lifestyles than men. White, non-Hispanic adults are more likely to be physically active than Hispanic and black, non-Hispanic adults.

Health Benefits and Disease

[**Obesity** and **type 2 diabetes** are two common results of physical inactivity.] While obesity contributes greatly to type 2 diabetes, there are also individuals who are not even overweight, but due to their being physically sedentary, combined with poor nutritional habits and other behaviors like smoking tobacco and drinking alcohol, and interacting with genetic predispositions—some of which are much more prevalent within certain racial/ethnic populations—have developed type 2 diabetes as well. Current research studies that find sitting for most of one's waking hours is as harmful to health as habits like smoking. Even when exercising an hour each day, sitting for the rest of the day still has significant negative health impacts. People who drink, smoke, never exercise, spend most of their time sitting, and experience high levels of emotional and/or psychological stress are at much higher risks for hypertension, heart attacks, strokes, type 2 diabetes, some cancers, mental and emotional disorders, poorer quality of life, and earlier mortality. Physical activity can aid weight control, lower risks for heart disease and some cancers, strengthen the muscles and bones, and enhance mental health. While physically active people are not immune to disease, they lower their risks for many illnesses.

Injury Prevention and Cause

Research studies show that up to one half of all hip fractures could be prevented by engaging regularly in enough **moderate physical activity**. Physical activity that bears weight strengthens the bones and prevents them from becoming porous, brittle, and more prone to breaking. Another consideration is that regular physical activity improves coordination, balance, and flexibility. Better coordination, balance, and flexibility can lower a person's likelihood of falling during everyday life activities as well as during sports and recreational physical activities. Stronger bones can prevent fractures in the event of a fall, while improved coordination, balance, and flexibility can avert many falls in the first place. Studies have also proven that people who are physically inactive in general sustain more accidents and injuries than people who are physically active. Children who are physically inactive risk higher stress, anxiety, and lower self-esteem and are likelier to smoke and take drugs. Sedentary workers are absent from work more than active ones.

Healthy Lifestyle

Because most American students today do not receive PE at the frequencies or durations recommended for optimal health, they must engage in **physical activity** outside of PE classes and outside of school. To constitute physical activity, brisk walking or other pursuits must use energy by moving the body at a level of intensity sufficient to raise one's body temperature to feel warmer, and to cause one to breathe somewhat deeper than normally. Some students who live close enough can walk to and from school daily. They can play intramural and outdoor sports at school. Outside school, they can vacuum the house, wash the car, cut the grass, do gardening, clean up their rooms, and help their parents with other housework. These combine the benefits of contributing to smooth household and family functions with being more physically active for better health. Students can ride bicycles, go swimming, dance, and take weekend nature walks as more physically active forms of recreation than playing video games or watching TV. Experts recommend that children and teens build up to at least an hour of moderate physical activity most days of the week, while adults should aim for at least a half-hour most days.

Health-Related Physical Fitness

There are five major **components of physical fitness** that are directly related to health:

- **Cardiorespiratory endurance**. This is the ability of the circulatory system, i.e., the heart and blood vessels; and the respiratory system, i.e., the lungs, trachea, bronchi, pharynx, larynx, and diaphragm, to supply the muscles and the rest of the body with oxygen during continuing physical activity over time.
- **Muscular strength**. This is the greatest amount of force that any given muscle can generate during a single attempt.
- **Muscular endurance**. This is how long a given muscle is able to continue to perform an exercise or activity without becoming fatigued, i.e., becoming unable to perform the movement anymore.
- **Flexibility**. This is the ability to move the joints of the body through the full range of motion, e.g., when bending, turning, twisting, stretching, reaching, contracting, extending, etc.
- **Healthy body composition**. This refers to the ratio of lean muscle tissue to fatty tissue in the body. The amount of muscle should be greater in proportion to the amount of fat, though there should be at least enough fat to enable normal body functions.

Kinds of Physical Fitness Training

Weight training, aka strength/resistance training, can use measured weights; exercise bands, exercise balls or other resistance gear; or one's own body weight. By exercising the musculoskeletal system, resistance training improves neurological control of muscle functions and enlarges muscle fibers. This promotes both muscular strength and muscular endurance—strength by increasing the maximum force a muscle contraction can produce, and endurance by increasing the maximum amount of weight one can lift repeatedly and/or the maximum number of repetitions one can lift the same weight. **Cardiorespiratory endurance** is not simply aerobic training, as it requires overload, accessing both aerobic and anaerobic energy systems through circuit/interval/other training. **Stage training**, e.g., a three-stage model, involves:

- Developing baseline aerobic fitness at 65-75 percent of maximum heart rate, gradually increasing intensity and duration up to 30 minutes two or three times a week.
- Raising intensity to 65-85 percent of maximum heart rate/14-16 RPE or, in other words, raising the level of intensity from "challenging" to "difficult." Work-to-rest ratios progress from 1:3 to 1:2, then 1:1, gradually increasing interval durations.
- Short, high-intensity exercises (like sprinting) alternating with active recovery (like jogging), at 65-95 percent of maximum heart rate/17-19 RPE, or boosting the intensity from "difficult" to "impossible." Transitioning from stage (2) to (3) can take 2-3 months or more.

Developing Flexibility

Flexibility not only improves muscular and aerobic training and sports performance and prevents athletic injuries, but also facilitates everyday life activities and prevents age-related mobility loss. **Flexibility training** releases muscle tension that builds up during workouts and reduces stress in working muscles; balances joint tension, improving posture; and makes muscles more pliable, decreasing injury risk. **Stretching exercises** should follow each workout, four to seven days weekly. Intensity should create slight muscular tension without causing pain. Instructors should remind learners to continue their breathing patterns throughout stretches. Duration varies according to individual motivation and needs, but generally should be at least 5 to 10 minutes per session. Instructors should design organized workouts to include stretching, as learners most frequently cut this short when pressed for time. **Static stretching**, done seated, is easy, safe, and (once learned) doable virtually anywhere without equipment or assistance; but limited in efficacy for competitive athletes or increasing flexibility in multiple ranges of motion (ROMs). **Dynamic stretching**, done standing, uses reciprocal inhibition of opposing muscles to develop active ROM, gradually increasing in intensity and speed. Best for athletes and as warm-ups for movement-based sports and activities, it should be taught and learned gradually with appropriate movements to prevent trauma from excessive ROM or speed.

National PE and Sports Organization's Definitions.

The National Association for Sport and Physical Education (NASPE)'s Council on Physical Education for Children (COPEC) identifies **quality PE** as both developmentally and instructionally appropriate for the actual children involved. This council defines developmentally appropriate PE practices as acknowledging the changing abilities of children for moving, and as promoting those changes. **Developmentally appropriate PE programs** are defined as addressing developmental status, body size, age, fitness levels, previous experiences with movement, and other various individual student characteristics. NASPE's COPEC defines **instructionally appropriate education** as including both research-based and experience-based best known practices in programs that give all children maximal opportunities to learn and succeed. The council identifies the result of a PE program that is both developmentally and instructionally appropriate as a "physically educated" individual. NASPE (1990) defined a physically educated individual as someone who has learned the necessary skills for performing varied physical activities, participates regularly in physical activity, is physically fit, knows the benefits and implications of engaging in physical activities, and values physical activity and what it contributes to healthy lifestyles. NASPE deems appropriate PE programs significant first steps in becoming physically educated.

Appropriate Vs. Inappropriate Practices

Appropriate PE curriculum enhances all students' physical, motor, cognitive, and affective fitness by balancing concepts, skills, games, educational gymnastics, and rhythm and dance experiences with an observable sequence and scope determined by goals and objectives appropriate for all students. **Inappropriate curriculum** is based on teacher backgrounds, preferences, and interests, e.g., mainly playing large-group or whole-class games without developed learning goals and objectives. Practices inappropriate for developing motor skills and movement concepts limit the number of activities, games, and opportunities for developing basic motor skills and concepts. Appropriate practices frequently offer students meaningful, age-appropriate opportunities to practice locomotor, non-locomotor, and manipulative motor skills, developing confidence in their ability to perform these. Students also develop functional comprehension of body awareness, spatial awareness, effort, relationships, and other movement concepts. Practices inappropriate for promoting cognitive development through PE do not give students opportunities to integrate PE with classroom, art, music, and other school experiences; and do not enable students' learning to move while moving to learn. Appropriate practices design PE activities considering both physical and cognitive development by enabling students to analyze, communicate, question, integrate, apply concepts, and attain multicultural worldviews, thereby integrating PE into the whole educational experience.

Inappropriate Vs. Appropriate Practices

PE practices **inappropriate for promoting affective development** include teacher exclusion of activities that help students develop social skills, and overlooking opportunities to help children understand emotions they experience from PE participation. **Appropriate practices fostering affective development** include purposely designing and implementing activities through the school year, enabling students to collaborate, cooperate, and develop emerging social skills and positive self-concepts; and helping every student feel and appreciate joy and satisfaction from participating regularly in physical activity. Inappropriate approaches to fitness concepts include requiring participation in fitness activities

- 48 -

without helping students understand why. Appropriate approaches include designing activities that aid students in understanding and valuing significant physical fitness concepts and how these contribute to healthy lifestyles. Inappropriate uses of physical fitness tests include testing twice yearly, only as required by states/districts, or to qualify students for awards; requiring testing without students understanding why or what their results imply; and/or requiring testing without sufficient conditioning or preparation. Appropriate practices include conducting ongoing fitness assessment to help students understand, maintain (or improve), and enjoy physical well-being; sharing results privately with students and parents to develop knowledge, competence, and understanding; and preparing students for tests as part of ongoing PE programs.

Principles of Cardiorespiratory Endurance

PE teachers should explain to students that **cardiorespiratory fitness** is considered the most important component of physical fitness because it indicates effective functioning of their hearts, lungs, and blood vessels. They can tell them the heart is a pump with two sides: the right side supplies blood to the lungs, the left sends blood to different body systems. The vascular system provides body tissues with blood, which carries oxygen and carbon dioxide through the bloodstream. Cardiorespiratory fitness lowers risk of cardiovascular disease—America's foremost cause of death. It also reduces body fat and raises energy. PE teachers should encourage students to do all they can to avoid dying from **cardiovascular disease**, particularly if their families have histories of heart disease and/or diabetes. Cardiovascular disease screening measures total cholesterol, LDL, HDL, and triglycerides, which directly affect heart disease risk. Teachers should have students exercise aerobically, continuously using large muscles, to improve cardiorespiratory fitness, three to five days per week, at 60-85 percent of maximum heart rate, for 20-60 minutes continuously. Good exercises include walking, jogging, cycling, swimming, rowing, in-line skating, spinning, step aerobics, and dancing aerobically to music sustained at the necessary intensity.

Fitness Testing and Cardiorespiratory Endurance

According to the National Association for Sport and Physical Education (NASPE, 2010) position statement, PE programs not only develop student physical skills and cognitive understanding about physical activity to inform physically active, healthy lifestyles, they also teach students the significance of **health-related fitness**. NASPE states that, for students to achieve these goals, they must acquire knowledge about health-related fitness components, and a required part of that learning process is the assessment of those components. A philosophy of fitness testing includes that **purposeful measurement** is a necessary part of quality PE, and fitness education is a component of the PE curriculum conforming to exercise physiology standards. Additionally, **assessment** and **measurement** should be integrated with instruction. Moreover, educators should develop plans for applying individual student fitness data to inform their instruction. **Cardiorespiratory endurance** can be tested in elementary schools using a mile or half-mile run, e.g., the PACER (Progressive Aerobic Cardiovascular Endurance Run) Test. Measurements are number of PACER laps run, and time in minutes taken to complete a mile. Some schools require assessment twice yearly (beginning and end), but require instruction and practice throughout the school year. Baseline and subsequent data enable monitoring student progress.

Cardiorespiratory Endurance Safety

When exercising to develop greater **cardiorespiratory endurance**, students need not engage in strenuous activity. Teachers should start them slowly doing activities they enjoy, and supervise them in gradually increasing the intensity of their pace. Activities to improve cardiorespiratory endurance should elevate the heart rate for an extended duration of time, but at a safe level. These include activities like walking, bicycling, or swimming. PE experts say it is impossible to overemphasize the importance of drinking water before, during, and after exercising. Sweating during exercise depletes the body of fluid and electrolytes, which can disrupt heart rhythms, so hydration and rehydration are paramount. It is also important to pay attention to the heat index—i.e., the effect that higher humidity has of raising the actual temperature to a functionally higher heat—when exercising outdoors, and modify workouts accordingly. Not only does humidity make temperatures effectively higher, it also prevents perspiration from evaporating, which keeps bodies from cooling off efficiently and can result in overheating, heat exhaustion, and heat prostration. Clothing unsuited to the weather can also cause serious health problems.

Benefits of Flexibility Training

Flexibility is the ability to move the body freely. It encompasses two parts: **range of motion (ROM)**, which is the extent of direction and distance that one's joints are able to move; and **mobility**, which is the ability of the muscles to move with restrictions around the joints. By pursuing flexibility training, one realizes benefits including increasing one's range of motion; decreasing one's risks for becoming injured during physical activities by making muscles more pliable, less stiff, and less prone to pulls, tears, ruptures, sprains, etc.; decreasing the soreness of muscles following exercise by keeping muscles more relaxed and looser; and enhancing overall athletic performance by using less energy for body movement through having more flexible muscles and joints. Flexibility not only improves sport performance, it also facilitates activities of daily living like lifting objects or children, squatting down, reaching high shelves, getting out of bed, and turning fully to see behind oneself when backing up or parking a car.

Stretching Exercises

Stretching is an equally important part of fitness as strength and aerobic capacity, although some people often overlook it in training programs. Stretching before and after performing other conditioning exercises promotes flexibility and prevents stiffness, soreness, and even injuries. Before stretching, one should always warm-up. Injuries are more likely from stretching cold muscles. One should stretch the whole body, not just selected parts. Each stretch should be held for 15 to 30 seconds or more, but should *not* include bouncing, which can cause injuries. One should stretch until one feels some mild tension in the muscle or the joint, but not actual pain. Pain is a signal to stop whatever one is doing. When resuming, do not stretch as far, as hard, or as quickly; or stretch in a different manner or direction. While stretching, one should never hold one's breath, but should always continue to breathe normally.

Different Basic Full-Body Stretches

Arms above head, palms up, stretch arms upward: stretches forearms, front upper arms, chest, and upper side muscles. Arms behind back, hands turned inward, stretch arms backward: stretches chest, shoulder, upper arms. Raise arm, bend elbow, place hand on the back. With other arm, grasp opposing elbow, pull upward toward opposite side: stretches outer upper arm, side, and back on raised-arm side. Arms outspread at sides below shoulders, move arms inward, stretching chest, shoulder, front and back arms. Sit with one leg straight, one knee bent upward, lower leg across straightened leg, foot on floor. Turn upper body away from crossed leg, placing hands on floor to side: stretches ribcage, leg, and outer hip. Sit with knees bent outward, as low to floor as possible, feet together, clasping feet with hands: stretches hips, inner thighs. Sit, legs together straight in front, feet flexed. Lean forward, stretching hamstrings. Stand, one hand touching surface; bend opposite knee behind; pull ankle up with same-side hand, stretching quadriceps. Bend from hips/waist; touch toes, stretching backs of legs, lower back. Hands on wall, one foot back, step forward with opposite foot: stretches back lower leg. Perform all one-sided stretches on each side.

Muscular Strength and Endurance

Muscular strength equals how much force one can produce within one effort. **Muscular endurance** equals how many times one can repeat a movement before muscles become too fatigued to work. As examples, the amount of weight an individual can bench-press signifies that person's muscular strength; the number of times that individual can bench-press that weight repeatedly before fatiguing indicates that person's muscular endurance. The two are not necessarily equal in the same person. Some people can lift enormous amounts of weight, but only a few times, showing high muscular strength but low muscular endurance. Some people can lift a lesser amount of weight, but can repeat it many times, meaning lower muscular strength and higher muscular endurance. Others are high or low in both muscular strength and endurance. People can develop both muscular strength and muscular endurance through strength training, e.g., lifting weights or using resistance, by both executing many repetitions of the same action, gradually increasing the number of repetitions; and also gradually increasing the amount of weight or resistance used. One may build muscular strength and endurance in all muscle groups of the body, or concentrate on specific muscles or muscle groups.

Upper-Body Muscular Strength and Endurance

In lifting weights, one can work each arm **individually** using dumbbells, or both arms **together** using barbells. One thing to remember is that training each arm individually can result in slightly different levels of muscular strength and endurance in each arm. To begin workouts for the arms, use a general strength-training routine. Starting with weights of 20 pounds or lower, lift them 12 times; 12 repetitions (reps) equal one set. Do two or three sets of 12 repetitions each. As this becomes easier, start to lift heavier weights in small increments. Also gradually increase the number of sets performed. Increasing the weight builds muscular strength. Increasing the sets builds muscular endurance. One excellent exercise to increase upper-body muscular strength and endurance is doing push-ups. These build the pectoral muscles in the chest, the triceps muscles at the backs of the upper arms, and the deltoid muscles at the fronts of the shoulders. Even a few push-ups can be difficult for people lacking upper-body strength. Perform 10 repetitions, beginning with only one or two sets. Increase by two repetitions per week. Building upper-body strength enables more forceful arm extensions for bench-pressing, swimming, throwing, and more push-ups.

Lower-Body Muscular Strength and Endurance

Among the best **lower-body and leg exercises** are squats and lunges. These increase strength and endurance in the gluteus maximus, gluteus medius, gluteus minimus, and tensor fasciae latae muscles of the buttocks; the hamstrings along the backs of the legs; the quadriceps at the fronts of the thighs; and the gastrocnemius and soleus muscles in the calves. Strengthening these muscles improves running speed, power, distance, and stamina. A variation of squatting and lunging is to perform these holding dumbbells in both hands to increase weight resistance. To build muscular strength and endurance in the buttocks and legs, do three to five sets of 10 squats and/or lunges per set every other day. Some trainers recommend engaging in boxing and martial arts as sports that require high intensity and increase muscular strength and endurance. Striking opponents or punching bags with force requires muscular strength; going through 12 rounds in a boxing match requires endurance. While martial arts can involve the hands, arms, legs, and weapons, these sports also require strength and endurance to win. Learning both boxing and martial arts involves combinations of various cardiovascular, strength-training, and mental conditioning activities.

Body Composition

Body composition is basically the ratio of fatty tissue to non-fatty tissue, especially lean muscle tissue, in the body. For people who are overweight, improving their body composition entails both decreasing their total proportion of **body fat** and increasing their total proportion of **lean muscle tissue**. For people who are underweight, it can include both gaining some body fat and also more muscle tissue. For people with normal weights and without excess fatty tissue but lacking muscular development, it involves increasing the proportion of lean muscular tissue in the body. While isolation exercises work only one joint at a time, **compound exercises** use movements that require articulations of multiple joints at a time. Compound exercises are best for improving body composition. Compound pushing exercises improve upper-body composition through resistance movements of the arms and shoulders. Those using horizontally loaded resistance include push-ups and weighted flat, incline and decline bench-presses, which work the pectorals, triceps, serratus, and lateral deltoid muscles. Exercises using vertically loaded resistance include the shoulder press and military press, which work the anterior deltoid, upper pectoral, and trapezius muscles.

Aerobic Exercise

While strength training increases muscle and decreases fat, **aerobic training** is also effective for decreasing body fat. **Visceral fat**, surrounding the vital organs and concentrated in the abdomen, is more of a threat to health than subcutaneous fat, found elsewhere just below the skin. Recent research finds that high-intensity exercise reduces more visceral fat than moderate-intensity exercise. The "HIIT" method stands for "high-intensity interval training." **High-intensity interval training** involves exercising at high intensity and also to develop endurance. It can include running, sprinting, climbing stairs, running up and down stadium steps, or any other aerobic exercise performed at intensity levels of seven out of 10 or above. An example of high-intensity interval training would be running on a track, road, path, or treadmill at 70-95 percent of maximum capacity for 30 seconds to 5 minutes; resting for a duration equal to or greater than the exercise duration; and repeating the interval, for a total of approximately 22 minutes, at least three days of the week.

Safety Practices to Observe

Before beginning any kind of exercise program, one should discuss it with a doctor or **healthcare provider(s)** to ensure types and amounts of exercise are safe for one's individual health, and learn whether s/he advises avoiding any particular activities because of specific health conditions (e.g., heart conditions) and/or previous injuries (e.g., not using arm poles while walking on a treadmill following a recent shoulder or upper-back injury). Then one should also have a consultation with a **personal trainer** who can assess body composition and develop an individualized training program targeting types of conditioning most needed and body parts needing contouring and what kinds, e.g., building muscle, increasing definition, reducing fat, changing shape, etc. Everybody should always warm-up for at least 10-15 minutes first. After warming up properly, they should then perform stretches with all muscle groups and joints to increase flexibility and lower risks for injuries. People should not eat large meals immediately before exercising, but they should eat a small meal 2-3 hours before, or a snack 30-60 minutes before. Drinking water before, during, and after working out is imperative.

- 52 -

Muscular Endurance

- The **continuous tension** form of muscular endurance makes demands on the muscles to be under continuing tension for extended durations of time. Some continuous tension activities appropriate for middle school students include tug-of-war, isometric muscle contractions, extremely slow muscle contractions, isolation exercises, compound exercises without lockouts, beginning weight training, and supervised mountain climbing or wall climbing.
- The **repetitive dynamic contraction** form of muscular endurance requires repeated muscle contractions over time periods. Some middle-school activities include running, bicycling, swimming, rowing, skating, and weight training involving many repetitions and/or supersets using the same muscle.
- The **prolonged, intense contractions with short rest periods** form of muscular endurance involves contractions for longer durations with brief recovery periods between bouts. Some activities include playing football; handball; ice hockey; and weight training that involves circuit training (going from one exercise or machine to another in a circuit), performing multiple sets of repetitions, and/or performing multiple different exercises to work the same muscle.

4-9 Gymnasium or Outdoor Activities

Body core strength provides a foundation for all sports and physical activities. Here are some gym/outdoor activities with core-strengthening exercises for grades 4-6 and 7-9. Equipment includes one basketball, volleyball, soccer ball, or medicine ball per student; jump ropes; folding mats; ribbon sticks, scarves, pom-poms; exercise bands; and masking tape. Have students warm-up first and then choose partners and balls. Teachers review exercises for core strength and stability. Considering any student physical limitations or injuries, teachers offer variations and/or have students suggest variations. Exercises include abdominal crunches with feet on floor, feet raised 90 degrees, and elbow-to-opposite-knee; V-sits (legs and torso form a V); twisting V-sits; same-sided hand-to-heel touch sit-ups; bicycles; hip raises; dolphin kicks; side planks; alternating leg-lowering from 90 degrees; and "superhumans" lying prone, raising opposite arm and leg alternately. Partners alternate: one performs, one gives feedback. Students may roll dice to decide repetition numbers, or repeat to muscle fatigue. Individual students record activities and repetitions they completed. Use these for future reference to monitor progress. Ribbon sticks, scarves, pom-poms and exercise bands can help some students extend their movements. Teachers encourage students to practice their favorite activities every 15 minutes for 30 seconds while watching TV, doing homework, or using computers.

K-6 Gymnasium Activity

This **creative dance activity** for grades K-3 and 4-6 builds endurance and develops spatial awareness and concepts. Equipment needed includes audio player, recorded music, and pathway signs. Teachers review space concepts of direction and pathways, e.g., combining locomotor movements with directions. Teachers call out forward, backward, and sideways directions for students to take while moving around the gym; then combine a locomotor pattern and direction, e.g., walking backward, skipping sideways, galloping forward, etc. Teachers draw these patterns on pathway signs and post on the walls. Teachers point at pathway pictures and have students move using these, first using two body parts and then three, for example, straight, zigzag, small curves, larger curves; small spirals, larger spirals. Teachers lead students around the gym in a large spiral pathway. Have students move in pairs to pathways they choose; have some pairs demonstrate. Have students combine three or more pathways and directions to create "movement stories." Remind them to notice others' movements, shoulder-check while moving backward, and avoid collisions. Have some students demonstrate stories and others identify directions and pathways included. Use music with strong beats during story creation and presentation. For more

- 53 -

complexity, have students add shapes (square, rectangular, circular, triangular, figure-eight, or favorite letter, for instance) into stories.

Improving Overall Physical Fitness

When students who have been inactive want to lose weight and/or become more physically fit, their initial enthusiasm assures their motivation to pursue these goals; however, they must be counseled to **moderate** their eagerness to obtain results quickly or they will strain their muscles or overwork their entire bodies. Particularly when they are not already conditioned, they must be warned not to begin at high intensity or repeat initial workouts obsessively. These practices cause injuries, derailing fitness efforts early. Students should be taught to begin **slowly**, paying attention to their bodies' feedback; when they feel ready, they can increase their intensities, speeds, repetitions, and durations gradually, a little at a time. **Incorrect form** is also a hazard for inexperienced exercisers. They should begin working out in front of mirrors to observe and modify their body positions as needed. Teachers and trainers can help correct form. Students should determine they are using proper form before increasing the speed of their repetitions. Another consideration is **not focusing overly on body parts**. Students may think exercises to tone and build specific muscles will give them their desired appearance; however, regular exercise combined with healthy nutrition more effectively shape bodies overall.

Safety and Efficacy for Strength Training

- Never hold your breath, which can cause lightheadedness, dizziness, and fainting.
- Never lock elbows, knees, or other joints; this produces tremendous stress and can cause injuries.
- When lifting barbells, always use bar collars.
- Concentrate on lifting and lowering weights slowly with control to maximize effectiveness and prevent injury.
- When using free weights, always have a spotter to help prevent injuries and with using correct form.
- When using free weights, always keep both hands at equal distances from the middle of the bar. Unequal distances can stress and injure one side of the body.
- Never overly bend or twist the spine; this can cause lower back problems and injuries.
- While using weights standing up, always keep the knees slightly bent to prevent undue stress on the lower back.
- When doing leg exercises with weights or resistance, always keep the knees in alignment with the toes to avoid leg injuries.
- Always replace weights so others will not trip over them. Always place weights on the correct racks so others do not mistakenly pick up the wrong weights.

Biomechanical Principles

Using **biomechanics** correctly ensures safety. For example, lunges with knee aligned over ankle are safe; lunges extending the knee past the ankle are mechanically incorrect and unsafe. Consider individual differences, e.g., a healthy 18-year-old female can safely do a squat-jump, but a 66-year-old female with osteoporosis cannot. **Biomechanical changes** informing ineffective, inefficient, or unsafe movements include: movement pattern changes, indicating fatigue and compensation with other body parts; body weight shifts, indicating fatigue or excessive difficulty; forward body flexion, indicating fatigue preventing muscles from overcoming gravitational pull; and flexed or bent joints, shortening muscles to be ineffective and inefficient, also indicating fatigued working muscles. According to the force-length curve, muscles generate their greatest force when slightly stretched or just past resting length. To choose safe, effective, and efficient exercises, incorporate walking, cycling, and other natural movement patterns. Repeat the same movements during and between lessons. Design lessons and programs in logical sequences or increments. Minimize degrees of freedom, i.e., number of joints involved. Minimize intersegmental coordination, i.e., different simultaneous arm and leg movements, such as an overhead press plus a squat. Select bilateral exercises for equal, opposite workloads. Distribute forces evenly across the body to minimize impact point. Apply forces horizontally or parallel, not vertically or downward to the body.

Physical Fitness and Activity

A definition of **physical fitness** that applies to most people rather than only to professional athletes is being able to actively complete all of one's daily living tasks without becoming overly tired and still having enough energy to pursue leisure activities for enjoyment. **Physical activity** should include both planned, structured activities, and movement that is integrated into daily life as an essential part of it. Regularly engaging in physical activity and exercise are not only required for being athletic, but for basic well-being and health. To be effective and safe, any comprehensive physical fitness program should incorporate the three major components of

- **aerobic exercise**, to promote cardiovascular health, endurance, and to manage weight;
- **resistance training**, which decreases risks for lower-back injuries and pain, improves posture, builds strength and muscular endurance, and also manages weight; and
- **flexibility** to stretch the muscles and move the joints, which prevents sore muscles, decreases the chances of injury, and maintains and/or improves the range of motion of the joints and the mobility of the muscles.

Aerobic Activity Levels

In fitness plans for most individuals, **aerobic activity** at a **moderate level** is recommended to add up to 150 minutes, or 2.5 hours per week. Aerobic activity at a **vigorous level** is recommended for half that duration, i.e., 75 minutes per week. Individuals may also choose to combine or alternate moderate and vigorous aerobic activities for equivalent durations. During activities at moderate intensities, people are able to speak but unable to sing. During activities at vigorous intensities, people can only utter a few words before needing to pause for breath. Examples of moderate-intensity activities include walking briskly, 3 mph or faster; bicycling at less than 10 mph; playing doubles tennis; doing water aerobics; ballroom dancing, and dancing in general. Examples of vigorous-intensity activities include running, jogging, race-walking; bicycling at more than 10 mph; playing singles tennis; swimming laps; aerobic dancing; doing heavy, continuous gardening that raises the heart rate; hiking with a heavy backpack or uphill; and jumping rope.

Personal Fitness Plan

To **assess** individual current status, define fitness goals, and identify what one is able or willing to do to achieve them, identify the following: current age; indicators of the current body fat, e.g., a "six-pack," a small belly, or a large belly; and an index of current strength, e.g., one can do a few push-ups and pull-ups, at least 10 good push-ups and five good pull-ups, or at least 20 good push-ups and 10 good pull-ups. Define a **fitness goal**, e.g., wanting people to perceive you (a) are trim and healthy, (b) must work out, or (c) must compete athletically. Define how soon you want or need to accomplish this goal, e.g., in a few months to a year, 1-2 years, or 3-6 years. To define what you are able or willing to do, identify whether you have about 2-4 hours, 5-10 hours, or 11-21 hours weekly to devote to fitness. Nutritionally, are you willing to substitute a few healthy for unhealthy foods, or consistently avoid junk food and eat produce, whole grains, and lean protein? Or eat six small meals daily and follow a strict dietary plan? Individuals should also identify their available exercise equipment and partners.

Health-Related Fitness

PE programs and teachers instruct students not only in sport skills, but also in the significance of **health-related fitness**. PE teachers need to help students develop both comprehension cognitively and competence physically to engage in regular physical activity to enable them to follow physically active, healthful lifestyles. To do so, students need to learn about health-related fitness needs, principles, and goals. One required component of this learning process is the assessment of fitness through **testing**. Some examples of fitness tests often used to assess elementary school student fitness include measuring the number of push-ups, curl-ups, and chin-ups they can do, and how well they can repeat these to a beat, to assess muscular strength and endurance. To assess flexibility, PE teachers may measure how far in inches a student can reach while sitting and how far s/he can stretch. To assess cardiorespiratory endurance and aerobic capacity, a common measure is how many laps a student can run, and the time in minutes it takes a student to run a mile or a half-mile.

Fitness Assessment Data

Fitness assessment data furnishes students, teachers, parents, and other stakeholders with student fitness feedback. Comparing baseline to subsequent data enables PE teachers to **monitor student progress**. PE teachers can also use fitness testing data to inform their curriculum development decisions about which program content will best address students' strengths and needs. Students can make use of their own fitness testing data to inform measurable goals they set for personal fitness plans. PE teachers can use fitness testing results to individualize and differentiate their instruction for each student to help them achieve their goals. Fitness assessment data can also be used **motivationally**: identifying skill improvements and attaining goals give students incentive to live active, healthy lives. When PE teachers conduct authentic fitness assessments, the results inform the context for the curricula and activities they plan. This helps students comprehend the reasons for PE activities, rather than assuming PE is simply playing games. Student motivation for physical activity; understanding of how to evaluate and improve personal fitness levels; self-assessment, data analysis, and development of personal fitness goals and plans are also enabled by using fitness data.

Conducting Fitness Assessment

According to the National Association for Sport and Physical Education (NASPE), **fitness assessment** is one of the components of the continual process of enabling students to comprehend, maintain, improve, and enjoy physical fitness that PE teachers should use. PE teachers should physically prepare students in each fitness component and testing protocol of the assessment instruments used to ensure safe participation. Teachers should do everything needed to establish non-threatening, private, encouraging, and educational testing circumstances. For example, they should explain to students what each test is designed to evaluate. They should encourage students to use test results as springboards for personal progress, not to compare themselves with others. Teachers should ensure the privacy of students and parents when sharing test results and not post these publicly to compare. They should use these results as tools to help students and parents develop individual goals and strategies to sustain and improve fitness measures. Teachers should also report student progress regularly to students and parents. Students should be informed immediately after testing of their scores, and use these during instruction throughout the school year. Parents should receive student fitness reports following completed assessments.

Personal Fitness Programs

Statistics show that half of all people who embark upon exercise programs **abandon** them within only six months of beginning. Therefore, personal trainers recommend assorted techniques to adopt that will

- 56 -

increase the likelihood of sticking with an exercise program long enough to make it a **permanent lifestyle change** and reap its benefits to health and well-being. One technique is to identify the best **location** for exercising. Students who do not get enough exercise through school PE classes need to choose places best suited for them. Some will find working out at a gym offers fewer distractions and better facilities, equipment, and trainers; others will find exercising at home more convenient. Distantly located gyms decrease the likelihood of attendance. Students should also identify the **time(s)** with the most convenience and fewest distractions for exercising; and the activities they enjoy most because the more convenient and fun a program is, the more likely they are to continue it. Starting exercise at overly high **intensities** and/or durations predicts dropout. Those who work out with more experienced partners may also overdo it.

Establishing and Monitoring Fitness Goals

Adults and students alike should set **fitness goals** that lead to long-term changes in lifestyle and are realistic. Goals should include both **results** and **behaviors**. For example, jumping 1 inch higher by the next sport season and losing 12 pounds within three months reflect outcome goals. Exercising every weekday at 7:30 p.m. for 20 minutes is a behavioral goal. To set suitable behavioral goals, students should understand the underlying objectives. Students can have far more control over accomplishing behavioral goals than outcome goals, so they should focus on attaining those target behaviors. If they do not meet short-term outcomes by their original goal deadlines, they should not let this discourage them. When they do accomplish outcome-related goals, students should change their behavioral goals accordingly. If they are not sure they can meet behavior goals consistently, or if they find more effective ways of meeting their objectives, students should re-evaluate their fitness plans.

Motivation and Commitment to Fitness

Planning specific workout times and establishing a **routine** helps physical activity become a habit. Students can enter these in their smartphone or tablet calendars like appointments; set alarms to remind them when to exercise; and pack workout bags or lay out exercise clothes and gear in advance. If they sometimes don't feel like exercising, they can agree with themselves to do just a short, light workout. Once prepared and warmed up, they will often become motivated for a full session. They should not give up hope if they miss a session, but reevaluate their fitness behavior plans, adjust strategies to prevent future omissions, recommit, analyze past barriers and identify new strategies to surmount them, and make backup plans for unexpected events or situations. Doing a variety of activities and exercises maintains interest. This includes fun activities like playing sports, kayaking; practical ones like walking dogs, yard work, walking to the store; and trying out new activities. Planning activities for the week or month helps. So does changing workouts according to changing interests and moods. Music, TV, and/or reading while walking, jogging, or cycling prevent boredom. Partners provide social support. Pedometers, stop watches, heart monitors, etc., and logging activity in writing or on digital devices help monitor progress.

Diet, Physical Activity, and Health

Regular physical activity aids in weight control; strengthens the heart, blood vessels, lungs, muscles, bones, and joints; and lowers risks for heart disease, stroke, diabetes, and various cancers. However, physical activity must be combined with good **nutrition** to be most effective. In fact, improper nutrition can even undermine any benefits of physical activity. For one thing, the body requires fuel to be physically active. People who eat too little and/or eat food that is not nutritious will not have enough energy to exercise. For another, foods high in refined sugars and flours and saturated fats will actually cause fatigue, depriving a person of energy and motivation to be active. In addition, people who want to build muscle cannot do so through strength training alone; they must eat lean proteins to supply the amino acids that are the building blocks of muscle. Foods high in refined sugars and flours and saturated fats are also very high in calories. Exercising, even vigorously for hours, is usually insufficient to burn as many calories as one can easily consume from the junk foods, fast foods, and restaurant foods so prevalent in modern society. Improper nutrition can derail the health benefits of physical activity.

Physical Activity, Weight, and General Health

To lose weight, you must expend more calories than you consume. In other words, weight loss requires a **calorie deficit**. Although most people lose weight by reducing the calories they eat, research evidence also finds regularly engaging in **physical activity** necessary for maintaining that weight loss. This explains why so many people who do not engage in enough regular physical activity regain weight after losing it. Even when people have lost weight, if they are physically active on a regular basis they lower their risk of diabetes and cardiovascular disease beyond the risk reduction afforded by weight loss alone. To put the relationship between diet, exercise, and weight into perspective, consider that a Big Mac from McDonald's has about 550 calories. A person who weighs about 150 pounds would have to run at a speed of 5 mph for an hour to burn that many calories. Few if any people who just ate a Big Mac will want or be able to run that fast for that long. Moreover, its high saturated fat content, refined white flour, etc. all contribute to cardiovascular disease, diabetes, and cancers.

Deficiencies in Nutrition and Physical Activity

According to the Centers for Disease Control and Prevention (CDC), **physical inactivity** and **poor diet** are major causes of chronic non-communicable diseases, from which hundreds of thousands of people die every year. In addition to deaths, disabilities caused by strokes, obesity, diabetes, and osteoporosis are the results of improper nutrition and sedentary lifestyles. The Healthy People initiatives have found that almost two-thirds of Americans eat too much saturated fat, three-quarters do not eat enough fruit, and more than half do not eat enough vegetables. People who are inactive physically have nearly twice the probability of developing heart disease as people who are active regularly. This makes physical inactivity approach high blood pressure, high cholesterol, or smoking cigarettes as a risk factor for heart disease. However, physical inactivity is a more prevalent risk factor than any of those others. Sedentary people who are also obese and have high blood pressure, and hence have multiple risk factors, can especially benefit from becoming physically active.

Diet for Healthy Weight

According to the US Centers for Disease Control and Prevention (CDC) and the federal Dietary Guidelines, a **healthy diet** should place the most emphasis on fruits and vegetables, whole grains, and fat-free or low-fat dairy products. It should also include lean protein sources like beans, fish, eggs, nuts, poultry, and lean meats. It should eliminate or limit trans fats, saturated fats, salt, added sugars, and cholesterol. In addition, a balanced diet should not contain many more or fewer calories than an individual needs every day to function optimally. Eating fresh produce in season, especially produce grown locally, is best. When favorite fruits are out of season or unaffordable, they are available frozen, canned, or dried. One caveat is to avoid canned fruits with heavy, sugar-laden syrups and find those canned in their own juices. If fresh vegetables are unavailable, many are flash-frozen at their peak nutritional value without added sodium or fatty sauces. For canned vegetables, avoid those with added sodium. Some ways to enjoy vegetables more include steaming them; adding different herbs, which provide flavor without salt or fat; sautéing in non-stick pans with a little cooking spray; and trying a new or unfamiliar vegetable every week.

Weight Management Strategies

The healthiest diets involve **balance** rather than completely eliminating foods we enjoy. Many people's favorite "comfort foods" happen to have high caloric, sugar, and/or fat content. To lose weight and/or

- 58 -

maintain weight loss, it is not necessary to give up these foods entirely, though. One strategy is to indulge in fattening foods, but less often. For example, instead of every day, eat them once a week, or even once a month. Not eating high-calorie foods as frequently reduces overall calories. Another strategy is enjoying fattening foods in smaller portions. For example, if a favorite comfort food is a candy bar, only eat half of it or buy it in a smaller size. Manufacturers offer many miniature, "snack size," or "fun size" candy bars. Sometimes taste and texture provide enough enjoyment rather than amount. Another strategy is comfort food "makeovers." For example, macaroni and cheese can be remade with skim milk instead of whole milk, low-fat cheese, and less butter. Some people incorporate healthier foods to lower calories while adding fiber and nutrients, e.g., cauliflower in macaroni and cheese, puréed spinach or beets in brownies, etc.

Maintaining Current Weight

Some individuals are not overweight, but will need to plan to avoid gaining weight. Others are overweight, but currently not ready to lose weight. In either case, **weight maintenance** has the benefits of preventing many chronic diseases, as well as minimizing the need for future weight loss. The number of calories needed to maintain weight varies individually. Variables affecting this include height, weight, gender, age, levels of physical activity, and muscle-to-fat ratio. Muscle tissue burns more calories than fatty tissue, even at rest. Thus some people have higher basal metabolisms than others; these people can afford to consume more calories without gaining weight. Some of this body composition is natural, some lifestyle-related. More physically active people burn more calories and can eat more than sedentary people. To maintain current weight, it is useful for people to weigh themselves regularly. It is easier to lose a gain of 2-3 pounds discovered sooner than 10 pounds discovered later. If weight creeps up, it helps to self-examine changes in physical activity and eating. People can keep food diaries, activity logs, and use numerous available digital apps for self-monitoring.

Participating in Physical Fitness

Experts say that, to be healthy, children and teens need to engage in **moderate physical activity** for around an hour a day, adults around half an hour a day, about five days a week. But most Americans fall far short of these parameters. Increasing the frequency and duration of physical activity improves health even more. People who want to lose weight or maintain their weight loss may need 40-90 minutes of physical activity daily. Modern conveniences plus school and occupational work primarily done seated interfere with physical activity. Lack of financial resources is another obstacle. People living in socioeconomically disadvantaged communities lack not only money, but often also accessible community recreation facilities like safe outdoor parks, indoor recreation centers, facilities, equipment, and clubs or other social groups focusing on physical activities. There are solutions, however. For time, physical activity like walking can be divided into small, 10-minute sessions three times daily. For motivation, family outings, free or low-cost group activities, and walking and exercise partners offer social support.

Discuss Some Factors That Encourage Physical Activity in Communities and Families

Research finds people are more likely to engage in physical activities for recreation when they are located **near their homes** and are **free or inexpensive**. Even in communities containing beautiful state parks and other natural areas, citizens still prefer recreation that is closest to home and most affordable. People are more likely to exercise regularly when they live within 1 mile of a recreational facility. Another factor affecting physical recreation is safety. People who ride bicycles and walk or jog for recreation often must use public roads and streets, where motor vehicle traffic threatens their safety and discourages their participation. Some communities have obtained funding to create local bike, walking, and/or jogging paths separate and safe from road traffic. Because low-income families are less apt to enjoy access to recreational facilities, experts recommend that establishing free or low-cost facilities in low-income communities would make an appreciable difference in their physical activity levels, improving their health and enjoyment in life.

Physical Activity Levels Among Diverse Populations

Experts recommend that **local government offices** should work together with members of their **communities** who represent people with disabilities, low incomes, and culturally and ethnically diverse backgrounds. Incorporating the input and insight these community members can contribute, they can **collaborate** to make organized plans; identify, secure, and prepare or renovate suitable sites; construct community recreation facilities; and staff, operate, and manage them. When families have access to recreational facilities that are close to their homes and provide safe environments, appropriate space and equipment, and beneficial social interaction, they are much more likely to engage in physical activity for recreation, benefiting their physical, mental, and social health and well-being. Some neighborhoods have organized local walking groups and activities in ethnically diverse communities. These combine greater physical activity with safety and social interaction. Residents report greater neighborhood pride and ownership and stronger sense of community. Mexican-American citizens have reported in focus groups that they value family-based physical activities. For culturally competent responses, recreation facilities should organize family exercise programs rather than individually targeting women, men, seniors, youth, etc.

Physical Activity Addresses Stress

One way in which **physical activity combats stress** is by directly reducing it. Moving at moderate intensity long enough to increase the heart rate, breathe more deeply, work the muscles, and break a light sweat releases **endorphins**. These hormones, named from the Greek meaning "the morphine within," produce a naturally occurring "high," or sense of euphoria. Endorphins also alleviate physical and mental pain. People feel physically and mentally relaxed after expending energy; working the heart, lungs, and muscles; and perspiring and releasing toxins. Family and friends often observe someone they know well seems and feels much more "mellow" after exercising. Worries and negative attitudes are frequently dissipated by exercise. Another way physical activity affects stress is by improving the ability to **cope** with it. While some stressors are inherent in life and cannot themselves be eliminated, people's attitudes toward them can change markedly through being physically active. Increased physical strength, stamina, and flexibility afford greater senses of personal competence and empowerment. Increased blood circulation enables clearer thinking, hence more effective problem-solving. Enhanced physical and mental health synergistically improve capacities for dealing with life's challenges.

Enjoyment and Challenge

Enjoyment:
- A high school boy never interested in traditional intramural and team sports offered in PE classes sees a brochure on kayaking and decides to enroll in lessons at a local outdoor adventure training company. He finds navigating rapids thrilling and enjoys interacting with nature.
- Some low-income urban kindergarteners have done unstructured running, jumping, etc., and played simple games like Simon Says at home, but never learned any physically active games with rules. Their teacher introduces them to a variety of games wherein they must walk, run, change directions, link arms, jump, tumble, do extensions; throw, bowl, and fetch balls; touch things, etc., following teacher directions and rules. They enjoy these new experiences.

- 60 -

<u>Challenge:</u>

- A middle school girl can only do a few sit-ups. Her PE teacher assigns 30 sit-ups to alternating pairs. While spotting her partner—a pretty, thinner friend she admires, she sees the effort on her face with each sit-up. She is inspired to complete all 30 during her turn. A high school student has run 500-yard dashes, but never a marathon, and doubts her ability. Her PE teacher encourages her. After training regularly for three months, she successfully completes a full 26-mile race.

Social Interaction and Healthcare Expenses

Social interaction:

- Two high school girls have free periods at the end of the day and don't want to wait for the bus. They decide to walk to one of their homes instead. During the 3-mile trip, they enjoy conversing and interacting in the outdoors more than on a noisy, crowded school bus.
- A boy in elementary school gets good grades but is socially introverted and lacks physical self-confidence. His parents offer to enroll him in Little League baseball. As he learns and succeeds he gains confidence, teammates applaud and encourage him, and he makes new friends.

Healthcare expenses:

- A diabetic child's mother is overprotective about exercise. The school nurse and PE teacher collaborate with her on a plan for regular blood sugar testing during the school day, suitable exercise, and appropriate snacks before and after exercising. As a result, her family doctor reduces the child's insulin dosage.
- A PE teacher, collaborating with a dietitian and school nurse, designs a safe fitness program for an obese high school student. With significant weight loss, his type 2 diabetes symptoms abate. He needs less medication and fewer doctor visits; as a result, his parents' health insurance co-pays decrease.

Self-Concepts and Self-Esteem

International Council for Sport Science and Physical Education President and professor Margaret Talbot has written that challenging physical activities like sports and dance are powerfully influential for helping **youth** "learn to be themselves." She finds that, when presented appropriately, such activities teach young people to question assumptions they have held that limit them, and to perceive themselves and their potentials anew. In *Run Like a Girl: How Strong Women Make Happy Lives* (2011), Mina Samuels writes that once she discovered running, she not only gained self-confidence, but she found she was stronger than expected. As a result, she perceived herself differently, as someone with greater potential and a bigger future who could take risks and push herself—not just in sports but other life areas—by competing with herself rather than others, and setting and meeting higher expectations and standards for herself. Psychologists find physical self-worth, sense of autonomy and self-efficacy enhanced through developing competence in sport skills. Studies have found elementary, high school, and Latino students benefit with higher **self-esteem** from school sports participation and other physical activity.

Mental and Emotional Well-Being

Many research studies find improvements in **mood**, with fewer symptoms of **anxiety and depression**, resulting from physical activity. Experiments have compared participants with major depression, giving some psychotropic medication and others an aerobic exercise intervention. The exercisers demonstrated more significant improvements and lower relapse rates than those taking the drugs. Other research has shown that walking programs increase positive mood. Six-month resistance training programs have decreased anger, tension, and confusion while elevating moods in participants. Investigators comparing the effects of yoga, dance, or lecture on participants' psychological well-being found significantly lowered negative affect and stress perception in the groups with the physical activities. Large-scale studies with adolescents find correlations between increased leisure-time physical activity and decreased symptoms of depression. In addition, research with 4th-grade Hispanic children from low-income families has found their self-esteem and cardiovascular fitness increased while their depression decreased when they participated in an aerobic intensity physical activity program.

Self-Management Skills

Self-assessment skills enable: self-evaluating fitness and interpreting results, e.g., choosing and self-administering good fitness assessments; goal-setting and plan-making; and success, new thinking, and learning skills. Self-monitoring skills entail keeping records, enabling viewing one's behavior more objectively and accurately, and gauging progress toward goals. For example, if you cut calories yet aren't losing weight, record-keeping can reveal you are eating more than you thought. Keeping progress records also promotes adhering to fitness plans and programs. These skills supply information and feedback, help change beliefs, aid planning and goal-setting, and raise success probabilities. **Goal-setting skills** are particularly important for beginners at behavior change. They enable establishing achievable, realistic future objectives. For example, success is more likely for someone wanting to reduce fat with a process goal to eat 200 fewer calories and burn 200 more calories daily than an outcome goal to lose 50 pounds. These skills facilitate planning and feedback, build confidence, change attitudes and beliefs, and increase enjoyment and success. **Planning skills** enable independently designing fitness programs, reinforcement, self-confidence, success, and enjoyment. **Performance skills** enhance competence, self-confidence, attitudes, success, and enjoyment. An example is learning stress-management and relaxation skills. Balancing attitudes enhances planning; goal-setting; beliefs; and enjoyment, e.g., emphasizing exercise's positive aspects, not its negative.

Management, Motivation, and Communication

Nonverbal Communication

Nonverbal communication is used in combination with **verbal communication** among both hearing and deaf people. While sign language is non-oral and non-auditory, it is largely verbal in that many ASL signs represent words. While some ASL signs are more expressive of emotions or concepts than specific words, these still accompany word concepts along with other nonverbal components, just as with spoken language. Other nonverbal components include eye contact, facial expressions, body posture, physical gestures, and contact by touch. Touch communicates not only people's comfort levels and feelings, but also their personality characteristics. For instance, a warm hug communicates something quite different from a light pat on the back; a firm handshake conveys different things than a limp one. For hearing people, the volume, tone, and pitch of their voices are additional components of nonverbal communication. They express emotions, nuances not included in words, and meanings. When people use sarcasm or irony, their tones contrast with word meanings. Visually, for both hearing and deaf people, clothes and home decor are further nonverbal communication forms that influence others' perceptions and judgments.

Primary Functions of Nonverbal Communication

Five primary functions of **nonverbal communication** identified by social psychologist Michael Argyle (*Bodily Communication,* 1975, 2nd edition 2010) are to express feelings; to communicate interpersonal relationships; to support verbal interactions; to reflect personalities; and to perform greetings, farewells, and other social rituals. Often the beginning of an intimate or romantic relationship begins more effectively with eye contact across a roomful of people than with initial verbal overtures. Nonverbal communication accompanies and interacts with verbal communication. Facial expressions, vocal tones, and physical gestures can reinforce verbal meaning. For example, saying "Congratulations," accompanied with a genuine smile, reinforces word meaning and conveys its sincerity. In some cases, nonverbal communication contradicts verbal messages, as when someone says he or she loves another person but avoids eye contact. In PE activities, even if teachers have instructed students in verbal techniques like calling for a catch in baseball, it can be difficult to hear others' voices or locate individual callers during public games with noisy spectators. Football spectators, cheerleaders, and helmets can interfere with players' hearing each other, coaches, and referees. Students out of breath from exertion can have difficulty calling. Thus nonverbal communication becomes even more important.

Verbal Communication

Verbal communication is any kind of social interaction using words, whether they are spoken, written, or signed. Therefore, sign language among deaf people is included in verbal communication. Not only spoken conversations, but listening to news reports on TV, reading the newspaper, and sending and receiving text messages on smartphones are all examples of verbal communication. As pointed out by a LiveStrong author (Lucas, 2014), as humans, our ancestors were pack animals, hunting and gathering collectively and interdependent with each other for survival, safety, and company. Verbal communication figures prominently in the overall communication we rely on for social, business, financial, physical, and psychological well-being through interpersonal interactions and relationships. While other animals and prehistoric humans communicated through vocal sounds that expressed emotions and signals like warnings, alerts, etc., humans now differ from other animals by having developed the organized systems of sounds that make up spoken and written language; moreover, today humans have technology that enables virtually instantaneous verbal communication regardless of physical location or distance.

Communication Between Coaches and Athletes

To share their experience with athletes, coaches must be able to **communicate** with them to give them information enabling effective training and helping athletes perform better. For athletes to initiate the proper actions, coaches must communicate well with them. At the same time, though, the athletes need to receive, comprehend, and accept the information their coaches communicate. According to experts, coaches should ask themselves several fundamental things about their communications with athletes:

- Whether they have athletes' attention;
- Whether they are explaining so athletes can understand easily;
- Whether athletes have understood what the coach has communicated;
- Whether the athletes believe what the coach tells them; and
- Whether the athletes accept what the coach says.

Though it initially seems in-person communication involves taking turns talking, smoothly flowing communication actually entails many additional verbal and nonverbal behaviors, including eye movements, body posture, nodding, smiling, laughing, frowning, touching, and many other things in addition to language. Downturned or glazed eyes and fidgeting communicate boredom; half-raised eyebrows show puzzlement, while fully raised show disbelief. Group posture indicates team mood and attitude toward the coach. Coaches need sensitivity to athletes' signals to control a team/group.

Communication Blocks Between Coaches and Athlete

According to an expert (Crookes, *Athletics Coach,* 1991), **communication blocks** between coaches and athletes can arise owing to different factors. For example, an athlete may perceive something differently than the coach does, so their viewpoints are not aligned, interfering with their communication. When a coach introduces a topic, athletes who are naturally action-oriented may jump to conclusions rather than waiting to undergo the process of listening, understanding, and accepting the coach's communication. Sometimes a coach tries to communicate something that an athlete lacks the knowledge required to understand. Some athletes may not be motivated to listen to the coach; some may not be motivated to translate the coach's communication into actions by the athletes. Some coaches may find it difficult to express certain things they want to communicate to the athletes. In situations when emotions become highly involved, they can interfere with the process of communicating information clearly and objectively. In some instances, the personalities of some coaches and some athletes may clash, which can also interfere with communicating effectively. Such communication blocks function reciprocally. Hence coaches must think carefully about the communication process.

Essential Communication Considerations for Coaches

Before **communicating** with athletes, coaches should consider

- WHY they wish to communicate;
- WHO they want to communicate with;
- WHERE and
- WHEN the communication should best be;
- WHAT they want to communicate; and
- HOW they will communicate it.

According to an expert in athletic coaching (Crookes, 1991), six elements of effective communication are:

- Present the information in a CLEAR way;
- Be CONCISE, not obscuring the message with long-winded speeches;
- Give CORRECT information and do not mislead athletes;
- Give COMPLETE information, not just parts of it;
- Be COURTEOUS, i.e., non-threatening and polite so as not to instigate conflicts; and
- Be CONSTRUCTIVE, i.e., present information positively, not negatively or critically.

Giving information in a **positive way** is more effective for encouraging athletes to make changes. To give athletes corrections in their techniques and actions, coaches should always lead with a positive comment. Recommendations for coaches include developing their verbal and nonverbal communication skills, giving positive feedback in coaching sessions, giving equal attention to every athlete, communicating consistently with athlete learning and thinking styles, and listening to athletes as well as talking to them.

General and Specific Feedback

General feedback is also called descriptive feedback; **specific feedback** is also called prescriptive feedback. General feedback can be socially reinforcing, but usually too vague to inform student improvement. For example, "Way to go!", "Good job", or "You can do it" praise the student but do not specify *what* the student did that was good; neither do they convey what else the student could do to improve. Prescriptive feedback tells students specifically what they are doing or should do. For example, "Good, you're stepping forward with the opposite foot when you throw" gives both positive reinforcement and specific information about what the student did correctly. To correct or improve student performance, most students need feedback with specific instructions like "Kick with the instep, not the toe," "turn sideways," or "follow through." These instructions are qualitative by describing the movement processes to perform or that are being performed. Prescriptive feedback, like its name, is analogous to a doctor's prescription to treat a diagnosed illness: as medication improves health or fixes health problems, prescriptive feedback helps students improve skill performance or fixes performance problems.

Situations Wherein Feedback is not Necessary

For students to learn motor tasks, **receiving feedback** is a necessary component. There are, however, some kinds of tasks that inherently provide **environmental feedback**, like seeing a basketball go through the hoop. While it is important for students to use correct throwing technique even when the ball does not go through, if it does, they may need less feedback from the teacher. With some skills, watching a demonstration enables students to see easily how to do it correctly; this also reduces need for teacher feedback. Whether a student needs feedback or the amount of feedback needed can be directly associated with student learning level. If a simple skill is easy to learn, or the student has enough experience with a skill, sometimes no feedback is necessary. Part of effective PE instruction is knowing when to provide feedback. PE teachers who give skill-related, specific feedback help students learn skills more quickly and efficiently. Effective PE teachers also organize their classes to afford required opportunities for practice, as well as giving students **skill-related feedback** when they need it.

Feedback and New Motor Skills

To apply knowledge of concepts related to using feedback in teaching students new motor skills, PE teachers should begin by **analyzing the skill** they want to teach. They should consider whether the skill will need verbal assistance. They should assess whether or not the environment can provide information to the students about whether they are performing the skill correctly. If the environment will give enough feedback to students learning the skill, PE teachers may allow this environmental feedback to suffice rather than adding their own feedback if it would be redundant. PE teachers should initially give performance-related cues to students to instruct them in executing the new skill. Where sufficient environmental feedback occurs, they can then let students learn from their own mistakes as they are practicing. Teachers should also help students to make critical self-evaluations of their own performance. PE teachers should also understand that when they are teaching skills wherein the students cannot view how they are performing relative to the task and cannot see their own body parts, and when they are teaching more complex skills, they must provide students with feedback.

Self-Evaluating Performance

PE teachers should initially give students **performance-related cues** when teaching new motor skills. Once students begin practicing, if the skills are not complex and they can see their own body parts or performance, they will learn through making and correcting errors. To help students make critical **self-evaluations** of their own performance, PE teachers can give students checklists that include photos of the skills, with the words used as cues next to the pictures. They can assign students to pairs or teams and have them check one another's performance of skill components. Another useful instructional strategy is to record video of the students. As they watch the playback, teach them how to verbalize the critical parts of the skill. Then assign them to a group and have them watch the video, analyzing whether each member performed the skill correctly or not by calling "yes" or "no". By assigning students to give their own feedback, PE teachers not only enable them to learn the required task, but also enable them to perform it without depending on teacher feedback, making them more independent learners.

Congruent Feedback

Congruent feedback is not only specific and not general in nature, but also matches the cues that the PE teacher or coach has given students and athletes in advance of their practicing or performing a skill. For example, if the teacher or coach used a cue like "Follow through" when kicking a ball, swinging a bat at a ball, etc., instead of saying "Good job," which is too general, the teacher or coach says, "Good job following through," specifying that the student or athlete correctly followed through as an integral part of the action or task. The teacher or coach should match the feedback's wording to the cue, rather than using different words to describe it. This makes feedback **congruent** with the cue. Another advantage of congruent feedback is that it not only reminds the individual student of the cue while providing positive reinforcement for correct technique, but also serves as a reminder for the rest of the class or team, who have all been given the same cues. The sandwich approach involves first describing one thing the student or athlete did well, then identifying one thing to correct or improve, and ending with another piece of positive feedback. This way correction is sandwiched between positive reinforcements, making it more palatable.

Types of Feedback

Teacher feedback: PE teachers give students task sheets clearly stating criteria; teachers circulate, giving feedback. Advantages: students can work independently; teachers can give individual students specific feedback. Disadvantage: Giving all students feedback can be difficult. Teacher roles: Planning tasks, providing feedback. Student role: Deciding exactly when, where, and how to do the task. **Peer feedback**: PE teachers give clear task criteria, grouping students to evaluate each other's performance. Advantages: Teachers can circulate through the class; students learn through observing and analyzing others' movements; students develop their social skills; all students get feedback. Disadvantages: Some students may be unable to give good feedback; tasks must be sufficiently clear for students to perform independently. Teacher roles: Planning tasks; supplying specific criteria for performing each skill; observing student cooperation and collaboration and feedback skills; availability as needed. Student roles: Alternating between performing the skill and providing criteria-based feedback. **Self-feedback**:

- 66 -

Students view video of and evaluate their own performance. Advantages: Greater student independence; students learn to analyze their own movements. Disadvantages: Less-skilled students may be unable to self-analyze correctly. Teacher roles: Determining student self-assessment abilities, and the same as in peer feedback. Student roles: Executing teacher-planned tasks; self-evaluating their performance.

Task Cards and Technology

While teachers can design their own **task cards**, many are available online. Some are within different price ranges, but many are free of charge for downloading and printing. For Pre-K and elementary grades, teachers can laminate printed task cards and glue them to popsicle sticks. For example, there are task cards on Yoga for Kids for grades Pre-K through 3. Brain Breaks, by The Teacher Next Door, consists of a set of 100 task cards containing creative movement, exercises, and active games to enhance student learning for grades 1-6. Brain Breaks also offers a free set of Song and Dance Cards, which can be used flexibly for individual students, small groups, and whole classes from Pre-K through sixth grade. These task cards even include QR codes, which can be scanned using an iPad or iPod Touch. They provide kinesthetic activities to help refocus students' attention after classroom transitions. They require little equipment, help "break the ice," and build classroom motivation, gross motor skills, eye-hand coordination, creativity, and cooperation. These can help teachers with classroom management, provide indoor activities in bad weather, and help teachers with students who finish assignments early, as well as be fun for students.

Task Cards, Station Signs, Or Posters

When a PE teacher wants to teach a specific sport skill, e.g., how to dribble a basketball, **concrete visual graphics** are very helpful for communicating information. The teacher can use task cards, station signs, or posters, and set up stations using a minimum of equipment, like goals, a target, cones, and a basketball in addition to the cards, signs, or posters to guide students through a dribbling unit. Each station can involve completing a task of progressively greater difficulty. This way, students master one dribbling skill at a time. Progressing from one station to the next helps students attain **cumulative learning**. The visual cues provided by cards, posters, and signs are a great help to students with learning disabilities, reading difficulties, hearing impairments, or other cognitive, neurological, or physiological disabilities. In addition, all students benefit from the multimodal stimulation and cognitive redundancy afforded by accompanying spoken teacher instructions, physical teacher and student demonstrations, and student practice with visual cues. To make it even easier for teachers, PE task cards are available online for teaching dribbling and numerous other skills to various ranges of grade levels.

Bulletin Boards

PE teachers can use **bulletin boards** to engage students and illustrate teaching units. A time-lapse bulletin board is one creative application a PE teacher used with grades 3-5 studying balance. An actual bulletin board is not even necessary: this teacher did not have one, but simply taped together two large sheets of paper and hung them on the wall, labeled "BALANCE." He assigned students homework to bring in pictures showing or explaining balance. They could make drawings, find photographs, diagrams or artwork in magazines, papers, or articles, or find pictures online. In addition to grades 3-5, he even had kindergarteners contribute pictures. The teacher initially posted about a dozen pictures on the board to get it started and give students some examples and ideas. Over time, contributions increased until the board was completely filled with pictures, even overlapping. (Photos of the time lapse are posted on the PE Central® website.) The teacher reported this project was simple, yet successful. It supplemented the teaching unit, visually helped students understand many forms and aspects of balance, and engaged them in contributing to individual and class learning.

Music

The most obvious use of **music** is accompanying dance movements and choreography, since most dances are choreographed to specific music. However, music has many other applications in PE activities. For example, PE teachers can help students achieve even rates and rhythms of dribbling basketballs timed to musical beats. Practice, e.g., repeating chest passes and bounce passes against a mini-trampoline or wall, can be done to music, both prolonging the duration students can continue and helping them regulate speeds and intervals. Motivation to initiate and continue aerobic exercises is greatly enhanced by music with driving beats, which also help students control body movement rates and rhythms. Music facilitates precision in whole class, group, or team movements. **Tempo** directly accelerates movement for increasing speed and aerobic conditioning, and slows movement for control and cool-down phases. Teachers and coaches can define practice exercise parameters using music, e.g., having students or athletes complete however many of an assigned action they can while the music is playing. Music aids classroom management by stimulating movement and making activities more fun and interesting for younger students; playing favorite current songs also alleviates boredom and increases appeal for high school students.

Video Recordings

Physical movements are much more difficult to teach by simply describing them verbally (making them abstract and not visible), but much easier to teach by **demonstrating** them physically so students can see them. Demonstrations not only show which movements to perform and in what sequence, but also illustrate correct form and technique. When no student in a group has ever done something before, the PE teacher is the obvious choice to demonstrate. Instead of having to demonstrate the same movements over and over, the teacher can make video recordings of himself or herself demonstrating and play these for students. In addition to relieving teachers of unnecessary repeated exertion, videos can capture an ideal demonstration, eliminating variations among live repetitions and the possibility of an inferior demonstration when the coach has an "off" day. They can also be played by substitute or student teachers in the event of a teacher or coach's absence. When a student displays exemplary technique, the teacher can make a video with student and parent permission for other students to view, enabling them to relate to a peer demonstration.

Video Recordings and Classroom Management

Videos provide records proving exactly what happened at certain times and places. These can be valuable for class management. For example, if a dispute arises between or among students while the teacher was occupied with other students and unable to observe, video playback can inform the teacher, and eliminate false accusations and shifting of blame. Some PE teachers and coaches might choose to record their classes or sessions routinely for such purposes, similar to the way surveillance cameras keep records in business, public, and residential locations as security measures. Videos can also be used to help teach self-observation and self-assessment skills to younger children, cognitively limited students, and high school students. Students who have never viewed their own performance techniques or interpersonal behaviors are often surprised to see how they must appear to others by watching video playback. This feedback can be used to instruct students to change inconsiderate or aggressive behaviors, adopt more prosocial behaviors, correct athletic techniques, and learn more effective conflict resolution methods.

Expected Communication and Interaction

According to the Physical Education Standards of the National Board for Professional Teaching Standards (NBPTS), one standard is to create an **environment of respect and rapport**. This board states that to establish such an environment, exemplary PE teachers carefully select what they say and do to gain

- 68 -

rapport with their students and develop understandings with them to enable and maintain learning environments that are **productive** and without **bullying**. PE teachers should engage their students as partners in learning through making decisions collaboratively, inviting them to participate in establishing policies, procedures, and rules. PE teachers are expected to be sensitive to how they set tones with their students and to model behaviors for them that are constructive and positive. The standard gives the example that when confronting student behavior problems, teachers ask students to describe the characteristics of their behavior, articulate what made it disruptive, and identify how they could solve the problem. Such engagement is recommended for facilitating student ownership in classroom management and organization.

Discuss the expectations of some national standards for PE teachers for using mutual communication to show and elicit respect, and create high expectations.

The National Board for Professional Teaching Standards (NBPTS) includes in its Physical Education Standards the description that good PE teachers use **two-way communication** with students. Doing so accomplishes the dual purposes of showing that they respect their students' ideas and feelings, and showing their students reciprocally that the teachers also expect their students to be equally considerate of them in turn. The NBPTS PE standard for creating a respectful, supportive learning environment also requires that PE teachers involve their students in dialogue on an ongoing basis. This is for the purposes of giving students motivation for helping to sustain learning environments that welcome all students, and of furthering responsible student behavior. This standard also dictates that PE teachers regularly communicate to their students their high expectations. Expecting students to perform up to the full levels of their capacities not only promotes student achievement, but is also another way of communicating the teachers' respect for their students and for their abilities.

Respect for Students

Good PE teachers should **challenge** their students, not only physically but also **intellectually**. They can do this by assisting students in setting **goals** for themselves that promote discovery by and about themselves. Working toward these goals should also develop students' higher-order cognitive skills for analyzing, interpreting, synthesizing, and evaluating. For example, a PE teacher might assign a class of students to move an object from one place to another without dropping it. At first this might appear simple; however, considering the number of students on each team, the distance between the two points, the weight of the object to be transported, and similar factors entails cooperative strategizing among the students to enable them to attain their shared goal. Devising plays in football and other competitive team sports, and developing technical strategies in track and field events and other activities, require critical thinking and problem-solving skills. Good PE teachers not only know this, but also recognize that facilitating students' quality participation also fully engages students in their learning environments.

Encouraging Communication

Excellent PE teachers not only communicate their own **high expectations** for students, but also encourage students to develop and sustain equally **high expectations for themselves**. They do this by engaging students in conversations to explore students' comprehension of individuality, personal attitudes, effort, results of learning, and respect. As an example, a PE teacher might begin students' first class by talking about how students can set a goal to finish each class more physically educated than when they started. Further, the teacher can encourage students to think about what this goal means to each of them personally. Students can express their individual perspectives and interpretations of how they might realize this goal. PE teachers should also help students understand their learning objectives by structuring the learning activities they provide. For example, the teacher can write up an entry task on a whiteboard before class, enabling students to start the activity independently, which supports established high expectations regarding classroom procedures and routines. Good PE teachers understand that when students comprehend expectations, their resulting comfort levels contribute to enhanced learning environments and productivity.

Communicating Respectfully with Parents

When PE teachers post their **class rules** and distribute them to students at the beginning of every school year, they should also send copies of these same rules home to students' **parents**. It is a good idea to include a cover letter, politely asking parents to review the class policies and rules in order to ensure that their children understand them and parents are informed of them. With the advantages of today's technology, it can be more effective to email these to parents rather than giving them to students, which often results in their being crumpled up in backpacks and never reaching the parents. In their cover letter, PE teachers should also explain briefly but clearly to parents the importance of students' knowing and following all rules, especially in PE class, because if they do not, students can hurt themselves or others. This communication is also good preparation in the event of student behavior problems, disputes, or injuries ultimately involving parents: they are informed of the rules in advance and cannot deny knowledge or accuse teachers of not informing them.

Communicating Respectfully with Irate Parents

When irate parents wish to meet with PE teachers, they should do the same as school principals and other teachers: remain calm; prohibit out-of-control, non-adult behavior in their offices and classrooms; not allow parents to "unload" in the presence of their children; listen and acknowledge parent concerns; empower parents by inviting their contributions; show respect for parents and expect it in return; and engage them in a collaborative spirit of problem solving. **Respecting parents** goes a long way to defuse hostilities, which usually arise from parental concern and protective impulses toward their children. Parents become less defensive and aggressive when they realize their child's welfare and progress are equally important to the teacher and they are on the same side, not adversaries. PE teachers must also communicate respectfully with their **colleagues**. Sharing their expertise and knowledge with less experienced teachers establishes more effective working relationships, which support the students, faculty cohesiveness, and school, and make the teacher's life easier; looking down on less experienced colleagues only incites resentment and hostility, fragmenting the faculty. Conversely, PE teachers can learn from more experienced colleagues, and even defuse superior attitudes, by respecting them and inviting their advice.

Movement and Lifelong Physical Activities

Reaching and Grasping

Even before birth, fetuses display **arm and hand movements**—waving arms, making isolated finger movements, and using coordinated arm-hand movements like moving their thumbs to their mouths. Outside the womb, without the buoyancy of amniotic fluid, newborns must contend with gravity. Beginning with jerky extensions and flapping of the arms, they develop successful **reaching** for objects by 4-5 months. Detailed motion analysis reveals that infants initially problem-solve by moving their hands to targets individually. More sedentary babies must transcend gravity to raise their arms, while more active babies must damp inertia to control spontaneous, continuous arm-flapping. Both only open their hands into fitting shapes after touching objects. By around 8 months, babies can adjust their hand shapes prior to object contact, informing themselves visually about object shapes, sizes, and orientations. While visual information about object properties and locations is critical to adaptive planning of arm and hand movements, babies can **reach and grasp** as successfully in the dark as in light, so they need not see their arms or hands to guide them—likely because kinesthetics and proprioception work for body parts but not separate objects.

Using Hand-Held Tools

After babies have mastered the **motor actions** involved in reaching and grasping objects, they can apply their skills to achieve rewarding results. They learn to differentiate **textures**: they will bang hard objects against hard surfaces because this makes noise, but will not repeat banging soft objects against soft surfaces as it makes no noise. Infants are observed to test different combinations of objects and surfaces to determine which is noisiest. At 9 months, babies typically can bang on surfaces with spoons, but they take several months longer to develop the **fine motor control** for using spoons in the complex operation of scooping and bringing food to their mouths. Cognitive developmental psychologist Jean Piaget first described how older babies differentiate their reaching and grasping skills into instrumental actions to attain their goals. For example, around 8 months, babies reach and pull a cloth to move a toy on the cloth closer. Older babies lean forward, holding sticks, to extend their reach for objects. Toddlers rake in out-of-reach objects using canes as tools. They demonstrate comprehension of the tool-target relationship by turning the canes functionally.

Walking Development

Newborns may already have **inter-limb coordination**, as demonstrated by their crawling, swimming, and stepping reflexes. After developing the locomotion skills of crawling, babies go through several transitional upright stages of pulling up, balancing while standing, and sideways cruising while holding onto furniture for support. These transitional stages culminate in independent walking. From babies' first steps, to toddling, to eventual adult-like walking around elementary school ages, children evidence dramatic **gait changes**. When babies first begin to walk, their feet are spaced widely apart, with their toes pointed outward. They hold their legs nearly straight, not bending their knees. They typically bend their elbows upward, with the palms of their hands facing the ceiling. They either set each foot down all at once or walk on their toes, instead of rolling the foot from heel to toe as adults do. As their bodies and brains mature, their body proportions change, their balance improves and they gain additional experience, their gait patterns gradually change until by around seven years old, they walk the way adults walk.

Maturational Considerations

Despite common PE class **segregation** of males from females, some experts find it appropriate to allow adolescents of both genders to participate **together** in physical activities without body contact that require agility and lower-body strength. Some examples of these include running, ultimate Frisbee, and capture the flag. For activities that need more upper-body strength, PE teachers and coaches should base their assignment of teams on the skill levels of the individual students to prevent them from injuring themselves and one another. Experts also point out the importance of evenly matching sports teams on the basis of levels of maturation and skills. That way, deficits in individual student skill levels are not as obvious, and all students have fun participating. Some examples of suitable activities include individual and/or partners' tennis, badminton, and competitive team activities like flag football. It is important for PE teachers and coaches to monitor student physical activities, and adjust them as needed to assure all students have competitive, positive, and enjoyable experiences.

Perceptual Exploration

Infants need visual information about the characteristics and locations of objects to reach and grasp, as evidenced by their intercepting moving objects, moving their opposite hand to the right place before object arrival. Researchers have observed a basic motor development need is coordination of **perceptual exploring** and **manual skills**. Newborns not only bring hands to mouths; when stretching arms out, they also turn their heads to maintain their arm view. As they grow, older babies bring not only fingers, but also objects to their mouths. They coordinate among visual, tactile, and oral exploration; looking at; reaching; grasping; touching; turning; and mouthing objects. Babies also must use balance control, even for simple reaching actions: extending one arm out from the base of support displaces the center of gravity, requiring counterbalancing through opposition. When infants' abdominal and back muscles are not yet strong enough to support them in sitting positions, they use their hands to achieve a "tripod" (three-point) balance. Once they sit independently around 5-6 months, this frees their hands to reach, grasp, and manipulate smaller objects. Within several more months, they can coordinate leaning with reaching to avoid tipping over.

Contribution of Perception

The process of absorbing, organizing, and interpreting sensory input—i.e., **perception**—is multisensory: information from all of the senses contributes to a child's motor behaviors in response to the input received. For example, when infants see a face and hear a voice, they turn their heads. From natural newborn waving and kicking, babies adapt to their environments by developing control over reaching for things; locomotion, i.e., learning to crawl, then walk, then run, etc.; and eventually learning complex skills for sports participation. **Developing infant motor behaviors** include control over eye movements to gaze at people and things, and control over head movements. As motor competence develops, babies use perceptual information to choose which motor actions to perform. Reciprocally, they get most of this perceptual information through motor movements of their eyes, arms, hands, and legs. According to how slippery, rigid, or sloped a surface is, they will adjust their crawling or walking. Changes in size, weight, muscular strength, and body fat from infancy to toddlerhood present perceptual-motor challenges as they practice various actions.

Kinesthesis and Equilibrium

Kinesthesis is the sense of the body parts' positions and movements. Muscles, tendons, and joints contain receptors enabling kinesthesis. We are able to know where all of our body parts are at any time, and in what manner and direction they are moving, through kinesthesis. **Equilibrium** is our sense of balance. This gives us information regarding where our bodies are in space. For example, we can distinguish whether we are standing up, sitting, or lying down; in an ascending or descending elevator; or riding a roller coaster through our sense of equilibrium. The vestibular system in the inner ear is the sensory system that provides equilibrium. Specifically, the three semicircular canals contain fluid. Whenever our heads move, this fluid moves along with the head. The fluid's movement stimulates hair cells/cilia in the semicircular canals. These receptors send impulses to the brain via nerves. The brain interprets these impulses to understand the movement, giving us feedback about it. Our brains interpret the combined feedback from kinesthesis and equilibrium for orienting ourselves in space.

Perceptual and Motor Behaviors

While research has long observed that the **developmental domains** are interrelated, recent research further reinforces the depth of **interdependence** among developmental domains, processes, and factors. Some researchers point out that cognition, perception, and motor behavior transpire in the context of culture, social relationships, experience, and emotion, affecting overall brain function and mental and physical health. Others also find **perception and motor actions** are not independent, but interdependent processes; they characterize these as parts of an action system. Very early strong motivation in infants to pay attention, obtain information, explore, and engage their physical and social environments is evidence that cognitive, perceptual, motor, emotional, and social domains of development are interrelated, demonstrated by visual tracking, head-turning, and reaching. One investigator has observed that infants do not reach for desired objects because of brain programming; rather, they match their movements to their goals and the specific tasks involved. As some define it, behavior equals movement. Psychology is the study of human behavior; perception and motor behaviors inform psychological development. Some researchers find excellent opportunities for studying infants' social cognition by observing how they use social information to guide motor behavior in unfamiliar or physically challenging situations.

Promoting Motor Learning for Sports

Researchers into education have examined whether learning **specific** academic subjects could expand students' **general** attentional and learning skills. Many have concluded the nature of learning is more specific, in that the mind functions in a very detailed manner by adapting to the particular information it experiences. They additionally find that improving any individual mental process seldom improves any other individual one. These conclusions have been applied to the subject of motor learning. Experimental studies have demonstrated that movement is very closely related to sensory stimuli. This indicates that specificity in physical training is necessary for attaining successful outcomes in motor learning. Prevailing scientific evidence shows that, for students to acquire motor skills, the most important factor in practice is practicing the actual target skill itself, rather than related skills or other skills. For functional sport motor skills to become permanent behavior changes, the stimuli presented must duplicate the energy systems and movements used in a designated sport activity. Therefore, researchers conclude actually performing a sport itself is the best training for learning the motor skills involved in that sport.

Training an Athletic Skill

A common consideration in teaching new athletic skills is whether to teach a skill as a **whole**, or to break it down into its component pieces and teach those **individually**. Although task analysis has proven valuable for some purposes to education, to acquire specific sport skills, whole training has been found superior to part training for motor learning. For example, in volleyball, to teach spiking the ball, the parts would consist of approach footwork, arm work, jumping, contacting the ball, and recovery. The whole of spiking would be all these elements together. A part of spiking would be contacting the ball alone, or jumping alone, etc. Investigators reviewing the literature could not find even one study showing better results from teaching individual parts of such sport skills, or teaching individual skill parts in progressive sequence. Much additional research corroborates the concept that volleyball and other athletic skills demanding high levels of inter-limb coordination are learned best through teaching and practicing the whole skill rather than the parts, or even progressive parts.

Teaching Methods vs Experience Levels

By studying **sports training methods** as they are informed by **principles of motor learning**, researchers have found that, while educators must structure learning environments according to their particular students' skill levels and information-processing abilities, the training methods they use should nevertheless be constant across students. Neuroscience informs that beginners are more limited in their ability to process information. Additionally, motor learning principles dictate a positive correspondence between the relative complexity of the regulatory stimuli educators use and of students' experience, and vice versa. The balance is such that, without enough novelty, motor learning will not take place, while too much novelty will overwhelm student processing capacities. Teachers can control the learning environment to accommodate beginners' lower processing abilities. For example, when teaching volleyball to 3rd-graders, they can limit the content by using a smaller court, fewer players, a lighter ball, and/or a lower net. As students gain playing skills, teachers can introduce more new stimuli, enabling student motor behaviors to progress in complexity.

Significance of Posture

In both classical and contemporary theories of motor development, the role played by **posture** is central. In classical theories, which attributed motor skills development to neuromuscular maturation, the gradually increasing erectness of babies' postures as they progressed in overcoming the effects of gravity was demonstration of the growth of control over actions in their cerebral cortices. In contemporary theories involving dynamic systems approaches and perception-action relationships, posture is equally important as action's biomechanical basis. Not only locomotor skills, but manual skills and even raising and turning the head all depend on having a **stable postural base**. Sitting up, crawling, walking, and every other developmental milestone in posture necessitates learning about new perception-action systems. In learning control over a new postural system, the first step is co-contraction of large muscle groups. This enables focusing attention on the movement's goal-directed aspects by freeing more resources. But movements initiated by co-contraction are energy-inefficient and jerky. With enough practice, babies learn to activate muscles in sequence and take advantage of the forces of inertia and gravity, allowing much lesser exertion of muscular force.

Influences of Maturation and Experience

While historically, scientists believed that genetically determined growth and development—i.e., **maturation**—was responsible for motor skill development, more recent research has uncovered evidence that the motor development process is not simply passive in nature, but is also **active**, as when babies engage in movement and physically explore their environments. As they develop physical abilities through growth and acquire motor skills through independent learning, maturation and experience and their interaction all influence motor development. Earlier motor skills like crawling and walking are more strongly influenced by **maturation**, though experience also clearly plays a part, as evidenced by babies' learning through experience in early attempts, errors, failures, repetitions, and eventual success. Later, more sophisticated motor skills like playing basketball or juggling are even more influenced by **experience**, instruction, and social factors as well as genetic predispositions. While early motor skill development follows similar sequences and timing across different cultures, cultural differences do influence the rates at which motor skills develop. For example, babies sit, stand, and walk later in cultures where mothers carry them more, and earlier in cultures where parents train them early in these skills.

Promoting Psychomotor Learning

Some instructional methods PE teachers can use to promote student psychomotor learning include the **task/reciprocal method**. In this technique, the teacher uses stations to integrate the students' learning of specific tasks into the learning setup. Another is the **command/direct method**. In this style, teacher-centered task instruction is utilized: The PE teacher gives students clear explanations of the learning goals, explains the skills to be learned, and then demonstrates these skills for the students. The PE teacher then gives the students time to practice the new skills. During their practice, the PE teacher monitors their progress frequently and regularly. Another instructional method PE teachers can use to promote psychomotor learning is the **contingency/contract approach**. In this type of instruction, the PE teacher offers specified rewards to students, which are contingent upon their completing the indicated tasks. This behavioral method reinforces psychomotor behaviors, i.e., increases the probability of students' repeating them, by rewarding the behaviors.

Development of Children's Motor Skills

- **Muscle tone** during contraction and at rest varies among children. Hypotonia is low muscle tone, causing floppiness, weakness, and poor balance; hypertonia is high muscle tone, causing stiffness and difficult movement. Children with Down syndrome may have hypotonia, while those with cerebral palsy often have hypertonia.
- **Strength** is relative force of muscular contractions against resistance. Children with weak muscles may have difficulty achieving motor development milestones.
- **Endurance** enables children to sustain exertion over time, entailing multiple factors including muscle tone, strength, cardiovascular and pulmonary function, and motivation. Children with low endurance may be able to step up one stair but not climb a whole flight.
- **Balance** while stationary and while moving results from vestibular equilibrium interacting with sensory information, including sight, proprioception, muscle tone, and strength.
- **Motor planning** coordinates systems controlling perception, movement intensity, speed, and sequencing in the complex and frequently intuitive process of executing steps in physical activities.
- **Sensory integration** is interpreting environmental sensory input correctly and responding with appropriate motor activity. Children's response thresholds vary along a continuum among ranges of understimulation, average stimulation, and overstimulation.

Effects of Experience on Motor Patterns

Neurophysiological studies have found the brain has **plasticity**; i.e., both its structures and functions can be modified by various influences, such as behavioral training and other new learning. **Neuroplasticity** affords great promise for improving abilities in people with neurological damage or deficits, and those wanting to enhance their cognitive processing skills. Furthermore, some researchers have found specific **motor experiences** determine the place and character of plasticity in the corticospinal system. For example, training in motor skills stimulates generation of new synapses, enhances synaptic potential, and restructures movement representations in the motor cortex. Training in endurance generates formation of new blood vessels in the motor cortex, but does not change number of synapses or organization of motor maps. Strength training changes activation of spinal motor neurons and generates new synapses in the spinal cord, but does not change motor map organization. All three types of training modify spinal reflexes that rely on each task's specific behavioral requirements. These findings show acquiring skilled movements causes neural circuits in the motor cortex to be reorganized to support producing and refining skilled movement sequences.

Helping Students Acquire Motor Skills

PE teachers not only need to know the process of motor development thoroughly, they moreover need to understand the **principles** whereby their students learn and transfer new information to progress in learning motor skills and refining them. **Instruction and practice** are critical: without these, the extent of children's motor skills development is determined only by their natural talents and abilities. But when PE teachers give students structured, frequent practice, their motor skills development improves. In motor skills development, **student self-assessment** is a tool that can have powerful impact. When PE teachers require students to assess their own abilities and skills, students are encouraged to reflect about their current levels of skill; they become more motivated to advance these levels, and assume control over their development processes. **Observational learning** is a key principle of PE because students learn motor skills more easily by observing their correct performance demonstrated by teachers than they can by trying to follow verbal directions. It is easier to reproduce physical movements we see than imagine and produce them from what we hear.

Principle of Feedback

Input from teachers and coaches is vital for students to learn motor skills. Student motivation and interest are enhanced by **positive feedback**, while student recognition and correction of errors are enhanced by **negative feedback**. When students learn motor skills, these are temporarily saved in short-term memory. Positive feedback supports transfer to permanent, long-term memory. It not only encourages, but also helps students remember all aspects of their performance. Negative feedback is not only corrective, but also motivational: when students and athletes do not improve their technique over time, they lose motivation. Students receive **internal feedback** through kinesthesia and proprioception. When they produce movements, they receive sensations and information from their muscles, joints, and vestibular (balance) systems. They receive verbal and visual **external feedback** from teachers and coaches. External feedback that improves internal feedback by enabling students and athletes to establish kinesthetic references for correct movements and techniques is called **augmented feedback**. Extrinsic feedback includes knowledge of performance, and information about performance and technique. Studies find feedback timing equally important as feedback content. Positive feedback is crucial to beginners for successfully learning skills. Beginners may be bored by negative feedback, but corrections and results are very important to advanced students and athletes.

PE Techniques and Strategies

For students to develop greater **spatial awareness and coordination**, they need both maturity and plenty of practice. In their lessons, PE teachers should concentrate on activities that require vision, hearing, and/or touch; that are sequential in nature; and that children enjoy performing. It is very beneficial to students for PE teachers to discuss the specific steps for performing fundamental skills with them. For example, running; hitting and catching a ball; dribbling a basketball, making a basket; and setting a volleyball are all skills and activities that PE teachers can break down into incremental steps and teach them one step at a time. Instructional strategies that are recommended include first introducing a skill to students; having the students practice the skill using a variety of equipment and in a variety of settings; modifying games to incorporate practice of the requisite skills; implementing lead-up games containing these practice modifications; and then, after enough practice, giving students the opportunity to use the skills they have learned and practiced in the contexts of real games.

Spatial Awareness

Spatial awareness involves consciousness of and decisions about changes in objects' positions within three-dimensional space. The sequence of developing spatial awareness has two phases:

- recognizing object locations in space **relative to one's own body**; and
- locating multiple objects in space relative to each other, **independently of one's body**.

PE teachers can apply the concept of spatial awareness to class activities by instructing students to move toward and away from, behind and in front of, over and under, next to, inside, and outside various objects. They can provide hoops, balls, boxes, etc. as objects in various sizes and shapes. These activities develop spatial awareness, particularly in younger children or students with spatial awareness deficits. PE teachers can assess student body awareness by observing them play Simon Says; asking them to touch their body parts; make straight, twisted, and round shapes with their bodies; and fit them into variously-sized spaces. They can enhance body awareness by having children touch one body part to another, twist their necks, nod heads, wiggle noses, open mouths, close eyes, shrug shoulders, bend elbows, clap hands, snap fingers, bend knees, stamp feet, and wiggle toes.

Define Effort Awareness.

Effort awareness refers to an individual's knowledge of time, force, and balance and how these are related to physical movements and athletic activities. According to the findings of research studies, movement concepts are interrelated and interactive with the concepts of space, direction, and speed. When students understand these concepts, they will be able to move so as to avoid collisions with other people and/or objects, and they will have self-confidence in their ability to move effectively. In order to understand a sport and perform it successfully, a student or athlete must incorporate the movement concepts of vision, space, direction, and speed. For example, when a student plays basketball or soccer, s/he has to determine what the appropriate amount or distance of personal space is among players. In addition, these movement concepts are all connected with one another. For example, a student playing a sport has to coordinate speed and direction in order to change or maintain his or her pathway without losing speed. This consists of the abilities to perform ably within space and to change one's motion.

Management, Motivation, and Communication

Family Life Education

In some states, **family life education elements** are included in health and physical education classes required for graduation or diplomas. For middle and high schools, health and PE core curriculum content standards in some states include content regarding **human sexuality and relationships**. Education departments provide for parents who object to this content based on their cultural, religious, or moral beliefs by incorporating a policy that their children may be excused from those parts of the courses if parents furnish the schools with a signed statement that this content conflicts with their personal beliefs. In these cases, the schools provide excused students with alternative instructional content and activities that they determine are in alignment with their state's PE core curriculum content standards and their local health education curricula. Parents' written statements must explain to school principals or administrators how the content conflicts with their beliefs. Once administrators clarify school programs with parents, students may be excused, but must complete agreed-upon, assigned activities; e.g., taking a course in nutrition and foods, a PE class, or an independent study project, in place of a human sexuality course, to meet core curriculum content standards for comprehensive health and PE.

Being Sensitive to Various Beliefs

Although the standards set by state education departments for comprehensive health and PE afford a structure for their local school districts to follow, each school district is also responsible for maintaining a balance between aligning its curriculum with the **state standards** and also taking into account and fulfilling the **diverse needs of its student population**. In many American states, conditions of constant change in demographic profiles are increasingly the norm these days. With such continual flux, it is not realistic to expect any one teacher to know about all of the cultural beliefs, traditions, and expectations of every group represented in his or her school. As a result, school districts have the duty of collaborating with their community-based cultural and religious organizations to build cultural and religious sensitivity as a continuing endeavor. Some states have established networks to help school districts to find and access organizations specializing in expertise related to this subject. As an example, the state of New Jersey's Department of Health and Senior Services has developed a Network for Cultural Competence, with a website where educators can locate and contact groups with resources promoting cultural knowledge and responsiveness.

Culturally Relevant Curriculum

The National Association for Sport and Physical Education (NASPE, 2009) has indicated the increasing importance for PE teacher preparation to include **cultural diversity** in pedagogy. While research into general education offers more plentiful instances of cultural relevance, some investigators point out its comparative dearth in physical education. Some authors recommend methods for establishing equitable PE practices relative to race, social class, gender, and sexuality. Some focus more on evidence of versions of unintentional racism in PE. However, less research is available into **culturally relevant physical education (CRPE)**. Past studies have shown that teacher practices did not become more culturally sensitive as a result of taking courses in multicultural education. Others cite factors like communicating with students having limited English-language proficiency (LEP), the local relevance of various physical activities, and curricula including diverse representations and languages as challenges to PE teachers in attempting to design urban PE curricula that are culturally relevant.

Fitness Education

Fitness education is a part of a total PE program, directed toward helping students gain information and higher-level comprehension of both the processes of physical activity habits and health lifestyle, and the products of good health, wellness, and health-related physical fitness. The **Fitness Education Project team** formed by the National Association for Sport and Physical Education (NASPE), after reviewing current literature and consulting with nationwide professionals with expertise in pedagogy and content specialties, PE district curriculum materials, and state and national PE standards to gain insights, produced a comprehensive **Instructional Framework for Fitness Education in Physical Education (IFFEPE)**. This document's purpose is to guide educators in designing and providing fitness education by informing them as to what students should know, understand, and be able to do at each grade level from Pre-K through college. The IFFEPE's authors developed it based on the assumption that all students, regardless of age, gender, ethnicity, or cultural background, can attain healthy levels of physical fitness through engaging regularly in moderate to vigorous physical activity.

IFFEPE

The National Association for Sport and Physical Education (NASPE) created a **Fitness Education Project** and a team dedicated to it. This team studied the current research into fitness education and conferred with experts in fitness education content, instruction, curriculum, and standards across the country. Based on the information they acquired, the team developed a comprehensive **Instructional Framework for Fitness Education in Physical Education (IFFEPE)**. This resource is a set of materials to help students by guiding PE teachers and others in designing current, coherent, sequenced, integrated fitness education curriculum and instruction. Full or partial lessons from the IFFEPE can be incorporated in established PE curricula to meet grade-level fitness content. Its benchmarks enable measurement of values, knowledge, and skills requisite to competence, development of courses or curricula, or curricular inclusion of applicable domains. IFFEPE content is holistic, treating all areas as important to include in fitness education. It is designed for all students, and allows educators plenty of the creativity and instructional innovation fitness education requires. PE teachers, fitness leaders, administrators, and curriculum coordinators can use it to identify desired fitness education learning experience results, and to tailor content to meet diverse student needs on program, local, or state levels.

Adapted Physical Education

Under the federal Individuals with Disabilities Education Act (IDEA), students with qualifying **disabilities** receive special education and related services and have IEPs (individualized education programs). Special education includes PE. If a student's disability requires adaptations to participate in PE, the student must receive **APE**. While therapeutic recreation (TR), physical therapy (PT), and occupational therapy (OT) are related services, PE and APE are not related services, but instead are direct educational services according to federal law. APE is aligned with PE in terms of curriculum purposes. In defining APE, the IDEA includes motor fitness, physical fitness, fundamental motor patterns and motor skills, individual and group games and sports, lifetime sports, aquatics skills, and dance skills. These are the same skills as in PE, but individualized in design to meet the unique needs of students with disabilities. Student difficulties with physical mobility, functional independence, or motor performance that impede participating and benefiting from PE should receive APE. PT, OT, and TR may additionally be recommended for some students, but are not substitutes for or interchangeable with APE.

Benefits of APE

The federal Individuals with Disabilities Education Act (IDEA) mandates a **free and appropriate public education (FAPE)** to students who are eligible for special education services in the **least restrictive**

environment (LRE) possible. This includes physical education services. Students who cannot participate in or benefit from regular PE services because they have limitations in functional activities, motor activities, or physical mobility are therefore required to be given APE services, which are adapted to enable them to participate in and benefit from PE. Some of the benefits of APE to these students include developing functional, developmentally appropriate motor skills in young children that enable them to play and participate in educational environments with non-disabled peers; promoting an active lifestyle that incorporates physical activity; developing basic motor skills needed to participate with peers in sports and games; improving the self-image and self-esteem of students; gaining skills that increase mobility, physical independence, self-help, self-sufficiency, and independent living; and reducing health-related complications.

APE Can Improve Historical Practices

Historically, students with **disabilities** have often been excused from PE classes or assigned timekeeper, scorekeeper, or other **sedentary** roles. This reinforced assumptions that persons with disabilities must be physically passive and contributed to obesity and shorter lifespans for disabled individuals. The APE goal of over 50 percent moderate-to-vigorous physical activity (>50 percent MVPA) equals the regular PE goal. Alternative activities should not be sedentary. Educators should collaborate with students, parents, administrators, other professionals, and community members to develop active APE programs. APE can modify PE activities to enable students with disabilities to engage successfully in games, rhythms, exercises, and sports. Mainstreamed students can participate in APE within regular PE classes or in self-contained classrooms. Teachers can provide individualized PE instruction within group settings. Teaching, skills, and activities should be differentiated for each student's unique capabilities as much as possible. Students with disabilities may practice and demonstrate functional physical fitness through alternative means. For example, a non-ambulatory student could demonstrate sufficient upper-body strength for throwing a basketball at an eight-foot-high basket, or a student with limited motor, physical, and cognitive skills could demonstrate sufficient aerobic endurance for playing a modified soccer game for 10 minutes before having to stop and rest.

Movement and Lifelong Physical Activities

Develop Body and Spatial Awareness

To help students develop **body awareness**, PE teachers can instruct them to touch or point to their various body parts, form their bodies into different shapes, and to fit their bodies into differently sized and shaped spaces. These can both assess and develop body awareness. To assess and develop **spatial awareness**, PE teachers can provide differently sized and shaped objects like boxes, balls, hoops, etc. and have students move around, over, under, into, out of, in front of, in back of, and toward and away from them. To help students develop understanding of force, PE teachers can place targets at varying distances and have students throw beanbags, balls, or other objects at the targets. They can prompt students to notice how much force they must use to reach nearer vs. farther targets, and discuss use of relatively too much and too little force. Another exercise is to have spotters (carefully) positioned behind each student, and have students forcefully throw or otherwise propel wind-resistant objects like swim fins away from them to observe how this forces their bodies backward. This can also be done in swimming pools.

Concepts of Direction and Level

PE teachers can help students develop their understanding of the **spatial concept of direction** by instructing them to move to the left, to the right, forward, backward, up, down, and diagonally in space. They can prompt students to be aware of their own kinesthetic feedback that tells them in which directions they are moving. Activities that develop **rotation skills** also help children's awareness and control of the directions in which they are turning. Locomotor "car" activities for children that involve taking turns walking in pairs, one behind the other with hands on the front child's shoulders, can include having the front child "steer," changing walking directions. This develops the front child's skill in controlling **direction**, and the back child's skill in following directional changes. Rotation activities for middle childhood using equipment can involve exploring moving in various directions. Students learning to fall sideways should practice doing this in both directions. PE teachers can direct students to notice the high, middle, or low levels of their bodies or body parts during movements. When teaching how to land safely from falls by rolling sideways, PE teachers can have students practice with falling from different levels.

Pathway, Energy, Time, Speed, and Force

PE teachers can help students develop understanding and control of **pathways of movement through space** by having them walk and run in a circle, a zigzag pattern, a serpentine pattern, etc. They can also help students develop concepts of **planes in space** by having them move along circular, vertical, or horizontal pathways. To help students understand different types of **energy** required in different activities, they can have them perform short-term, high-intensity activities like lifting weights and sprinting, and explain these use fast-twitch/type II/"white" muscle fibers; and longer-duration, lower-intensity activities like distance running and bicycling, and explain these use slow-twitch/type I/"red" muscle fibers. The latter require more aerobic/oxygen-using energy whereas the former do not use oxygen and cannot be repeated once muscles fatigue until rested and replenished. PE teachers can have students run or perform other movements at different speeds to understand the roles of **time** and **speed** in movement, and have them practice increasing and decreasing the rates of their movements to gain control over speed. They can teach students how force, time, and speed interact during running as they must modify their stance time and peak force/impact time to change running speeds.

Measuring Torque

Torque is the rotational version of force. In other words, torque represents how much a given force can make something or someone rotate or turn. **Large torque** is strong rotation; **small torque** is weak rotation. In the US/English system, the unit of torque measurement is the foot-pound; in the SI system, it is the Newton-meter (Nm). With torque represented as T, force as F, and the perpendicular (right-angle) distance from the force's action line as $\perp$d, the formula for measuring torque is T=F$\perp$d. A practical example to illustrate how torque operates is to imagine two skaters on ice. One skater has longer arms and the other has shorter arms. Each skater's body is equal to a rotational axis. If both skaters extend their arms horizontally and a third person pushes on each skater's arm, this will cause the skaters to rotate. Each skater's arm length equals the quantity $\perp$d, i.e., distance between the axis (skater's body) and force. Equal force will make the longer-armed skater rotate faster because the longer arm creates greater torque.

Biomechanical Summation of Forces

Summation of forces is to attain maximal force with any movement that uses multiple muscles in a manner that enables generating the maximum force possible. Thus the total amount of force is a sum of the total individual muscles when these are added together. The **general principle of the order of use** is that larger, stronger muscle groups in the center of the body initiate power, and smaller muscles in the extremities are used for coordination and finer movements. The largest, heaviest body parts are slowest and move first; smaller body parts are faster and move last. Force is both simultaneous and sequential. To attain maximal force, use as many body parts as possible. **Sequential force**, e.g., of body, then arm, then forearm, must be well-timed: if these follow too early or late in the sequence, they are ineffective. For example, the summation events in kicking a football are: body weight is transferred forward with the abdominals leading, the hip moves forward, the leg trailing, abdominals and quadriceps move the thigh forward, quadriceps and calf muscles straighten the lower leg, and calf muscles snap the foot.

Center of Gravity

The **center of gravity** is the point at which a single force, of magnitude mg, meaning the weight of the system or body, would have to be applied to a rigid system or body in order to achieve an exact balance of the rotational and translational effects of the gravitational forces that act on the parts of the system or body. Put another way, the center of gravity is the point at which the weight of a system or body can be considered as acting. Although there is a minuscule difference between the center of gravity and the **center of mass**, they can be considered as the same for all practical applications. Therefore, center of mass is considered a synonym for center of gravity; however, center of pressure is not a synonym. In terms of the human body, its center of gravity is not fixed at any certain location in the anatomy. The location of the human body's center of gravity changes in accordance with the positions of the various body parts. The symbols used for center of gravity are C of G or COG.

Kinetics and Running.

Most sports require running speed—to outrun opponents in races, as a running start to develop enough takeoff velocity for jumping distance or height, to get to a base before being tagged, to evade tacklers, etc. Although speed-walkers can attain high speeds via an unusual gait that drops the hip with each step, running typically has faster speeds than walking. **Kinetics** is the part of biomechanics involving the study of movement and the forces that produce movement. The definition of **running** is a gait that includes an aerial phase when no body parts contact the ground or floor, with no external forces on the body (excluding gravity and wind resistance). Runners must modify the stance phase (when contacting the ground) to change speeds. A force plate measures running forces according to Newton's third law of motion (for every action there is an equal and opposite reaction): foot force produces a downward, backward force vector; the ground produces an upward, forward force. The force plate measures this ground reaction force (GRF). Faster running requires shorter stance time plus higher peak forces. Force = impulse / impact time; impulse is relatively constant. Bent knees extend impact time, reducing joint forces and injuries.

Biomechanics Concepts and Principles

The concept of **force-motion** states that when we produce or change movement, unbalanced forces act upon our bodies or objects we manipulate. **Force-time** states that substantial changes in motion are produced over time, not immediately. **Inertia** defines the property all objects have of resisting changes in states of motion. **Range of motion** is the overall extent of motion a person uses in a movement, described through angular or linear movement of the body parts. **Balance** is an individual's capacity for controlling his or her body position in relation to a base of support. The **coordination continuum** means the goal or purpose of a movement determines the most effective timing of segmental movements or muscle actions. For example, people extend their hips, knees, and ankles concurrently to lift a heavy object but use more sequential movements in the kinematic chain, from legs to trunk to arms, in overarm throwing. **Segmental interaction** means that forces operating in a system of rigid, lined bodies are transferable through joints and links. **Optimal projection** means there is a best range of angles of projection for given goals or purposes in most human throwing and propelling of projectiles.

Learning Objectives of Biomechanical Principles

When PE teachers instruct students how to apply **biomechanical principles**, students learn to produce and control force in ways that make their movements safer and more effective. For example, on the topic of effects upon objects, PE teachers can instruct students in applying the **concept of force** relative to how objects move in space. Learning objectives could include calculating and showing how the movements of projectiles are affected by the application of force; explaining and demonstrating how absorbing force increases their control over objects in sports activities, like collecting a soccer ball, bunting a softball, or catching a football; and explaining and demonstrating how efficient movement reduces the likelihood of injuries during various sports activities. For example, in soccer, kicking the ball using the instep rather than the toes can prevent injuries. On the topic of balance, PE teachers can instruct students in analyzing the concept of balance during complex movement patterns. As an example, a general learning objective could be for students to explore how their center of gravity affects their balance and performance during various movement activities.

Locomotor Skills

Among motor skills, one major category is **locomotor skills**. Locomotor skills are movements wherein we use our legs and feet to move our bodies from one location to another. The basic locomotor skills children develop, in the approximate order they usually learn them, are: walking; running; hopping; jumping; skipping; galloping; sliding, i.e., galloping sideways; and leaping. Most normally developing children typically learn to walk around the age of 1 year. They usually have learned to run, hop, and jump by the age of 2 years. They begin to learn how to gallop, skip, slide, and leap around the age of 3 years. Young children will need to be provided with plenty of opportunities for practicing, though most of them find practicing fun during early childhood. They also will need their parents to provide them with some instruction to acquire the basic locomotor skills, which they do not necessarily just learn on their own.

Basic Locomotor Skills

Here are some tips for parents to help their young children master the basic **locomotor skills**. **Walking**: Tell children to walk with straight, smooth steps and swing their arms in opposition to their feet. Have them practice different walks, e.g., on tiptoe, low with bent knees, fast and slow, robotic and liquid, etc. **Galloping**: Tell children to use one foot as "leader" and the other as "follower," alternating sides. **Jumping**: Have children keep their feet together, pushing and landing with both feet. Have them try jumping rope; see how high they can jump, how many times in a row, and how quietly they can land. **Hopping**: Have children see how quickly and slowly they can hop, and whether either side is harder. **Side-sliding**: Tell children to spread their arms, lead with one foot, and rise in the middle. **Leaping**: Have children lead with one foot and leap over an object, landing with the other foot. **Skipping**: Tell children to march, raising one knee high and hopping on the other foot—step/hop, step/hop, alternating sides.

Fundamental Elementary Motor Skills

Some **fundamental motor skills** critical to learn in **elementary school** include running, jumping vertically, leaping, dodging, kicking, overhand throwing, catching, ball bouncing, punting, forehand striking, and two-handed side-arm striking. Some examples of the overhand throw as applied in advanced form in specific sports include baseball and softball pitching, tennis and badminton serving, throwing a javelin, volleyball passing, and basketball shoulder passes. Some examples of the two-handed side-arm strike as applied in advanced sports-specific forms include swinging a golf club, hockey stick, or baseball bat; forehand drives in tennis, badminton, disc golf, squash, or table tennis (ping pong); and cut shots in volleyball, golf, or pool. Running, vertical jumping, kicking, and catching should be introduced in kindergarten. Running, vertical jumping, and catching should be mastered in 2nd grade, kicking in 3rd grade. Overhand throwing, ball bouncing, leaping, and dodging should be introduced in 1st grade. Ball bouncing, leaping, and dodging should be mastered in 3rd grade, overhand throwing in 4th grade. Punting, forehand striking, and two-handed side-arm striking should be introduced in 2nd grade. Punting should be mastered in 4th grade, forehand and two-hand side-arm strikes in 5th.

Non-Locomotor Skills

Whereas locomotor skills involve moving from one location to another using the legs and feet, **non-locomotor skills** are motor skills that do not involve moving among locations. Non-locomotor skills involve little or no shifting of the base of support, and do not cause changes in position. Lifting a weight and squeezing a ball are examples of non-locomotor skills. Some other common movements that involve non-locomotor skills are balancing, swaying, turning, twisting, and swinging. **Bending** is movement around a joint between two body parts. **Dodging** is sharply avoiding a person or object, e.g., by leaning away or ducking. **Stretching** is extending or hyperextending the joints to straighten or lengthen the body parts. **Twisting** rotates the body or body parts around an axis having a stationary base. **Turning** is moving the body through space in a circle, releasing the base of support. **Swinging** involves circular or pendular movements below an axis of the body or body parts. **Swaying** is like swinging, but above an axis. **Pushing** is applying force against a person or object to move one's body away or move the person or object away. **Pulling** is exerting force to move people or objects closer to one's body.

Non-Locomotor Skills Grades 1, 2, and 3

In **grade 1**, teachers introduce non-locomotor skills like bending, twisting, curling, and swaying involving a broad range of joints by discussing weight transfer, arm-leg opposition, and other mechanics involved. Teachers have students imitate elephants swaying and trees swaying in wind. Teachers assign small groups to develop warm-up routines using these skills, identify joints used, and name each movement. In **grade 2**, teachers introduce and demonstrate the motions, pair students to perform warm-up and cool-down activities requiring two people using these movements, and have students identify joints and major muscle groups involved and identify exercises targeting each joint in a warm-up routine. In **grade 3**, teachers introduce and demonstrate the skills, work on building student comprehension of principles of improving flexibility, discuss which joints can move, and list exercises targeting each joint in a fitness

- 84 -

routine. Teachers design a fitness routine for students to improve range of motion in specified joints, connecting the different movements; and pair students to perform these and improvise exercise that equally stretch opposing muscles in specified joints. Teachers have individual students create and lead warm-up and fitness routines in class.

Non-Locomotor Skills Grades 4,5, and 6

In **grade 4**, teachers review non-locomotor skills and discuss their importance in physical activities, including bending in tucked, pike, squat, forward, and backward positions; stretching before physical activity, including identifying muscle groups to stretch in warm-up and cool-down; static balancing, with 1-part to 4-part bases and in gymnastic routines; and dynamic balancing, including turning in dance and games and flopping from sitting, kneeling, and standing positions. Teachers guide paired students in mat exercises, have them create routines targeting multiple muscle groups, and have all students perform these. In **grade 5**, teachers review; have students develop skills further through individual and group activities; perform bends, stretches, and rolls on mats; and create warm-up and cool-down routines, and lead the class in performing these. Teachers invite a physical therapist or other professional to discuss stretching and injuries caused by improper stretching. In **grade 6**, teachers review; have students explore non-locomotor movements on mats, pointing out specific movements discovered; assign pairs or small groups to create warm-up routines, recording and displaying activities and muscle groups included on posters; assign homework of short reports with diagrams explaining the relationship of stretching and injury prevention; and emphasize more independent student movement development.

Manipulative Or Object Control Skills

Manipulative or object control skills are the category of motor skills that involve using objects. They include both fine motor skills, as in buttoning buttons, zipping zippers, fastening and unfastening clasps, twist ties, etc.; using crayons, pencils, pens, and other writing, drawing, and painting implements; using spoons, forks, and other eating utensils; and gross motor skills, as in swinging a baseball bat, a tennis racket, a jai alai cesta, a jump rope, a golf club, a bow and arrow, etc. The actions included in manipulative skills include pushing, pulling, lifting, swinging, striking, throwing, catching, kicking, rolling a ball, volleying, bouncing, and dribbling. A consideration to keep in mind when young children are first learning manipulative skills is not to expect them to be perfectly accurate, for example hitting a target, throwing directly to another player in a game, or catching a ball thrown to them. Children must first master the throwing, catching, hitting, kicking, or other action before they can develop accuracy as well. It can help to have children practice the movements and techniques with imaginary objects to begin, and then progress to real objects.

Manipulative Movement Activities 5 years

Teachers can put hoops on the ground or hang them from doorframes or trees with rope for young children to practice throwing things through them. Parents can develop **throwing skills** at home by having children throw rolled socks into laundry hampers or baskets. When they succeed, have them take one step further back for the next throw. Teachers and parents can use pillows or cushions to set up courses (with or without children's participation), placing empty boxes, wastebaskets, buckets, etc. as "golf holes." Have children take turns throwing beanbags into the holes. Children can crumple paper into "snowballs"; adults tape these up and give baskets of them to two groups of children. Mark a line between groups with rope, tape, or chalk. On a signal, children throw "snowballs" over the line for 30 seconds, see who has the fewest snowballs left, switch teams, and repeat. Have children clean up by throwing snowballs into baskets. Adults can cut centers out of empty plastic food tubs to make rings, and have children try to toss rings over plastic bottles. Have children try to toss coins onto paper or plastic plates on the floor or ground. Let children throw a ball trying to knock a stuffed animal off a stool.

Manipulative Movement Activities 5-12 years

Older children can practice throwing for **accuracy** or **distance**. Here are some activities to practice throwing for distance.

- **Force Back:** Students face one another in pairs, throwing a ball toward the other as far as they can. The thrower's partner catches or retrieves the ball, throwing it back from where it landed.
- **Three Court Ball:** Assign students to two equally-numbered teams. Each team has one-third of a court and a tennis ball. Students try to throw the ball into the middle third of the court and have it bounce over the other team's goal line.
- **Scatterball:** Use a baseball diamond or any field with several bases arranged in a diamond, circle, square, or other enclosed shape. Divide students into two teams: throwers and fielders. Throwers take turns, one at a time, throwing balls as far away as they can. Then each thrower runs around bases until told to stop. The fielders catch or retrieve the balls thrown and collect them in a basket, bucket, or other receptacle. Switch teams and repeat. The team scoring the most runs wins. Students can also practice catching by throwing and bouncing balls or beanbags in pairs, groups, and teams.

Playing Baseball, Basketball, and Football

Baseball requires locomotor skills for players to run to the bases after a hit, and to run to catch fly balls. It requires non-locomotor skills as players twist their bodies to field the ball, catch the ball, and when batting; lean backward or forward to field balls, lean or bend down to catch low or rolling ground balls; reach out to tag runners out before they reach a base; and go through the movement sequence of pitching that involves leaning back, twisting, raising one leg, etc. Catchers also move their bodies while squatting to catch pitches without changing their base of support. Baseball additionally involves manipulative skills for pitching, catching, fielding, and batting. **Basketball** involves the locomotor skills of running and jumping; the non-locomotor skills of leaning, stretching, and bending; and the manipulative skills of dribbling, passing, catching, and throwing the ball. **Football** involves the locomotor skills of running, and sometimes jumping over other players; non-locomotor skills of bending in the huddle and twisting when dodging tackles; and manipulative skills of holding, passing (throwing), intercepting, and receiving (catching) the ball.

Playing Tennis, Volleyball, and Golf

Tennis involves the locomotor skills of running, walking, and jumping over the net at the end of a match. It uses the non-locomotor skills of bending to pick up a ball, stretching and twisting to prepare for a serve; and stretching, bending, leaning, and twisting and reaching to return the ball in a volley. It uses manipulative skills for swinging the racket to hit the ball when serving and returning. **Volleyball** uses the locomotor skills of walking to take and rotate positions, and running to reach the ball; the non-locomotor skills of stretching, reaching, twisting, and bending to reach the ball in high and low positions; and the manipulative skills of serving the ball using the fist, spiking the ball from above with the palms of the hands, and hitting the ball from below with the fists. **Golf** uses the locomotor skill of walking; the non-locomotor skills of twisting and turning to swing, and bending to retrieve the ball from the cup, green, trap, etc.; and the manipulative skills of swinging the club to hit the ball, retrieving the ball by hand, and writing down scores.

Locomotor, Non-Locomotor, and Manipulative Skills K-6

Fourth-graders should run and change direction dribbling a basketball or kicking a soccer ball. **Fifth-graders** should integrate skills by changing speeds and directions to evade defenders while dribbling a basketball, running with a football, or kicking a soccer ball; or consistently and strategically moving to open spaces to receive passes in small-sided games. **Sixth-graders** should run and leap over consecutive cones or other obstacles without stopping. **Kindergarteners** should be able to volley beach balls or balloons to themselves five successive times and hit balls or balloons up 9-12 inches continuously with different body parts. **First-graders** should be able to vary their striking force and volley 6-10 times upward, alternating left and right palms. **Second-graders** should be able to volley with partners using both hands, and volley underhand while walking forward c. 20 feet. **Third-graders** should make and catch forearm passes to themselves, and volley to partners using overhead passes. **Fourth-graders** should serve underhand or overhand with correct form, and consistently volley using forearm passes to themselves. **Fifth-graders** should serve underhand, overhand, pass overhead, and forearm pass; show correct overhead volleying form against a wall; and consistently serve volleyballs over nets 6 feet high or walls from 15 feet away. **Sixth-graders** should return volleyballs with forearm passes at least 6 feet high.

Softball vs. Baseball

A variation of baseball, **softball** uses a smaller infield and a larger ball. Two main rule differences from baseball are that, in softball, pitching must be underhand; and regulation softball games have seven innings rather than nine as baseball does. Softballs are 11-12 inches in circumference, which is 3 inches bigger than baseballs. Infields have bases 60 feet apart, not 90 feet apart as they are in baseball. Two types of softball are slow-pitch and fast-pitch. **Slow-pitch**, the kind most often played, has 10 players per team. Slow-pitch softball sometimes uses a ball larger than the usual 12 inches. Slow-pitch softball requires the pitcher to throw the ball in an arcing path. It also does not allow bunting the ball or stealing bases as baseball does. **Fast-pitch** softball has nine players per team, the same as baseball. As its name indicates, it requires faster pitching than slow-pitch softball. Fast-pitch softball also permits bunting and stealing as baseball does. In both slow-pitch and fast-pitch softball, an underhand pitch is required. Pitching distances required are from 46 or 43 feet for men, 39 feet for women, and 35 feet for girls. This contrasts with baseball's 60.5 foot pitching distance.

Rules and Practices of Soccer

Soccer fields are rectangular, with a goal at each end. Soccer teams have 11 players, who score by kicking the ball into the opposing team's goal. Some competition rules stipulate a minimum number of players per team, commonly seven. Only goalkeepers are allowed to touch the ball with their arms and/or hands while it is in play, and only in their penalty areas in front of the goals. Goal posts are 8 yards apart. Outfielders are allowed to contact the ball with their heads and/or torsos in addition to their feet. Whichever team scores more goals by the end of the soccer game is the winner. For tied scores, a draw is declared; there is a penalty shootout; or extra time is designated, depending on the format of the competition. Soccer has 17 official game laws. Soccer balls are 27-28 inches around, weigh 14-16 ounces, and are inflated to pressures of 8.5-15.6 pounds per square inch (at sea level). Adult pitching distances are 110-120 yards long and 70-80 yards wide internationally, 100-130 yards long and 45-90 yards wide non-internationally. Soccer/association football's highest governing body is **FIFA** (Fédération Internationale de Football Association), which organizes the World Cup every four years.

Characteristics of Tennis

Tennis is played with rackets strung with cord hitting a small, felt-covered, hollow rubber ball over/around a net in the center of the court to the opponent's side. Courts are clay, grass, asphalt, concrete, or acrylic, and sometimes carpeted indoors. Nets are 3 feet high in the center, and 3 feet 6 inches high at the posts. The object is preventing opponents from returning the ball within bounds. Returning the ball within bounds earns a point. Tennis is played by opposing single players or doubles (teams of two). One player, behind the baseline between sideline and center mark, serves the ball.

Receiver(s) can be anywhere on their side of the court. Legal services must clear the net without touching and go diagonally into the opposing service box. A "let," a serve hitting the net before landing in the service box, is void and retaken. Serves falling wide or long of the service box or not clearing the net are faults. Touching the baseline or extension of the center mark with one's foot before hitting the ball is a foot fault. Two consecutive service faults (double faults) give receiver(s) the point. Legal returns hit the ball before two bounces. Players and teams cannot hit the ball twice consecutively. During rallies, legal returns can hit the net.

Track and Field

Track and field is a sport that encompasses a number of different competitive athletic activities that involve running, jumping, and throwing skills. Among **running events**, it includes sprinting (short, fast running contests), middle- and long-distance races, hurdling (jumping over barriers while running), and relay races. Included among **jumping events** are the long jump (a horizontal distance jumping contest), high jump (a vertical height jumping contest), triple jump, and pole vault (clearing a high bar by propelling one's body with a pole). **Throwing events** include the shot put (swinging and flinging a small, heavy iron shot for the maximum distance), javelin (throwing a long, spear-like projectile for distance), discus (throwing a flat, disc-shaped projectile for distance), and hammer throw (throwing a hammer-like projectile for distance). Track and field also includes events that **combine** multiple sports into a single contest, such as the heptathlon combining seven events, the decathlon combining ten events, and others. Athletes win running events with the fastest time, and jumping and throwing events with the longest heights or distances. Major track and field competition activities include the International Association of Athletics Federations (IAAF) governing body's World Championship, and the Olympics.

Volleyball

Volleyball teams have six players, scoring points by grounding the ball on the opposing team's court, and extensive rules. Serves are from behind the court's rear boundary line with the hand/arm, over a net. The receiving team must keep the ball airborne within their court and return it to the serving team's court. Players can touch the ball up to three times; one player cannot touch the ball twice consecutively.* Grounding the ball on the opposite court is a "kill," winning the rally for that team, which gets a point and the serve beginning the next rally. A team loses a rally by committing a fault. Faults include: catching and throwing the ball, *double hit, four consecutive ball contacts by one team, making the ball touch the floor outside the opposite court or without clearing the net first, touching the net (a net foul), and crossing the boundary line while serving (a foot fault). Common volleyball techniques include spiking and blocking (both requiring vertical jumping skill), setting, passing, offensive and defensive roles, and specialized player positions.

Dribbling and Shooting Basketballs

Kindergarteners should be able to twirl a hula hoop and roll it on the floor. They should be able to drop a ball and catch it at the peak of its bounce. They should be able to dribble a ball continuously with their dominant hand. **First-graders** should be able to juggle two scarves, pass beanbags hand to hand between their legs in a figure 8, and dribble a ball with their dominant hand while moving. **Second-graders** should be able to dribble a ball around stationary objects, and dribble a ball with both left and right hands while standing in place without losing control. **Third-graders** should be able to circle a hula hoop around the waist without using the hands; juggle three scarves or plastic bags in a cascading pattern; and dribble a basketball in a figure-8 pathway, alternating dribbling hands, to the opposite sides of cones set 10 inches apart.

Dribbling and Shooting, Throwing, Catching, and Rolling Skills

For dribbling and shooting, **4th-graders** should be able to demonstrate a bank shot with a basketball, and dribble the ball around obstacles with good ball control while changing directions at a jogging speed. **Fifth-graders** should be able to juggle small objects like beanbags, tennis balls, etc. in a cascade pattern; dribble a basketball with good control while changing speeds and directions around defensive opposing players who must walk and not use their hands; and demonstrate a basketball layup using the opposing foot on takeoff while moving continuously throughout. **Sixth-graders** should be able to shoot a basketball from anywhere on the court behind the second hash mark*, demonstrating good form. *PE teachers may want to vary the distance they use to assess this skill. **Sixth-graders** should also be able to demonstrate good skills for handling basketballs. For throwing and catching, **kindergarteners** should throw and catch beanbags to themselves and catch teacher-thrown (7-9 inches) foam balls from 5 feet. **First-graders** should roll a tennis ball and scoop up a slowly rolled tennis ball in their hands; throw small, soft balls with hand-foot opposition; and consistently catch big (4-9 inches) balls self-tossed above the head.

Throwing, Catching, and Rolling Skills

Second-graders should catch small, soft tennis/yarn balls at peak, self-tossed above the head; throw balls 7 inches and larger against walls from roughly 8 feet away and catch them before they bounce; and underhand-toss small balls with correct form and accuracy to targets or partners from 15 feet. **Third-graders** should demonstrate correct form in a two-handed overhead/soccer throw, pass balls to slowly-moving partners using chest and bounce passes, catch balls while slowly traveling, and overhand-throw small balls using correct form to partners and targets from at least 20 feet. **Fourth-graders** should throw and catch footballs, Frisbees, and other sport-specific balls or objects with correct form; consistently scoop up rolled balls with hands using mature form (knuckles on ground, pinkies together), moving laterally to get ahead of the ball; and play "keep-away" and other small-sided, low-level throwing-catching games. **Fifth-graders** should throw and catch footballs, basketballs, and other sport-specific balls within skill combinations, e.g., catching, dribbling, and passing to moving teammates; and throw lead passes including chest bounce, overhand, and underhand to moving teammates with mature form and accuracy. **Sixth-graders** should accurately throw and catch footballs, basketballs, and other sport balls to and from partners in dynamic situations with mature form, and advance balls down playing areas passing back and forth in small-sided games.

Striking With Implements

- **Kindergarteners**: Balance beanbags or objects on rackets and paddles while walking; hit balls off batting tees using implements.
- **First-graders**: Strike beach balls or balloons forward using short implements while walking 20 feet without letting them hit the floor; strike four times without their hitting the floor using short, light implements (e.g., lollipops).
- **Second-graders**: Bounce, then strike balls at walls or targets; strike beach balls or balloons with imple-ments over low nets to partners without their touching the ground or floor; consistently strike balls upward with only one bounce.
- **Third-graders**: Successfully hit balls or objects from close-proximity "soft tosses"; bounce and strike small foam tennis balls with soft, controlled forehand across the gym or into large areas; use long-handled implements to strike objects on the floor or ground to targets.
- **Fourth-graders**: Successfully hit self-tossed objects with one bounce; volley or rally objects using implements over nets and low barriers; receive teacher hockey passes and shoot to targets from about 10 feet.

- **Fifth-graders**: Successfully strike underhand teacher-pitched (3-5 inches) whiffle or foam balls; repeatedly hit balls forehand or backhand against walls at close range; bounce and hit small foam balls with soft, controlled backhand into large areas; dribble and shoot at goals with continuous action using long-handled implements.
- **Sixth-graders**: Successfully strike underhand-teacher-pitched softballs; serve balls without bouncing consistently at target areas; and give-and-go using long-handled implements.

Manipulative Skills Involving Kicking

- **Kindergarteners**: Dribble a soccer ball slowly with both feet while walking; approach stationary balls and kick with high follow-through without stopping; kick stationary balls with any foot part with high leg backswing and follow-through.
- **First-graders**: Dribble medium/large balls with either foot, walking/jogging; kicking balls with solid contact, high follow-through; approaching stationary balls, kick without stopping with high follow-through.
- **Second-graders**: Dribble balls using both feet, jogging; trap balls when stopping; show correct form kicking balls using insteps; kick slowly-rolled balls to kickers with solid contact and high follow-through.
- **Third-graders**: Dribble soccer balls using feet insides/outsides, running at varying speeds; pass balls to partners or targets using inside-foot kicks somewhat accurately and consistently; punt balls, with or without a bounce, using correct form, 15 feet or more most times.
- **Fourth-graders**: Dribble around stationary opponents or objects without object contact or ball loss; trap teammate-rolled balls; dribble and instep-kick moving balls at large goals.
- **Fifth-graders**: Dribble around lightly resistant, moving opponents; punt soccer balls and/or footballs 30 feet or more with two- or three-step approaches; make lead passes while dribbling with inside-foot kicks to moving teammates.
- **Sixth-graders**: Change speeds and directions to evade opponents while dribbling soccer balls; trap balls from different speeds and heights; show competency with soccer dribbling and inside-foot passes in "keep-away" games.

Recreational Activities

For people to engage in recreational activities, they must have **free time** when they are not occupied with working, activities of daily living, sleeping, or social obligations. Historically, people had less leisure time than they do today: they needed more time to survive physically and economically. With industrialization, higher standards of living, longer life expectancies, and more commercially offered recreational activities, people now have more **leisure time** available. Although some perspectives see leisure as spare time, others see it as an essential part of civilization and personal development because it enables people to reflect on the realities and values they overlook during daily life activities. Leisure is viewed as both a reward in and of itself and a reward for work, or even the purpose of work. Today, leisure has come to be seen as reflecting a nation's character and values: the United Nations Universal Declaration of Human Rights considers leisure a human right. Recreational activities are pursued for purposes of pleasure, healthy lifestyles, social interaction, competition, physical and mental rehabilitation, and other therapeutic and preventive medical purposes.

PE Competencies Grades 1-2

- **Body awareness**: demonstrate body movements (flexion, extension, rotation) and shapes. Walk, run, skip, and slide. Stop at boundaries with control. Quickly, safely change direction without falling. Throw underhand, roll, and dribble a ball. Identify walking, running, galloping, skipping, hopping, jumping, leaping, and sliding.

- **Space concepts**: Demonstrate directions, pathways, levels, and ranges during activities; p~ locomotor skills while changing these; apply them in simple activities or games (moving to dou~ tagging, etc.).
- **Movement quality**: Understand and apply energy and force, time, flow, balance concepts to psychomotor skills, e.g., starting and stopping without falling; bending knees to lower center of gravity; showing understanding of hard and soft, tense and relaxed force variations; controlling personal force, e.g., in tagging, striking; demonstrating fast and slow movement; moving to simple beats and rhythms; following simple, teacher-led rhythmic movements; combining jumping and turning, bouncing and catching; showing smooth transitions between dance or rhythmic movements.
- **Health-related fitness elements**: Begin identifying physiological exercise effects like faster breathing and heart rate; define the four health-related fitness components in their own words. Additional competencies include movement-related problem-solving skills, awareness of personal responsibility for individual wellness, self-confidence and success, safe behavior for self and others, and appropriate social interactions.

PE Competencies Grades 3-6

- **Grades 3-4**: Describe movements identifying body parts and actions. Identify basic muscle groups and movements. Show awareness of body part relationships (opposition, unison, sequence). Demonstrate leaping, alternating leading foot. Apply space concepts in movements with others. Balance on various equipment with control. Show an understanding of static and dynamic balance. Show comprehension of how bodies create and absorb force. Choose forces appropriate to tasks. Control personal and manipulative force, like dribbling while walking and running. Demonstrate slow, medium, and fast movement. Move with tempo changes. Incorporate various equipment into rhythmic patterns and movements. Combine up to three movements with or without equipment, e.g., jump-roping routines. Demonstrate smooth transitions among sequential motor skills, like running to jumping. Solve movement challenges combining concepts of force, time, and balance, e.g., gymnastics routines. Define, apply, and assess the four health-related fitness components.
- **Grades 5-6**: Identify specific muscle groups and movements. Combine body movements and shapes. Identify major skills in beginning gymnastics, dance, and sports. Recognize similar skills in different activities. Perform movement sequences. Adjust force for tasks projecting objects, using various equipment. Adjust body movements for speed changes. Combine movement concepts and motor skills in series.

PE Competencies Grades 7-8

Give partners and groups constructive feedback; solve more complex problems with larger groups in simple movement challenges. Describe body movements using more advanced terminology. Show an understanding of body part relationships in performing more complex skills. Identify major skills involved in more complex gymnastics, dance, sports, and/or related activities. Recognize similarities in the use of space in tactics, dance, gymnastics and other advanced activities. Perform more complex movement sequences like low/high ropes exercises. Keep time to music while performing steps and patterns in a variety of dance styles. Adjust movements with partners or groups to a beat. Combine speed, force, directions, levels, and pathways in a dance routine, a sport tactic like dribbling against a defender, or other complex series of movement concepts and motor skills. Demonstrate mature form in various basic skills; adjust skills to more complex situations, e.g., throwing and hitting to different locations. Assess personal performance on Fitnessgram or other nationally accepted instrument. Monitor heart and respiratory rate, perceived exertion, recovery rate during and following activity. Understand basic FITT principles. Play by rules, show appropriate sports conduct, officiate small-group games, appropriately assume leader-follower roles, cooperate with others, show appreciation for appropriate feedback, interact with others from diverse backgrounds.

PE Competencies Grades 9-12

Recognize personal strengths and weaknesses and develop strategies accordingly. Give partners and groups critical, specific feedback to improve skills and efficiency. Describe body movements using advanced terminology. Identify similar skills in different activities, like volleyball spikes and tennis/badminton smashes. Apply space concepts applicably in varied activities, e.g., dance or gymnastic floor routines and set plays and other tactics in sports games. Recognize similar uses of space among different advanced activities. Apply balance skills in various activities like yoga, skiing, Tae Bo, and volleyball. Demonstrate competency choosing and performing skills in several new activities, e.g., territorial team sports, wall and net sports, target sports, run-scoring games, rhythmic activities, and outdoor adventure or recreation activities. Choose, perform, and apply knowledge and skills proficiently in two different kinds of sports or physical activities. Regularly participate in physical activities to attain and maintain personal activity goals. Assess, refine, maintain comprehensive personal fitness plans based on nationally accepted assessment. Adjust activities according to knowledge of physiological effects. Analyze characteristics of sports and activities. Persevere to achieve higher performance levels. Anticipate and correct potentially dangerous outcomes (spotting, refereeing, and belaying). Evaluate competition by quality, not results. Show self-discipline and self-direction. Respect feedback and revise actions. Develop leading and following skills. Include diverse others. Help others.

Participating in Sports with Disabilities

Depending whether an individual has acquired a **disability** later in life or has had it from birth, some individuals will not have had experiences with sports early in life. This presents one **obstacle** to sports participation later and throughout life. Another common problem for people with disabilities is people in their communities, schools, and organizations lacking awareness and understanding of how to include persons having disabilities in sports events they organize and manage. Limited community resources, programs, and opportunities to acquire training, participate, and compete affect people with disabilities. This limitation sometimes results from the aforementioned lack of awareness and understanding about inclusion methods; and sometimes also exists despite community awareness, understanding, and desire, e.g., when funding and support are still missing. Lack of accessible gyms, buildings, and other facilities is another barrier. Dearth of accessible transportation interferes with attending sports events to participate. Social and psychological barriers include parent, teacher, coach, and even disabled people's attitudes and beliefs toward disability and sports participation. Inadequate access to information and resources is another obstacle.

Current Opportunities for Those with Disabilities

Associations and organizations in the world devoted to accommodating **athletes with disabilities** have grown markedly from the 1970s until now. Many of these are international groups. People with disabilities in some nations also have more opportunities now than in the past for participation in PE in schools, community associations, clubs, and casual recreational activities. In the arena of competitive sports, opportunities include disability-specific and sport-specific world championships; the Parapan American Games and other regional tournaments featuring multiple sports; certain Olympics Games events designated for athletes with disabilities; similar such events in the Commonwealth Games; and additionally, some athletes with disabilities compete against non-disabled athletes in some mainstream competitions. Internationally, 18 or more games now exist for athletes with disabilities. Among the three biggest international competitions, the Special Olympics offer year-round opportunities for training and competition to people with intellectual disabilities at every level; the Paralympic Games include intellectual disabilities, cerebral palsy, spinal cord injuries, amputations, visual impairments, and other disabilities; and the Deaflympics offer competitions for deaf and hard-of-hearing athletes.

Sports for People with Disabilities

Research evidence in recent decades shows that quality of life and functional abilities are improved for people with **disabilities** by participating in **sports and other physical activity**. Studies have found that physical well-being and health are enhanced across disability groups by participation in physical activity and sports. General affect, as well as physical fitness, are seen to improve through sports and physical activity in psychiatric patients diagnosed with anxiety and depressive disorders. Research studies have also established correlations between physical and sports activity and increased self-esteem, social awareness, and self-confidence in people with disabilities, which can contribute to their empowerment. Also in recent decades, a major focus has developed on including and integrating people with disabilities into mainstream sports. This has resulted in many new opportunities for them to compete or participate. Disability sports participation also contributes on a global scale to national identity and nation-building. After natural and man-made disasters, sports participation helps to rehabilitate people with disabilities.

Physical Benefits of Recreational Activities

Participating in **recreation** can enhance an individual's **physical health and wellness**. This is especially true of participating in **outdoor recreational activities**. According to the findings of research studies, people who are often active in recreation offered at state parks are found to make fewer visits to the doctor, to have lower body mass indexes (BMIs, i.e., the ratio of their weight to their height), and lower systolic (the top or first number) blood pressure than people who are not active in such recreational parks activities. Moreover, a State Parks report from California (2005) has shown that recreational activities outdoors constitute some of the best opportunities for people to increase the amounts of exercise that they get. In addition, another research study (2001) has found that the amounts of physical activity in which people participate in their communities are directly influenced by how many recreational facilities are available in their area.

Effects of Recreational Activity

The relationship between **physical and mental health** is reciprocal: Not only does physical wellness promote better mental health, but mental wellness also can have an impact on physical well-being. When people participate in physical, recreational, and leisure activities, it gives them a sense of control over how they spend their time. This is important to busy people who often feel overwhelmed by all of the obligations they must meet. It also offers relief from those required duties in the form of having fun instead of only doing things they have to do. Leisure activities give people opportunities to achieve balance in their lives. Recreational activities help individuals manage stress more effectively, and they decrease symptoms of depression. Parents benefit their children by participating in leisure activities as they model healthy ways of managing emotions and addressing stress for them. One State Parks report (California, 2005) found that simply remembering a past outdoor recreation can elevate one's mood.

Leisure Recreation

Research studies investigating the effects of **leisure recreation** have found that quality of life is improved by finding balance in life, and one important way people can find such balance is by allocating some of their time for leisure and recreation. In addition, physical recreation is especially related to enhancing **self-esteem**. People who participate regularly in recreational activities are more likely to report greater satisfaction with their lives. Greater life satisfaction is implicated significantly in better mental health. Better mental health is in turn associated with better physical health. As overwhelming evidence of this, in a 2000 study by the American Recreation Coalition, 90 percent of respondents who regularly engaged in recreational activities reported satisfaction with their physical fitness and health. A sharp contrast was the 60 percent of respondents not regularly engaging in recreational activities, who reported dissatisfaction with their fitness and health. Such benefits make recreational therapy (RT) important in rehabilitation programs. The American Therapeutic Recreation Association highlights RT benefits to recovering addicts, psychiatric patients, seniors, and children including better body function, improved cognitive function, stress management, and accelerated healing from medical conditions.

Rhythmic Movement

The **elements of rhythm** include beat, duration, tempo, accent, meter, phrase, rhythms, and polyrhythms. **Beat** is the underlying pulse that can be heard and counted in music, percussion, and rhythmic movements like tapping toes, clapping hands, snapping fingers, dribbling basketballs, etc. **Duration** is the length or span of time covered by a beat. **Tempo** is the speed or pace at which music and rhythmic movement proceeds, from slow to fast and everything in between. **Accent** is additional emphasis on one or more beats. **Meter** is the rhythmic organization/time signature of music. For example, the 4/4 time signature means there are four beats to each measure and the quarter note gets one count. The 6/8 time signature means there are six beats to each measure and the eighth note gets one count. Just as a phrase in language is a combination of words, a **musical phrase** is a combination of beats, which can be longer than a single measure. **Rhythms** are combinations of beats, which may be equal in duration/interval ("1, 2, 3, 4") or uneven, mixing fast and slow beats and/or different durations. **Polyrhythms** are multiple rhythms played simultaneously in layers.

Rhythmic Movement Activity

"Brain Dance" (A.G. Gilbert, 2006), done to music from *Christy Lane's Authentic African and Caribbean Rhythms* (2000) is a warm-up activity for completing the eight motor patterns on the beat in sequence.

- **Breath**: Move arms up and down, coordinating with inhaling and exhaling.
- **Tactile**: To "wake up proprioceptors," i.e., raise awareness and sensation of location in space and body movement, brush, squeeze, tap, and slap body areas and muscles.
- **Core-distal**: Bring all body parts close to center, and then extend outward.
- **Head-tail**: Bring head and tailbone closer front and back; flex, extend, and laterally flex the spine, e.g., rounding, arching, and side-to-side "snake" movements.
- **Upper-lower halves**: Move only the upper body and arms bilaterally first, then move only the lower body and legs bilaterally.
- **Body-side** (left/right halves): Move the left arm and leg together, then move the right arm and leg together.
- **Cross-lateral** (diagonal body division): Make movements in opposition, e.g., lifting the left knee, touching it with the right hand and vice versa, crossing the midline.
- **Vestibular** (inner ear): Disrupt and restore balance by moving off-balance and then stopping, using movements like rocking, spinning, etc.

Teaching Rhythm

The "hip-hop" activity (Cardinal, 2013) gives students practice in **changing duration** among regular time, half-time, and double-time, plus emphasis on **beat and phrasing**. Recommended musical selections are Pachelbel's *Canon in D* and Jay Sean's *Do You Remember*. Teachers lead students in tapping two fingers together to music, lightly so as not to influence classmates or overwhelm the music, first in half-time, then regular time, and then double-time. Students then repeat each step individually for practice. Then they repeat tapping while marching in place (non-locomotor), then while walking (locomotor) with full motion through each beat's duration—first at half-time; then when the teacher says "Hip," speeding up to regular time; when the teacher cues "Hop," slowing down to half-time; when the teacher says "Hip-hip," speeding up two levels to double-time; and when the teacher says "Hop-hop," slowing down two levels to half-time. Each is performed for two 8-counts, rotating from half-time to regular time to double-time, back to half-time, etc., including full range of arm movements. Tapping-and-walking combinations begin with just walking half-time, then walking regular time while tapping half-time, then walking double-time while tapping regular time, then walking half-time while tapping double-time, etc.

Accent and Phrasing

An activity (Cardinal, 2013) that emphasizes **accent and phrasing** involves bouncing pinky balls on different beats within a measure or phrase, first while standing (non-locomotor and manipulative) and then while walking (locomotor, non-locomotor, and manipulative). Teachers instruct students to stand and bounce balls on the "1" of each 4-count phrase, then on the "2," then on the "3," then on the "4," practicing repeatedly before changing beats. After enough practice, teachers have students do this while walking. They can then give them different combinations of bouncing with walking, such as step, bounce, step, bounce; bounce, step, bounce, step; step, step, bounce; bounce, bounce, step; etc. Teachers can give students music with a 4/4 time signature and then change to 3/4 (waltz) time music, 2/4 time, etc. The most challenging transition is from the "4" to the "1" count without stopping while walking through space. Recommended music includes: *Beer Barrel/Pennsylvania Polka* from *Christy Lane's Let's Do Ballroom* for 2/4 time; *Edelweiss* from the same source for 3/4 time; *Mad World* by Tears for Fears or the cover by Michael Andrews & Gary Jules for slower 4/4 time; and *Viva la Vida* by Coldplay or *I Gotta Feeling* by The Black Eyed Peas for faster 4/4 time.

Creative Movement and Dance

According to the National Association for the Education of Young Children (NAEYC – Dow, 2010), within the art form of creative movement, the words "**dance**" and "**movement**" are interchangeable. The human body is this art form's medium. The basic elements of dance/creative movement are:

- the body, its parts and range of motion;
- space;
- time; and
- energy.

Teachers can vary these elements when teaching children, e.g., by assigning variations in body part movements like marching while touching knees; clapping; holding arms up high, with one knee straight and one bent, on tiptoes; lying on the back with legs/feet in the air; etc. They can assign spatial variations, e.g., marching high, low, backward, turning, or in a square; temporal variations, e.g., marching in slow motion or as fast as possible, for a designated number of steps and then freezing; etc. Energy variations include marching as if stomping through mud, as if stuck in quicksand, as if barefoot on hot blacktop, without making any sound, etc.

Various Forms of Dance

Ballet is the foundation for all other Western dance forms, so students taught ballet will be well equipped to learn other forms. The development of core strength, which is essential; the five foot positions; and many steps, turns, and jumps from ballet are shared by jazz, modern/contemporary, tap, and ballroom dance. Some additional techniques not taught in classical ballet include: pelvic rotations and ribcage isolations in **jazz dance**; torso contractions and extensions in **modern/contemporary dance**; loosening the ankles in **tap**, as well as "spanking" and other tap-specific foot movements; specific frames, holds, and other postures in the **Viennese Waltz** and quickstep in **ballroom dance**; specific turns, steps, and other movements in the cha-cha, samba, rhumba, pasodoble, and other **Latin ballroom dances**; and general techniques in ballroom dance bearing weight and leading more on the heels than the toes, and movement down, into the floor instead of up, away from it as in ballet.

Injury Prevention in Dance Education

Thorough warm-ups and cool-downs are critical. **Warm-ups** must have cardiovascular elements increasing body temperature, heart and breathing rates, blood circulation to muscles, muscle tone, joint flexibility, reaction speed, mental alertness, and motivation to move; and move major muscle groups and angular, gliding, and rotational joints, including internal and external hip rotations. **Cool-downs** lower body temperature, slow breathing and mind, deeply stretch muscles, reward the body for its exertions, and should be followed by recovery periods. Thorough warm-ups and stretching can prevent delayed-onset muscle soreness, cramps, sprains, and tendonitis. Avoiding muscle fatigue prevents inflammation and cramping. Hydration and keeping dietary electrolytes balanced also prevents cramps. Dance spaces should have clean and sprung wood floors, high ceilings, no obstacles, good lighting and ventilation, access to water, separate male/female changing rooms, and wheelchair and telephone access. If only concrete flooring is available, high-impact jumping and running must be avoided to prevent stress fractures. Teacher first aid training and kits are necessary. Student footwear must be appropriate to floor surfaces (slippery, dirty, etc.). Teaching and learning correct body alignment also prevents (or at least limits) injuries and promotes proper dance technique, more effective mechanical functioning, and more energy-efficient movement. Pilates, Feldenkrais, ideokinesis, and yoga improve alignment.

Types of Music in Dance

Classical ballet commonly employs **classical music**. Many classical compositions were written expressly for the purpose of accompanying ballets. For example, Tchaikovsky was well-known for composing ballet music, including *The Nutcracker, Swan Lake, Romeo and Juliet,* and *The Sleeping Beauty.* Modern classical composer Igor Stravinsky collaborated with choreographer Michel Fokine for Sergei Diaghilev's Ballets Russes production of *The Firebird* (1910). Cincinnati Ballet choreographer Adam Hougland created an opera ballet to Mozart's masterpiece *Requiem Mass in D Minor.* In ballroom dance, the Viennese waltz was/is traditionally performed to **waltzes** by classical Viennese composers like Johann Strauss; however, today's creative choreographers also use diverse contemporary music in 3/4 time, e.g., on TV's *Dancing with the Stars.* Latin ballroom dances traditionally used music specifically for each dance, e.g., rhumba, samba, cha-cha, pasodoble, tango, etc., but *DWTS* also uses other music with appropriate tempi and rhythms. Jazz and tap dances have often been choreographed to/for Broadway show tunes, but can use any compatible music. Contemporary dance choreography frequently interprets song lyrics or expresses **lyrical or evocative music**. **Hip-hop music** most often accompanies hip-hop dance.

Apparatuses Used in Gymnastics

Low parallel bars are 7 feet long, 15 inches high, and 18 inches wide for practicing hand balances. **Standard parallel bars** are adjustable hand rails, made of fine-grained wood, on uprights connected by oval-shaped pressed steel rails. **Rails** go under upright and are completely secured inside the base. **Bars** adjust from 3 feet and 9 inches to 5 feet and 3 inches high and from 15 to 18 inches wide. **Mats** are thick pads covered with canvas or other material, filled with 2 inches of kapok/felt, made in various lengths, widths, and grades, to protect gymnasts when landing or falling. A **side horse** is a cylindrical body with an approximately 14-inch diameter, covered in leather/other material, mounted on steel legs/base, with two pommels, i.e., handles, on top near the middle. Horse height is adjustable from 36 to 57 inches. A **spring board** is an inclined board about 6 feet by 22 inches, over a fulcrum about half its length. It is lightweight, usually made of ash, shod with rubber, and with its upper end carpeted in cork. It is used to spring off from for tumbling, horse and buck vaulting, and to parallel bars.

Types of Gymnastics

Olympic gymnastics are better learned outside school hours. **Educational gymnastics** have different, non-competitive purposes: to teach children to increase their skills for controlling and maneuvering their bodies effectively against gravity's force, on the floor and on apparatus, through learning experiences. It integrates movement concepts, e.g., body and space awareness, force and effort, movement qualities and relationships. It also integrates with skill themes, e.g., balancing, transferring weight, traveling, jumping, and landing. Children must experience these in isolation and/or in dance or game contexts before experiencing them incorporated into gymnastics. Under **traveling**, some introductory themes include travelling independently and safely, to/from and on/off apparatus, changing direction/level, on feet/hands, together/apart, and in shapes. Under **weight-bearing**, included are getting on/off apart, weight on hands, balancing on different surfaces and body parts, balancing and rolling, landing and rolling, changing feet relationships with weight on hands, and while balancing. In **weight transfer**, included are log/side rolling, forward rolls, jumping and landing, and back safety rolls. Under **relationship**, included are individual sequences; partner sequences together, apart, or side-by-side; and symmetrical and asymmetrical movements.

Basic Tumbling Terminology

Tumbling is a series of acrobatic, controlled large-muscle movements including flips, springs, rolls, falls, dives, twists, etc. **Tumbling stunts** can be on the mat, deck, or ground; semi-aerial, i.e., from the feet to the hands to the feet; or aerial, i.e., from the feet through the air to the feet going forward, backward, or sideways. **Mat stunts** include chest rolls, from a hand balance onto the chest; dives—from a running start, leaping into the air, ending on the chest, back arched, rolling downward; rockers on the stomach, back arched; forward/backward rolls, and sideward shoulder rolls. **Semi-aerial stunts** include front/back walkovers; barrel rolls; cartwheels; cradle rocks to back and shoulders; egg rolls/fish flops, backward to short head balance to shoulders forward, rolling down to chest, stomach, to standing; round offs, changing forward to backward momentum via inward half-turning; front, back, leaping, or one-arm handsprings; headsprings; and shoulder/neck springs. **Aerial stunts** include brandy/Baroni, a handless roundoff; somersault/side somersault/front flip with half-twist/back somersault; spotter, landing on the takeoff spot; cutaway, landing behind it; gainer—backward somersault landing ahead of the takeoff spot; layout; tuck; whipback; bounders; alternates; and Rudolph (brandy with full twist). There are others for doubles and triples.

Intermediate Movement Themes 4-7

Here are some **intermediate themes** for grades 4-7 educational gymnastics lessons. For **traveling**: moving into and out of balance, and jumping with turns. For **weight bearing**: balancing while curling, stretching, twisting, or otherwise changing body shapes; partner balances; counter-tension (away); platform balance; and counter-balance (together). For body shape: the body shape in flight. For **relationship**: partner matching and copying, small group sequences, and using the partner as an obstacle to move over and/or through. For **traveling into and out of balance**, there are five steps in a learning experience.

- Run and jump onto a vaulting surface.
- Run, placing hands on the apparatus, and land on the same spot.
- Repeat (2), but add a roll upon landing. Practice roll progressions for the backward safety roll.

- Change the relationship of the feet while performing various vaults into the air; move into a balance.
- Hold the balance; then move into another balance.

Refinements for these steps are:

- Move into a balance.
- Take off with feet, and raise the hips as high as possible.
- Use a curved surface area; tuck tightly.
- Spread, cross, or bend the knees.
- Make the sequence parts flow.

Cooperative Games

In **cooperative games and activities**, students must work together to discover solutions to different challenges presented by the activities. Examples include activities to develop communication skills, teamwork skills, and problem-solving skills. One cooperative PE game activity for developing communication and teamwork skills is "Caterpillar Riot": Teams of 5 or 6 students stand in line, each wearing a hoop; hoops should touch. Each team is a "caterpillar." The goal is to collect as many objects from the floor as possible by moving the caterpillar forward. To advance, the rear player in each line steps into the hoop of the player ahead, picks up his or her empty hoop, and passes it to the front of the line. The front player puts the hoop down, stepping into it. Each player moves forward into the next hoop. Only the front player may pick up objects; other players must carry objects collected. When all objects are collected, the game ends. Builds include a preparatory race, advancing caterpillars without collecting objects; playing the full version; adding a time limit to the full version; and playing blindfolded.

Toxic Waste

To play "**Toxic Waste**": The equipment used includes ringette rings, foam balls, jump ropes, cones, and optional blindfolds. Teams of four students each have one foam ball sitting on top of a ringette ring with four jump ropes tied to it. The goal is for students to move the "toxic waste" foam ball from one end of the gym to the other without touching the ringette ring's ball, so students must utilize the ropes. If the ball falls, whichever team dropped it must return to the starting line and start over. After students play the original game, the teacher can add a build wherein one student on each team is blindfolded. After each round, the teacher blindfolds one more player, continuing until all players are blindfolded. One safety rule is that blindfolded students must walk, not run. After playing, the teacher can initiate student discussion by asking them questions such as, "To succeed in moving the toxic waste to the other side, how did you have to coordinate your movements as a team?" "What were the communication challenges in the game?" "How was your communication affected by having one or more players on your team blindfolded?"

Astronaut

One game PE teachers can have a whole class of children play is **Astronaut**, which involves running and dodging movement patterns and skills. It develops endurance, locomotor skills, non-locomotor skills, and group cooperation. The only equipment is one balloon per child. Teaching tips: The game is best played in a large, grassy area. Include short rest periods for young children, who tire quickly. Do not let children keep balloons afterward. To play, select four children as astronauts. The rest are Martians. Each astronaut has an air supply, i.e., an inflated balloon. On the teacher's signal, the Martians chase the astronauts, trying to destroy their air supplies by popping the balloons. Once all four balloons are popped, start over with four different astronauts. Repeat until all children have been astronauts. One variation is to add flags: once a Martian pulls an astronaut's flag, s/he must surrender the balloon to that Martian.

Four-Corner Cage Ball

Four-Corner Cage Ball involves kicking and crab-walking movements, and develops striking skills, arm and shoulder strength, and teamwork skills. Equipment is four cones and one cage ball. Divide the class into four teams, each forming one side of a square marked by cones. Number off each team; children must remember their numbers. Place a cage ball in the middle of the square. Call a number. All children with that number crab-walk to the cage ball; their goal is to kick the ball over the heads of another team. Other players, also crab-walking, can only block the ball using their feet. Any team having the ball kicked over their heads gets a point. Start again, calling new numbers. The object is NOT getting points. Teaching tips: With this competitive game, children may become excited, forget the rules, and block the ball with their hands. Teams can be given points for doing this if not for safety. For safety, no hard shoes or boots are allowed, and children should remove glasses. If outdoors on grass, carefully check first for debris. If running out of time without everybody getting a turn, extend boundaries as needed; call two or three numbers at once.

Outdoor Adventure Activities

Some exciting, fascinating, rewarding **outdoor adventure activities** include mountain-climbing; rafting; canoeing; kayaking; whitewater paddleboarding; sailing; driving powerboats; slacklining; rope-climbing; exploring mines; exploring caves; walking long-distance footpaths; backpacking; hiking; running; jungle treks; expeditions through primary rainforests; nature hikes and walks; exploring wild areas in four-wheel drive vehicles; and orienteering, which involves navigating a wilderness environment with a compass and a map, while also racing against others to reach a destination first. Some outdoor adventure enthusiasts pursue these interests close to home, which is most convenient and affordable, while others travel to other countries and exotic locations. Some altruistically-minded adventurers combine adventure expeditions to other lands with **team community service projects** when they arrive. Others find adventure experiences inspire photography, drawing, painting, writing music, writing literature, other artistic pursuits, or scientific/practical inventions. People unfamiliar with and interested in adventure can learn from experienced, credentialed instructors in the outdoor industry—as adventure school faculty or independent freelancers—many with websites advertising their services. In addition to teaching techniques and safety practices, instructors also mentor, motivate, and encourage learners; build their confidence and self-esteem; and foster their skills for teamwork, decision-making, and problem-solving.

Behavioral and Administrative Outdoor Adventures

Some of the courses offered in the area of **outdoor adventure** include leadership, group dynamics, risk management, conflict management, expedition planning, execution, and evaluation. Classes are offered in specific activities, e.g., backpacking techniques for beginners; slacklining techniques, including choosing the correct trees and avoiding damage to the trees used; learning to set up a line; and learning to stand and balance on a line before learning to walk on it. Multi-pitch climbing techniques include anchoring skills with gear anchors and multidirectional anchors, anchor builds, rappelling techniques, belaying directly off of anchors from above, belay station rope management, belay transfers, efficiently changing leaders, self-rescue techniques, and other hands-on learning. Some outdoor adventure schools and instructors use sports like paddleboarding in whitewater rapids while standing up as facilitation techniques for therapeutic recreation. They advocate these activities for being experienced in natural environments, including elements of perceived or actual danger, and providing challenges to participants. Beginning courses in kayaking techniques teach the basic strokes, e.g., the forward stroke, forward sweep stroke, and low brace stroke, starting in calm lakes. Once learners can paddle in straight lines, they can learn how to turn using the paddle as a rudder and use steering strokes.

Primary Safety Equipment

Football players need heavy shoulder, chest, and elbow pads to protect them from body contact injuries. Helmets are imperative to prevent head and brain injuries from collisions and blows. Recently the NFL began requiring players to wear knee and shin guards; PE teachers should have students follow this practice. **Baseball** does not require body contact through hitting or tackling like football. However, because it involves swinging hard bats and hitting and throwing balls which become projectiles, baseball players must wear helmets to protect against head injury. When traumatic brain injuries do not occur, getting "beaned" by a baseball is still extremely painful—even when wearing a helmet, let alone to an unprotected head. Being accidentally hit by a baseball bat can also seriously injure a student. **Hockey players** use angled wooden sticks, which can cause injuries. Ice hockey uses a small, dense, hard rubber puck, which can be very injurious if striking a player. Helmets, neck guards, shoulder and chest pads, elbow and forearm pads, and shin guards are included in hockey, plus heel guards on skates in ice hockey. Mouth guards are recommended in football and hockey to protect players from lost and broken teeth.

Risk Management and Safety

The *Outward Bound Wilderness First-Aid Book* (Isaac, 1998) is a manual of standard operating practices for **risk management and safety** in outdoor adventure recreation and education programs. Other outdoor education organizations offer similar books. Additional good resources include government education departments and recreation agencies, which have published outdoor activity risk management guidelines in many countries. Research studies published by various organizations provide data and narratives regarding risk management and incidents. For example, *Adventure Program Risk Management Report, Volume I* (1995) was issued by the Association for Experiential Education. The American Camping Association (ACA) and other outdoor associations have published guidelines, articles, and manuals describing risk management in rope challenge courses and many other specific adventure activities. Adventure Incorporated and others offer risk management specialists as consultants. The National Outdoor Leadership School organizes an annual Wilderness Risk Manager's Conference in America. Every developed nation offers outdoor and adventure risk management and first aid training courses, listed at www.outdoored.com. Professional Outdoor Education listservs also extensively discuss safety and risk management practices.

Benefits of Dance Activities

Dancing increases aerobic fitness, cardiopulmonary and cardiovascular fitness, endurance, muscular strength, muscular endurance, muscle tone, and motor fitness. It strengthens the bones through bearing weight and decreases risk of osteoporosis. It aids in managing a healthy weight. Dancing improves a person's flexibility, agility, and coordination. It enhances spatial awareness, balance, and sense of direction. People who learn to dance enjoy greater physical self-confidence, overall self-confidence, and self-esteem. Dancing improves mental functioning. It promotes better well-being, in general and psychologically. Because of the social interactions inherent in learning to dance, and dancing in classes, groups, and with partners, dance also improves social skills. Serious dancers become very physically fit; even those more casually involved in dance will get more physical activity, improving their health and well-being. Dance can be pursued competitively or socially. Inclement weather does not interfere with dance as it does with outdoor sports. Today there are many places to take dance classes or lessons, including dance studios, dance schools, fitness clubs, colleges and universities, university extensions, dance halls, community recreation centers, etc.

Learning Tumbling and Gymnastics

Learning **tumbling and gymnastics** skills and routines contributes significantly to children's development in many domains—not only in sport-specific skills, but additionally in academic performance and personality, psychological, and social development. Students meeting challenges in gymnastics, e.g., learning skills for performing on balance beams and parallel bars, gain self-confidence in their own abilities, which extends to school subjects and other life areas. Younger children think concretely, not abstractly; their lives are more physical than mental. The superior body movement and coordination they develop through tumbling and gymnastics give them much of their self-confidence. Children lacking natural talent to be "star" athletes in other sports benefit from success in tumbling and gymnastics as teachers can control the challenges and progress they experience. Students learn to overcome fears and to perform in front of others. The training required in gymnastics builds determination and a hard work ethic; its controlled environment and rules teach discipline. Physical strength and flexibility from gymnastics benefit student athletes playing football, basketball, baseball, and other sports. Athletes typically need more flexibility—which also prevents many injuries. Listening, following directions, taking turns, politeness, and respecting others are social skills learned in gymnastics.

Outdoor Adventure and Education

Outdoor learning in nature affords background benefits of increasing physical, mental, and spiritual health; personal and social communication skills; sensory, aesthetic, and spiritual awareness; sensitivity to one's own well-being; and the ability to exercise personal control. Outdoor learning in the natural environment can also have planned benefits when providers or educators determine or negotiate these. For example, through structured, well-planned, hands-on learning experiences, teachers and providers help students to develop their own self-esteem, take personal responsibility, cooperate with others, and respect others' needs. They help them develop better appreciation of the world and its peoples, which allows them to expand their personal horizons. They teach them to understand why people must establish and maintain sustainable relationships with the environment. They improve students' practical teamwork and problem-solving skills. And they foster knowledgeable, positive student responses regarding personal well-being and health. Outdoor learning allows bonus benefits as well through incidental learning and greater than expected value, which highly supportive learning atmospheres enable. Wider benefits include greater sustainability and other benefits for families, schools, sponsors, society, and future generations, who are all stakeholders in outdoor learning success.

Modified Movement and Dance Activities

According to experts (cf. Dow, 2013), all children can participate in most **movement activities** when they are modified. Each child can approach movement according to his or her individual abilities, experiences, and imagination. For instance, if a teacher gives children a greeting activity involving their waving various body parts, they can instruct children with physical disabilities to move their fingers, toes, eyelids, or tongues. When leading children in a jumping activity, if the class includes children in wheelchairs, teachers can instruct them to move their heads, shoulders, arms, and/or fingers instead of their legs. If the teacher is instructing children to form the shapes of alphabet letters with their bodies, s/he can guide children with physical disabilities to use their fingers or arms rather than their entire bodies. Children who are unable to do this can point to or hold up a picture or large shape of each letter to participate actively. Children of all/most ability levels can participate in dance stories by exploring and elaborating on characters and events in stories, poems, books, or songs through creative movement, including facial expressions.

Modifying Educational Gymnastics

Some gymnastics educators state that **inclusion** is not difficult because coaching practices should not really change: in providing opportunities according to individual student needs, **program competencies and strategies** can be preserved while maintaining awareness of **disabilities**. Educators have effected cultural changes by informing coaches at national championships that inclusion tools, tips, and other resources would become available. They find it necessary to raise awareness of and communicate social messages about inclusion before teaching technical elements of coaching students with disabilities. They advocate developing disability action plans. Some agencies and organizations offer funding to support such plans' strategies. Following awareness and education, educators identify the next step as requiring teacher or coach accreditation processes to incorporate mandatory training in inclusion management. They point out that high-performance coaches do this routinely when they assign unevenly-numbered teams and small-sided games and focus on developing specific tactics, techniques, and skills. An inclusive approach, they say, involves the same practices, but simply done for different purposes. Some experts use the **TREE** acronym and principle for modifying and challenging sports players according to individual ability: Teaching style, Rules and regulations, Equipment, and Environment.

Modifying Curriculum and Instruction

To provide inclusive PE environments, **modifications** are needed to make learning environments safe and meaningful for every student, enable all students' successfully learning appropriate PE skills, and eliminate mismatches between lesson content and student skill levels. To be appropriate, modifications must not make settings or activities unsafe for non-disabled students; not ruin activities or games by precluding fun; not overburden regular PE teachers; and enable safe, meaningful, and successful disabled student participation. **Curriculum modifications** include:

- multilevel selections of different learning objectives in the same domain
- objectives from different domains overlapping in the same activity
- different alternative activities.

Part (1) includes modifying tasks and equipment, e.g., for limited strength, speed, endurance, balance, or coordination; extending skill stations, e.g., holding basketball on lap tray, dropping ball to floor, slapping ball three consecutive times, dribbling while stationary or walking, or dribbling while jogging and or guarded; modifying instruction, e.g., in class format, teaching style, cues and signals, instruction and participation duration, setting, distracters, motivation level, direct instruction, movement exploration, and strategies intervention model. Part (2) includes cooperative learning; class-wide peer tutoring; teaching locomotor skills plus walking, dribbling, and 3-point shooting in a basketball game. Part (3) includes pull-out activities; concurrent multiple activities; and pocket-reference IEP objectives and RPE modifications, arrangements, and activities.

Adventure PE Adaptations

Experts identify the building-blocks of **adventure PE programs** as the core values of adventure education, which include: emphasizing non-competitive activities; participants' sense of accomplishment from successfully completing a specifically designed activity sequence; trust and cooperation fostered among co-participants; the communication participants exchange to attain their goals; the ability to implement activities at individual participant levels; the combination of enhancing strength, coordination, flexibility, and endurance while having fun; and the fact that activities require participants to cooperate with nature, promoting better appreciation and respect for the natural environment. **Adaptations** include allowing longer times to complete tasks, slowing activity paces, demonstrating activities visually and verbally, employing peer partner assistance, simplifying steps, modifying body positions, removing obstacles and distractions, increasing participation time by using stations, providing ramps, shortening course or activity distance, and using signing gestures along with verbal instructions. Special and regular education teachers must collaborate creatively to assess needs and find appropriate curriculum adaptations that both enable individual success and attain the school's/organization's and individual student's learning goals.

Planning, Instruction, and Student Assessment

Behavioral Development 5-6

Students in **grades 5-6** should show **self-confidence** by identifying PE activities that are personally challenging to them, identifying the skills they need to develop and/or refine personally to succeed, and choosing and practicing specific skills they need to improve. They should demonstrate **safety** for themselves and others and apply the appropriate etiquette in specific sports and activities, e.g., taking turns; avoiding personal fouls, like body contact in basketball; avoiding excessive force to the point of injury in football tackling and blocking; helping up fallen opponents; not teasing teammates or classmates for being out of condition; not celebrating opponent mistakes; not arguing with every call made by referees, umpires, or teachers; not insulting others; not denying fouls; avoiding inappropriate language; and shaking hands after contests. They should follow and help establish rules and procedures, show responsibility for their own actions and the capacity for receiving and providing honest feedback, show willingness to engage with others of different socioeconomic levels, contribute to positive group dynamics, and show cooperation by encouraging and supporting classmates and teammates with different skill levels and abilities.

Behavioral Development 7-8

Grade 7-8 students should demonstrate personal responsibility for their **individual wellness** by acquiring and identifying knowledge about the connections among exercise, nutrition, and fitness, and apply this knowledge in selecting activities for improving and maintaining their fitness goals. They should participate in lifelong and leisure sport or dance activities in and out of school to show they recognize the importance of physical activity to personal wellness. They should further their individual self-confidence and success through identifying how personal performance is affected by attitude, energy, and effort; set personal goals for attaining higher performance levels in challenging and new activities; and show positive attitudes about developing personal skills. They should show positive and supportive behavior to demonstrate safety for self and others. Appropriate social interactions demonstrating responsibility include: playing by the rules and not taking advantage of classmates or teammates; practicing proper sports conduct, e.g., accepting teacher, coach, and referee decisions without argument; and officiating in small-group games. Additional appropriate social behaviors and interactions include: showing appreciation for applicable feedback, being willing to work with others from diverse backgrounds, being able to adopt leader and follower roles as indicated, and cooperating with others within task activity structures.

Behavioral and Social Development 9-12

High school students should show recognition of personal responsibility for individual wellness by demonstrating they understand how personal traits, styles, preferences, and performance change throughout life, and applying this understanding to continually evolving fitness plans. They should also further their achievement and maintenance of personal fitness goals through regular participation in suitable physical activities. To further their self-confidence and individual success, they should be able to analyze the characteristics of the physical and sports activities they personally find challenging, rewarding, and enjoyable, e.g., they are high-risk, competitive, individual, group, socially interactive, aesthetically satisfying, etc. They should also challenge themselves in developing higher or new skill levels, and demonstrate perseverance in pursuing higher performance. By participating in related activities like spotting, refereeing, and belaying, they should demonstrate their ability to anticipate and correct consequences from physical activities that are potentially dangerous. **Appropriate social interactions** include: showing responsibility through sportsmanlike conduct; preventing dangerous outcomes; using quality of play, not results, to evaluate competition; displaying self-discipline and self-direction; revising their actions to show respect for feedback; exhibiting strategies to include diverse others in physical activities; recognizing and developing their leading and following abilities in group activities; and showing cooperation by helping others participate.

Leadership and Teamwork

When students must play a game or sport as team members rather than individuals, a **team captain** is often designated. This student must take responsibility for things like choosing team members; planning and organizing plays; developing tactics; providing motivation to team members; encouraging team solidarity; and getting team members to cooperate, collaborate, and function as a unit rather than a collection of individuals. Learning to perform these duties successfully will develop student leadership skills. **Teamwork** is also essential in sports. Purposes and benefits of team sports include winning contests, attaining shared goals, preparing for jobs and wider society, learning to build confidence and manage emotions, learning about oneself and others, and surviving and flourishing in large classes and schools. The power of numbers enables teams to accomplish things individuals cannot. When team members conflict with and/or work against one another, a team thus divided will more likely lose. Supporting each other and working together enables a team to win. Team members must accept their team roles, the team itself, its ground rules, and the individuality of their teammates.

Fair Play

In virtually all sports, **fair play** is a universal standard. Thus, when students learn sports in PE classes and activities, they are held to the same standards that adult athletes are to behave fairly by following the established rules of the game; not cheating by breaking or circumventing those rules; and treating their peers fairly by not taking advantage of their weaknesses, unfairly exploiting their strengths, or making fun of their shortcomings or difficulties. Sports have structures and rules to promote fairness. Playing sports can help young students learn to be fairer in their behavior, for example, by not choosing team members preferentially out of friendship or enmity; not rejecting students because they have disabilities or are shorter, slower, weaker, or have less experience; and not excluding students from diverse cultural, ethnic, or socioeconomic backgrounds. When students play team sports or games in PE, they must develop and refine skills for cooperating with others. When they respect and listen to others, help others participate, and work jointly as a team, they develop cooperative skills that will enhance their social interactions outside of PE activities in their schools, families, communities, current and/or future jobs, and everyday lives.

Good Sportsmanship

When students learn to play individual and team competitive sports, the meaning of **competition** is better construed as striving for excellence than exhibiting adversarial hostility. While individualistic American culture places great emphasis on competition in contrast to collectivist cultures' emphasis on cooperation, American sports also emphasize **good sportsmanship** and **fair play**. In this spirit, students should view other teams and individual competitors as worthy opponents rather than enemies, and the object of play as a challenge to exceed opponents' strategies and performance rather than a mission to destroy them or pound them into the ground. Good sportsmanship includes being a good winner by respecting opponents' efforts and acknowledging the competition they offer, and being a good loser by giving winners the credit they deserve for superior strategy and performance. Consideration promotes mutual respect and enabling healthy competition rather than antisocial or destructive behavior. Another element of sportsmanlike conduct is helping others, e.g., helping up an opposing player that has been knocked down. Supporting teammates teaches students to be supportive in friendships and workplace, family, and intimate relationships.

Student Respect for Peers

PE experts assert the importance of teaching not only information, skills, and strategies, but equally teaching **effective skills and objectives**. Without these, they say students, despite having the knowledge and skills, may not want to participate in PE activities. Values, attitudes, feelings, and interpersonal behaviors affect student motivation. Hence, the National Association for Sport and Physical Education's (NASPE) National PE Standards include "responsible personal and social behavior that respects self and others in physical activity settings" (2004). As role models, PE teachers should never show favoritism among students or marginalize students with lesser motor skills. They should also not limit the health benefits of PE activities for students with either lower or higher skills, but provide challenges to all levels. When designing PE activities and curriculum, teachers should deliberately include ways to teach respect for self and others, cooperation, teamwork, skills, and techniques. As examples, students can practice teamwork along with meeting individual and group goals during modified game play; students can learn to value safety for themselves and classmates while learning or practicing educational gymnastics skills and routines.

Peer Acceptance

Children and teenagers judge their own competence in large part through **social comparison** to their peers and **evaluations** from those peers. Moreover, students' beliefs of self-worth, approaches to motivation, participatory behaviors, and emotional experiences are all influenced by their peers. One type of relationship that researchers have investigated relative to student behavioral and psychosocial results in sports and physical activities is **peer acceptance**. This represents the extent to which members of a peer group like or embrace an individual, varying from rejection to popularity. Research has consistently revealed strong relationships between students' degrees of perceived physical competence and their degrees of peer acceptance. For instance, teens and children find competence in sports an important factor in peer group popularity and status. Investigators have found that students who are perceived as physically skilled by both themselves and their teachers were also rated as liked by their peers by both themselves and their teachers.

Practicing Inclusion of Peers

A common requirement in many PE standards is for students, particularly at the high school level, to demonstrate positive social interactions by including **diverse types of students** with them in their PE activities. Student diversity includes **disability**. Students with disabilities, especially physical disabilities, have historically been excluded from many PE activities because they could not participate in typical ways. However, modern federal laws mandate including students with disabilities in all aspects of education. One way students can include disabled peers is for PE teachers to instruct them to be peer facilitators, enabling them both to assist and participate. For example, non-disabled students can use hand-over-hand assistance to enable students with upper-body or limb disabilities to hit balls with bats and racquets; hit balloons with noodles; throw Frisbees at bowling pins; hit balls off tees at bowling pins; hit hockey pucks with hockey sticks; drive wheelchairs while dribbling balls with hockey sticks attached to the chairs; or catch whiffle balls, sponge balls, or beanbags in boxes. There are also many modified games wherein non-disabled students and those in wheelchairs or lacking upper-body control can participate together, and activities that include students with intellectual disabilities.

Understanding and Appreciation of Diversity

Experienced PE teachers have observed that students and teachers alike often suffer from **unrealistically stereotypical views** of diverse students. This is detrimental even when the stereotype appears positive. For example, many Americans view Asian-Americans as the "model minority" for being intelligent, academically successful, quiet, well-behaved, and hardworking. However, not every Asian-American is intellectually gifted, an excellent student, a model of good behavior, or even an English speaker. Making stereotyped assumptions can hurt such students by depriving them of needed behavioral and academic support. When teachers ask students the first thing they think of when they name Asian-Americans, students say "smart"; when they name African-Americans, students say "good athletes." Yet not every African-American person is athletic. Even in their own culture, some African-American students excelling academically may be stereotyped as "acting white." Educators call for the necessity for teachers to examine and challenge their own stereotypical beliefs, and understand their own diversity, in order to teach students to do the same.

Diverse Cultural Implications

PE teachers need to realize some **cultural differences** they will encounter when teaching diverse students. For example, Hispanic students tend to learn kinesthetically. While this is a natural fit with PE activities, some Anglo-American teachers who introduce new activities using verbal information may need to adjust instruction to begin with movements, which Latino students need to engage in learning. Hispanic and Asian students not raised in America are likely to avoid eye contact with teachers, and teachers should not demand it. Latino students may not be expressing agreement when they nod; their silence may not indicate understanding or agreement, but confusion or embarrassment. For all **English language learners (ELLs)**, teachers should include visual aids in demonstrations and employ peer facilitators to bridge language barriers. American teachers accustomed to encouraging competition must realize Latin, Asian, Native American, and other collectivist cultures frown on competing and value cooperating, and should accordingly deemphasize aggressive competition. Knowing what teachers expect of them makes Asian students more comfortable, as do cooperative learning environments; positive reinforcement benefits them. Culturally, they communicate nonverbally, e.g., leaning forward or backward; they rely on this more when they are ELLs.

Benefits Diverse Students Contribute

PE classes and teams incorporating students from **heterogeneous sources** benefit from a wider variety of contributions than those with narrowly homogeneous origins. For example, although American teachers and students might view the non-competitive cultural values of the collectivist traditions in which Hispanic, Native American, and Asian students have been raised as detrimental to winning in competitive team sports, this is not the only way to view them. Because they value cooperation for the good of the group, subsuming individual identity in favor of group identification, and helping others to promote collective harmony, students from these cultures can actually make better team players than some highly individualistic American students who behave more like high-profile athletes than they do like equal team members. Students from collectivist cultures are also more likely to engage in respectful sportsmanship than compete in overly aggressive ways. Deferring individual accomplishments and attention for being important parts of a group make them valuable contributors to team solidarity and success.

Diverse Cultures and Physical Activity

Asian cultures often have a **holistic** view of physical activity and sports. They value the connection between mind and body, and practice various sports and disciplines to develop spiritual awareness as well as physical skills. Yoga, tai chi, and the many martial arts are examples of Asian traditions combining physical and spiritual discipline this way. PE teachers should realize that Asian students previously accustomed to these traditions may view playing sports or games in PE for fun as irrelevant and spiritually unsatisfying, view playing them for aggressive competition as against their values of cooperation and group harmony, and view competing in sports for individual attention and fame as inappropriate. American cultural groups also view physical activity and fitness differently. Amongst the various sub-cultures in America, different body types may be considered as ideal or acceptable.

Personal Challenges and Satisfaction

Although mainstream American culture emphasizes competition in sports, students need not always compete to excel in PE activities. The concept of a "**personal best**" can be even more consistent with individual excellence, as it does not depend on comparisons or differences with other students and teams. Also, social psychologists studying achievement motivation have found students with a higher **internal locus of control**—i.e., they attribute their successes and failures to their own internal factors, not external influences—are more likely to maintain motivation to achieve more constantly across time, settings, and situations than those with a more external locus of control—i.e., they attribute their successes or failures to the help or interference of people, things, and events outside themselves. Students who strive to run faster than their last or current time, farther than their last or current distance; lift more weight or complete more repetitions; jump higher; and even in team sports, score more points than before, etc., compete with themselves, not others. Thus changes or differences in opponents will not affect their motivation or efforts. Also, in contrast with being on a losing team, students who achieve their own personal physical activity goals experience satisfaction regardless of what others do.

Competition and Achievement

When children are young and in earlier motor development stages, they may learn, practice, and enjoy running, jumping, hopping, skipping, balancing, etc., individually or in groups, but not **competitively**. As they grow, though, they will be exposed both in and out of school to running races to see who finishes first, experiencing their first taste of competition. Soon they will learn to play games and sports in PE classes. Individual activities include comparisons like who can hang from a high bar the longest, jump the highest and farthest, or make the most baskets, as well as run the fastest. While competitive themes pervade both individual and team activities, when students begin learning team sports, the inherent object is for one team to win by scoring more points, gaining more yards, making more runs or goals, etc. While some students may already have met "personal best" goals, if they find all their peers exceed them in certain activities, competition can motivate them to increase their **standards and efforts** accordingly. Because American education also compares academic achievement against national averages, PE competition and achievement can inform and transfer to other school subjects.

Positive Social Interactions

When younger children are first taught to play **organized games** with peers, they must learn to follow rules; take turns; share; cooperate with others; and refrain from hitting, kicking, biting, punching, and other antisocial behaviors. These are novel experiences to many youngsters. The structure and rules of organized games are ideal contexts to teach them to control aggressive behaviors; and to reinforce the pro-social, unselfish, helpful, and cooperative behaviors young children also naturally display at times. By participating in games, sports, dance, etc., older students learn not to reject, ignore, insult, tease, taunt, assault, or take advantage of peers; to offer helping hands when they need them; include peers with different backgrounds and abilities in physical activities; detect when and how to assume leader or follower roles; and include, invite, and help other students participate. When students improve their physical fitness, they gain self-esteem and physical well-being that often discourages incompatible habits like overeating, smoking, drinking, and taking drugs. Spending time being physically active leaves less unoccupied time for dangerous pursuits. Students interact socially through sharing sports, games, and dance instead of substance abuse or other risky behaviors.

State Educational Standards

A typical state standard in **physical education** is for students to understand the rules for a variety of physical activities, including games and sports. Some examples of the kinds of **benchmarks** that a state education department might specify for this standard are, for third grade: to identify the rules and procedures in specified physical activities, including games; for fifth grade: to demonstrate that they understand the rules that must be followed when participating in specified physical activities, including games; and for high school grades: to demonstrate the rules in complex versions of at least two different categories of movement forms in individual activities, dual activities, cardiorespiratory and aerobic lifetime activities, outdoor activities, team sports, aquatics, self-defense, yoga, martial arts, dance, and strength training and conditioning. For a standard of identifying the rules, procedures, and etiquette in a specified game or physical activity, a typical benchmark for fifth grade might be to demonstrate and explain the rules, procedures, and etiquette to follow when participating in physical activities or games; for eighth grade, to apply safe, effective rules, procedures, and etiquette for specific activities or games; and for high school, to analyze and apply the safe, effective rules, procedures, and etiquette for specific activities or games.

Fundamental Movement Skills (FMS)

FMS are significant to children's motor development, influencing physical, cognitive, and social growth. FMS are building blocks for games, dancing, sports, and other physical activities, as well as for lifelong interest in, motivation for, participation in, and enjoyment of active lifestyles. FMS have three categories: **locomotor**; **manipulative**; and **stability**, including rotation and balance. Rotation activities for young children include: Spinning, in both directions, eyes closed; slowly is equally good. Standing, bending, looking between legs; touching hands and head to the floor; waving to friends and throwing beanbags into hoops through legs; walking backwards looking through legs. Spinning inside a chalk circle or hoop lifted, while rotating the hoop. Pencil rolling: rolling on the floor with arms above the head, keeping fingers on a line, co-rolling with hands joined, or holding onto scarves. Lying stomach-down on slowly rotating office chairs. Novelty spinning on or in blankets, towels, cardboard boxes, or wash baskets in various directions. Sausage rolls: roll up children in blankets, sheets, or parachutes, and then unroll. Wheelbarrows: hand-walking with legs held, head lower than body (vestibular stimulation). Lying stomach-down on cylinders or exercise balls. Self-pulling or spinning on scooter boards using arms or ropes. Twirling to music while holding scarves.

Developing Rotation Skills

Older children can do **rotation activities** like these: On a vinyl or wood floor, spaced freely, have them spin around on their stomachs; on their bottoms, with or without using hands; on their backs; and standing. Ask what happens when they extend their legs and tuck their bodies. To improve rotation speed, provide smoother surfaces. Observe balance and change of focus. On grass, mats, or pads, have children rock forward, backward, shoulders to feet and back, from back to one foot, and up to standing. Ask what shapes they can create by rocking. Observe for slight spinal curve for protection. Using rolled mats or cylinders shorter across than children's leg lengths, have them sit cross-legged, feet together, tilt side to side, then rock, then come up into sitting position; sitting astride cylinders, rock side to side; challenge them to see how long they can stay on. Observe for neutral head position and controlled movement. Using equipment (ribbon balls or tennis balls in stockings or hoops, etc.) and music, teachers and students suggest individual and peer-led exploration and experimentation. Vary music speeds, body positions, and rotation planes. Explore different directions and heights with one piece of equipment. Design short movement sequences individually or in groups. Observe for loose grip, wrist action with small, fast movements, and arm action for large, slow movements.

Walking and Running 0-5

Musical Hoops: Give children hoops, have them dance to music and use varied locomotions, and jump into the nearest hoop when the music stops. Remove hoops each time until children must squeeze into hoops together. **Whistle Stop**: Children walk around, avoiding touching others; they freeze in place upon a whistle-blow. Change locomotion every time. **Movement A-to-B**: Have children take small or giant steps, run, turn while walking, walk heel to toe, jump, hop, tiptoe, crawl, roll, etc., between two points. **Traffic Lights**: Children imitate cars. Large red, green, and yellow cardboard circles are "lights." They run fast near green, walk slowly near yellow, stop instantly and jog in place near red. **Cars**: Children walk around in pairs, one child behind with hands on the front child's shoulders. The front child "steers," changing directions; they take turns. **Motor Bikes**: Children run or walk around, with feet shoulder-width apart and knees slightly bent; on a whistle-blow or other signal, they must stop, jump, and land as quietly as possible, holding their landings for three seconds. **Tail Chase**: With "tail" scarves tucked into their waistbands or pockets, children try to catch one another's tails, protecting their own tails while moving. When children catch others' tails, they give them back and keep playing. Vary locomotion, e.g., by jumping, to increase difficulty.

Walking and Running 5-12

As a favorite warmup, groups of four to five can play **Follow the Leader**. Regularly change the locomotor skill and leader. Another popular game is **Stuck in the Mud**. Teachers can vary locomotor skills; for example, the student can free the tagger "stuck in the mud" by running twice around the tagger and high-fiving him or her. Teachers can also vary the traveling locomotor skills used. **Buzz Off** is played like Stuck in the Mud, except when a player is tagged, he or she stands still, scratching as if bitten by an insect. To release the tagged player, two other players go to him or her, pass their hands over him or her, and say "Buzz off." In **Blob Tag**, two students holding hands try to tag others while remaining connected. Whenever they tag someone, that student joins the "blob." Once they have a "blob" of four, they break into two pairs and keep tagging until all students are joined in "blobs." In **Fast Cars**, students stand in a circle; each is given a car name (e.g., Toyota 1, Honda 1, Toyota 2, Honda 2, etc.). Whenever the teacher calls out a car name, students race around the circle and "park" in their original positions.

Throwing 0-5

Teachers can hang hoops from door frames or trees with rope for young children to practice **throwing** things through them, as well as put hoops on the floor or ground. Parents can develop throwing skills at home by having children throw rolled socks into laundry hampers or baskets. When they succeed, have them take one step further back for the next throw. Teachers and parents can use pillows and cushions to set up courses (with or without children's participation), placing empty boxes, wastebaskets, buckets, etc., as "golf holes." Have children take turns throwing beanbags into holes. Children can crumple paper into "snowballs"; adults then tape these up and give baskets of them to two groups of children. Mark a line between groups with rope, tape, or chalk. On a signal, children throw "snowballs" over the line for 30 seconds; see who has the fewest snowballs left, then switch teams and repeat. Have children clean up by throwing snowballs into baskets. Adults can cut centers out of empty plastic food tubs to make rings; have children try to toss the rings over plastic bottles. Have children try to toss coins onto paper or plastic plates on the floor or ground. Let children throw a ball trying to knock a stuffed animal off a stool.

Throwing and Catching 5-12

Older children can practice throwing for **accuracy** or **distance**. Some activities to practice throwing for distance include: "Force Back" – Students face one another in pairs, throwing a ball toward the other as far as they can. The thrower's partner catches or retrieves the ball, throwing it back from where it landed.

"Three Court Ball" – Assign students to two equally numbered teams. Each team has one-third of a court and a tennis ball. Students try to throw the ball into the middle third of the court and have it bounce over the other team's goal line. "Scatterball" – Use a baseball diamond or any field with several bases arranged in a diamond, circle, square, or some other shape. Divide students into two teams: throwers and fielders. Throwers take turns, one at a time, throwing balls as far away as they can. Then each thrower runs around bases until told to stop. The fielders catch or retrieve the balls thrown and collect them in a basket, bucket, etc. Switch teams and repeat. The team scoring the most runs wins. Students can also practice catching by throwing and bouncing balls or beanbags in pairs, groups, and teams.

Movement Principles

Impact when **landing** should be distributed across the greatest possible distance, area, or both; and joints should be bent when landing from jumps, for absorbing force. Learning cues for landing on the feet include landing with feet apart and knees bent. Children should land in a toes-ball of foot-heel sequence, and wriggle toes, pull in stomachs, tuck bottoms under, stretch arms in front, hold heads up, look straight ahead, and hold the landing three seconds. To land prone on hands or arms, they should hold arms shoulder-width apart, bend elbows, keep hands flat, spread fingers, hold heads up, keep bodies straight, and pull in stomachs to prevent back arching. Three phases of learning are: **Discovery** – children explore, show no stable support base, land flat-footed, and show little "give" in the knees. **Development** – children land from various distances or heights, realize the importance of shock absorption, show stable support base, land more consistently in toes-ball of foot-heel order, bend knees after heels touch ground, and rotate forward upon landing. **Consolidation** – Children show control and confidence landing in unpredictable or changing circumstances, show a wide support base, make controlled landings safely, and absorb shock through "give" in the hips, knees, and ankles.

How to Fall Sideways

This involves the movement concept or skill of rolling sideways for safely landing after **falling** from various levels. First, students fall from kneeling sideways, rocking onto their arm, side, and shoulder. They should try this in both directions. Then they roll sideways down a wedge to practice falling down a slope. Then, while moving, they fall, roll sideways, and then stand up and keep moving. This begins with walking, increasing the speed gradually to jogging, then running, and then with dodging. Students can pair up, shake hands in front support position, and then try to pull each other off balance. In "Tip the Spider," one partner in a pair on all fours is the spider. The other partner tips the spider onto his or her side by pushing on his or her closer shoulder while pulling on his or her opposite hand. Teachers should look for straight arms, hands facing inward to body, and even, soft surfaces. They can ask students when they might use this kind of landing, and what they must do to land safely when falling sideways.

Types of Feedback

One way to differentiate descriptive feedback from prescriptive feedback is that in **descriptive feedback**, the teacher tells the student what he or she observed the student doing incorrectly; in **prescriptive feedback**, the teacher tells the student what the student needs to do to correct the error the teacher observed. For example, with a basketball jump shot, if the teacher says, "You didn't follow through," this could suffice for a more advanced player who knows how to perform a follow-through correctly but just forgot or has not yet developed full automaticity with it. However, with a less experienced player who has not yet learned how to follow through or may not understand how to correct what he or she did, the above descriptive feedback example is not enough. Prescriptive feedback would involve specific correction instructions, e.g., "Flex your wrist harder when you let the ball go." This tells the student what to do to correct the jump shot. In order to give effective prescriptive feedback, PE teachers must know what the student did incorrectly (i.e., did not follow through) and provide a problem solution to correct it (i.e., flex the wrist harder upon releasing the ball).

Solicited vs. Unsolicited Feedback

Experts advise "When in doubt, be quiet" (Wrisberg, Human Kinetics). When athletes have internal feedback, **external feedback** is unnecessary. Studies find **solicited feedback** more beneficial than unsolicited feedback, and students can improve skills with comparatively little external feedback, requesting it less than 10 percent of the time in one study. Most requests are early in learning new skills. Athletes and students more likely want feedback with more technically difficult skills. Also, external feedback should not duplicate internal feedback; it should fill a need in the absence of internal feedback, e.g., when a student asks why he or she keeps making the same error. When teachers and coaches have developed good communication with students and athletes, they should be able to tell whether or not they need feedback; and students and athletes are more likely to request it when needed. Because problem solving is part of all learning, teachers and coaches help most by giving feedback about sources of pertinent internal feedback, like directing them to focus on body parts, positions, movements, and relationships. Early in practicing technique, program feedback has priority; later, when students and athletes have mastered basics, parameter feedback has priority. Letting students and athletes request feedback affords them more independent learning, and assures their motivation to hear the teacher's or coach's instruction.

Amounts and Types of Feedback for Enhancement

Experts advise keeping feedback **simple**, yet not **simplistic**. It should give students and athletes the most useful information pertaining to the moment or situation. This prevents student and athlete information overload and directs their attention to the most important things. For example, among kicking speed, direction, and leg-swinging rhythm, a student learning soccer may need performance feedback about only one, not others. Student and athlete experience levels also determine feedback amounts. For example, feedback about one or two specific performance aspects is enough for volleyball beginners, e.g., "watch the ball," "bend your knees," or "relax your hands." Students having learned basic movement patterns can apply feedback like "smoother and softer," knowing by then that this encompasses planning for ball contact, body positioning, and relaxing the hands. Program feedback should be simpler than parameter feedback: athletes typically find program adjustments harder than parameter adjustments. For example, program feedback for a football quarterback could be "flick your wrist a little more" for basic forward pass timing. Once the quarterback has developed more regular throwing patterns, complex parameter feedback like "add force, release the ball sooner" enables greater throwing distance. Summarizing and averaging feedback are additional ways to prevent information overload.

Frequency of Feedback to Students

Studies show skill development does not require **greater feedback frequency**; practice without external feedback can be more effective than with it. Researchers speculate that this forces learners to attend more to internal feedback and problem solve more independently. Also, overly frequent feedback can engender student or athlete **dependency** on external feedback. For example, if the teacher or coach tells a baseball outfielder after one throw to keep the ball lower, to follow through more after the next throw, etc., he or she will immediately apply each piece of feedback on the next throw. Such momentary corrections preclude stable performance, preventing players from learning about relationships between their actions and outcomes. Upon external feedback cessation, player performance tends to regress to earlier levels. Teachers and coaches can decrease feedback frequency whenever they observe students or athletes gaining proficiency. This can be early in practice with simpler skills and techniques, and once they show enough consistency with complex skills and techniques. If performance declines, feedback frequency can be raised temporarily until it improves. Feedback quality supersedes quantity. Research finds feedback need not be highly precise for effectiveness; e.g., "a little faster or higher" rather than "0.5 seconds average" or "15 feet high" will suffice. Beginners need only a general idea; more precision is indicated for advanced athletes' fine-tuning.

History of Aerobic Dance

U.S. Air Force exercise physiologist Kenneth Cooper, M.D. and physical therapist Col. Pauline Potts developed and named **aerobics**. Cooper observed some people with great muscular strength still performed poorly at endurance sports like long-distance running, swimming, and bicycling. He was first to measure ability to utilize oxygen in sustained performance, and to differentiate aerobic capacity from strength, flexibility, etc. He published *Aerobics* in 1968, including research-based walking, running, swimming, and bicycling exercise programs. This book arrived at a historically opportune time, as Americans were becoming increasingly sedentary due to modern conveniences. Once Jane Fonda released her exercise videos using aerobic techniques in 1982, aerobics became popular internationally. Today many gymnasiums and exercise and dance studios offer aerobics classes. With the goal of enhancing all fitness elements—cardiovascular fitness, flexibility, and muscular strength—aerobics exercises combine rhythmic dance-like movements that raise the heart and respiratory rates with strength training and stretching, typically to music with a strong beat. Classes are separated by complexity and intensity level according to student experience (e.g., beginning, intermediate, advanced). Class exercises are led by certified instructors with various specialty areas.

Lifetime Activities and Recreational Pursuits

Some high schools not only include **lifetime wellness** in their physical education departments, but even require students to complete a year of lifetime wellness courses as well as a year of physical education courses to graduate. Such schools identify their programs' primary goal or objective as ensuring that students become "health-literate" individuals. They define **health literacy** as characterizing a person who has critical thinking and problem-solving skills, is a self-directed learner, communicates effectively, and is a productive and responsible citizen. Lifetime wellness programs offer students ideas for wisely utilizing their leisure time, helps them acquire useful physical skills while developing positive self-images and self-confidence, and exposes them to a broad range of physical activities in which they will be able to participate throughout their lives. Some schools that espouse lifetime wellness take a holistic approach to health and lifetime physical activities. In other words, they embrace total wellness, encompassing individual physical, mental, emotional, and social well-being. They teach classes that gives students foundations of knowledge about health and wellness practices and issues. Standards and course content can include nutrition, disease prevention and control, substance use and abuse, mental health, safety and first aid, sexuality and family life, personal fitness, and related skills.

Adventure and Outdoor Pursuits

Two main purposes for **outdoor recreation** are:

- beneficial use, i.e., utilitarian value or social and physical rewards reaped through goal-directed individual or group activity; and
- pleasurable appreciation, i.e., experiences that enhance perceptual or spiritual development through engagement in the natural world and nature's processes.

Some goal-directed outdoor activities include mountain climbing, hill walking, caving (spelunking), canyoning, backpacking, hiking, canoeing, kayaking, and rafting. More general groups of these activities include horseback riding, snow sports, and water sports. While these activities can be emotionally, mentally, and spiritually rewarding, they are primarily physical. The physical and social outdoor setting can meet achievement needs, for testing endurance and stamina, improving or challenging skills, practicing, and excitement or adventure seeking; it can also meet needs for teambuilding and building social connections, risk-taking, survival skills, self-sufficiency, and physical health. Some examples of outdoor experiences that enhance perceptual and spiritual pleasure and appreciation, and may also be physically rewarding, include meditation, aesthetic contemplation, nature study, photography, painting, historical research, archeological research, paleontological research, and ethnography and research into indigenous cultures. People also pursue outdoor activities to relax, enjoy life, and find peace in nature, as alternatives to expensive tourism, and as an educational medium.

Martial Arts

Martial arts are standardized combat systems, practiced for various purposes including self-defense, competitions, entertainment, physical fitness, and physical, mental, and spiritual development. They date to over 4,000 years ago in China, and to ancient Greece in Europe. They may be classified by regional origins, e.g., Eastern or Western; historical/traditional or contemporary; intention/application, e.g., sport, choreography, self-defense, military, meditative, fitness, etc.; techniques used, e.g., armed/unarmed; or external/internal in Chinese tradition. Unarmed forms are generally classified as using strikes, grappling, or both. Western boxing, Wing Chun, and Kalaripayattu use punching strikes. Kickboxing, Taekwondo, Savate, and Capoeira use kicking strikes. Karate, Sanshou, and Muay Thai also use strikes. Judo, Sambo, and Hapkido use throwing types of grappling. Aikido, Judo, and Jujitsu use chokehold, submission hold, and joint lock types of grappling. Judo, Sambo, and wrestling use pinning techniques for grappling. Weapon-based martial arts include historical European, kobudo, silat, eskrima, and kalaripayat; single-weapon training martial arts styles like Japanese kendo (sword), kenjutsu, bojutsu (staff), and kyudo (archery); and modern Western martial arts and sports like fencing, singlestick, canne de combat, and archery.

Current Issues and Trends

Effective PE teachers must be knowledgeable about how **current issues and trends in their field**, in education in general, and in wider society influence how their physical education programs will be structured and the learning objectives they will encompass. Teachers must know about the **history** of physical education and sports and how they have developed and progressed, and the impacts these had and continue to have on teaching. They need to stay informed on an ongoing basis about new research findings and curriculum models. Moreover, they must assess these new developments carefully, and then adapt their teaching practices based on the information and insights they have gained. Good PE teachers stay informed of economic, political, and social issues in their local areas that affect PE, and are aware how their field is affected by these globally, nationally, in their states, and locally. They realize how the learning goals and objectives they develop and their own school and community roles are shaped by these factors. They consider student health issues, obesity, personal wellness, and other needs, and address these by adjusting their teaching **practices to promote students' being and becoming productive** members of society.

School Accountability

Ever since the 1990s, **school accountability** has become an increasing trend in education, requiring the establishment of **national standards** and the use of **nationally standardized assessment tests**. As in other subjects, it is an issue of debate concerning physical education. People who object to national PE testing do so on the basis that to enjoy physical activity as adults, youth must be able to enjoy it as students. They find that the motivation for lifelong participation in physical activity is not supported by standardized testing. On the other hand, people who agree with national PE testing find that it not only

- 114 -

helps students to judge their progress according to national standards for competence in PE skills and physical fitness, but also that PE should be given the same importance and be judged by the same standards and assessments that math, science, language arts, social studies, and other school subjects are.

Accountability in Physical Education

The **National Association for Sport and Physical Education (NASPE)** has offered some **guidelines** in response to differences in public opinion regarding the use of standardized testing to assess PE performance. These guidelines include an operational definition of a person who is physically educated and a set of benchmarks for PE competency at each school grade level. NASPE defines **physically educated** as being physically fit, being skilled in various physical activities, participating regularly in physical activity, being aware of the benefits of physical activity, valuing the contributions of physical activity to a healthy lifestyle, being respectful of diversity, and being socially responsible in action and behavior. However, the degrees of specificity and direction that are necessary regarding standards and assessments in PE still remain controversial topics. A recent trend in school programs as well as businesses is to use the term "**wellness**" in place of "health" and "fitness." Although wellness generally represents optimum well-being and health, its definition has been widened to encompass mental, emotional, social, environmental, and spiritual well-being.

Challenges

Some **recent and current issues** that present challenges and cause concern for educators in all subjects and schools in general include lack of adequate resources, lack of support for education from students' parents, overly large class sizes, teacher burnout, student discipline problems, violence, and drug abuse by students. These issues all have an impact on another issue that experts find the most important of all: the concern of educators for all **students' well-being and health**. These issues have the same impact on PE as on other school subjects. One issue that currently presents the greatest challenge to PE in K-12 schools is the way that curriculum time for PE instruction and activities has been decreased. Not only does this have a direct negative impact on the well-being and health of students, but it also poses a conundrum for educators who are expected to balance academic subjects and accountability requirements with considerations of what is ideal for students' education overall. Ample research shows both the health risks of being sedentary and the physiological and psychological benefits of exercise. Therefore, it is critical to every student's physical, cognitive, and psychological development to provide daily PE.

Identifying Goals and Objectives

Based on expert PE content knowledge and strong insights into their learning environments, good PE teachers **design their lessons** thoughtfully. When implementing them, they effectively demonstrate the concepts, pace the progressions involved, and apply teaching strategies to be appropriate to every student. They observe their students' progress and performance carefully, analyze and assess it accurately, and give them timely, positive feedback through applicable teaching opportunities. In designing instruction, PE teachers realize the progressive nature of student motor skill acquisition and sequence units and lessons accordingly. They identify suitable contexts in which to teach specific skills, and combine them with developing related complementary skills. Observing student ability maturation, PE teachers respond to emerging developmental changes. For example, a teacher can design catching lessons that begin with retrieving a rolling ball, progress to learning to control a bouncing ball, and culminate in fielding a flying ball. PE teachers enhance student skill development by analyzing skills on a continuum of task analysis, and focus on critical concepts and components in feedback to inform students. They supply students with opportunities to succeed at appropriately challenging difficulty levels, and with suitable amounts of time for practicing newly learned skills.

Making Modifications to Instructional Goals

PE teachers may initially set certain **instructional goals** for their students, but then encounter challenges in the forms of variables such as students' physical abilities, student cognitive abilities, different student learning styles, different student developmental levels, and diverse and specific student interests. Good teachers will have the flexibility and judgment to **modify** the goals to address these and other variables, and the expertise to modify their teaching strategies to be congruent with the new or revised goals. As an example, a teacher who has planned a lesson on throwing and discovers a wide range of skill levels within the same class might set up a series of learning stations. At one station, students with beginner throwing skills can practice throwing at a stationary target. At another station, students with intermediate throwing skill levels can practice making lead passes. At a third station, students with more advanced levels of throwing skills can practice passing to teammates while they are being defended.

Plan, Adapt, and Implement Lesson Plans

Effective PE teachers inform themselves of any **medical conditions** students might have, including those not obvious as visible or identified disabilities, and **modify** their instructional strategies so that all students learn the same concepts and comparable skills and meet similar learning objectives, but each in ways that address their unique individual needs. As one example, students with Down syndrome, metabolic diseases, birth defects, traumatic injuries, upper respiratory infections, rheumatoid arthritis, and head and neck surgery can all cause a condition known as atlantoaxial instability. This consists of an abnormality in either the bone or the ligament that allows too much movement where the first and second cervical vertebrae (C1 and C2), i.e., the atlas and the axis, are joined. When the spinal cord is also involved, this condition additionally produces neurological symptoms. A student who has this condition would not be able to execute a forward roll in tumbling, gymnastics, or other activities with safety. However, the PE teacher can enable the student to meet a comparable learning objective by performing a log roll instead.

Meeting Diverse Student Needs

PE teachers can avail themselves of various **modalities** to differentiate their instruction to meet their students' varying needs. For example, some students learn best when they see pictures, diagrams, or visual demonstrations before trying to perform movements themselves; teachers can use visual graphics to teach them. Other students have visual impairments, visual processing disorders, or simply more auditory learning styles; teachers can present them with more spoken, musical, and other sound cues, descriptions, and directions. For students with haptic learning styles, teachers can give them more physical, kinesthetic directions and descriptions. Students with strong reading-writing orientations will benefit when teachers give them descriptions and instructions to read, and have them write or type breakdowns, analyses, or explanations of the skills. PE teachers also develop and use task analyses, whole-to-part instructions, and cue words to explain and present the simpler pieces of more complex skills to help students understand and learn. They use developmentally appropriate metaphors and analogies. For example, they could compare golf putting to an elephant's trunk swinging for younger children, and to a pendulum's action for high school students.

Specific Game Rules

For a high school PE course that teaches a specific sport, e.g., volleyball, the course description might include that students will learn to use the knowledge and skills they acquired in earlier volleyball courses to lead their peers, which includes explaining the **rules**, the rationale for the rules, and identifying when and how the rules have been violated. Course content might also include for students to apply their knowledge of the game's rules through taking advantage of opportunities for peer coaching and officiating. Learning objectives for such a course could include that upon completing the course, students would be able to analyze and evaluate the rules associated with all course activities, as well as equipment, risks, and safety procedures. Another course learning objective could be that upon completing the course, students would be able to interpret and apply the rules associated with specific activities included in the course. Another objective could be to collaborate with peers in setting rules for discussions and decisions regarding presenting alternative viewpoints, reaching informal consensus, voting on essential issues, setting clear goals and deadlines, and assigning individual roles. Objectives like these would meet PE curriculum standards.

NASPE

NASPE states that the goal of elementary school PE programs that are developmentally and instructionally appropriate is to develop individuals with the confidence, knowledge, and skills to be **physically active throughout life**. NASPE joins leading child development and medical specialists in recommending that all elementary school-aged children receive a minimum of 150 minutes of quality PE weekly. The association indicates that instructionally appropriate PE practices address the development, changes in movement abilities, and individual differences of children. The design and delivery of elementary school PE programs and lessons must also consider children's past experiences with motor skills, sports, and cognitive and social development. In addition, PE lesson planning and selection of instructional strategies should reflect individual children's ages, physical maturation, fitness levels, and skill levels. Appropriate patterns of PE instruction should also integrate known best practices revealed through both teaching experiences and research studies, to the end of optimizing all children's opportunities to learn and succeed. National, state, and local PE standards should also be reflected in quality PE programs and lessons. PE teachers must evaluate student progress regularly, and adjust their progressions and lessons accordingly.

Overall Model Content Standards

One example of **high school PE model content standards** is the California Department of Education's:

- Students show knowledge and competency regarding motor skills, movement patterns, and strategies necessary for performing various physical activities.
- Students show knowledge of fitness concepts, principles, and strategies, and attain levels of physical fitness enabling performance and health.
- Students show they know psychology and sociology concepts, principles, and strategies applicable to learning and executing physical activities.

This education department has five model content standards for elementary and middle school PE. For elementary school, it emphasizes movement through time and space, individually and with partners; movement continuity and change; and object manipulation with speed and accuracy through time and space. For middle school, it emphasizes decision making, meeting challenges, problem-solving teamwork, and cooperative goal achievement. Instruction and learning are incremental in grades K-5 for developmental appropriateness, while consolidated and refined in grades 6-8. The rationale is that high school students, capable of higher-order cognition and more sophisticated skill performance, can integrate cumulative knowledge and skills. Hence the five earlier standards are combined into three high school standards, reflecting high school PE's culmination of PE in earlier grades.

Combining Various Instructional Strategies

One analogy from NASPE (in human kinetics) is comparing teaching to cooking: though teachers follow instructional recipes like chefs, they **combine** these with their own creativity and unique ingredients, whose combinations are influenced by judicious decisions to attain specific results. Teachers must take into account each student's unique aptitudes and abilities, the particular learning environment, the teacher's own instructional strategies and styles, and the teacher's own personality characteristics. Teachers cannot depend on a **single teaching method**, like chefs cannot depend on one excellent recipe to meet all diners' varying tastes and needs. They both need a repertoire of varied recipes. Before implementing any particular teaching style, the PE teacher must consider additional factors, including the content he or she will be teaching, whether the physical learning environment lends itself to executing particular teaching styles, the time required or allowed for implementing a teaching style, the amount of class time available, personal teacher style, and most of all, the students.

National Demographics

The **demographic patterns** across American schools are in a state of rapid change. As a result, student populations in our schools are becoming more **diverse** all the time. This diversity dictates that teachers, including PE teachers, must change their instructional practices to address the challenges presented by populations with increasing diversity. When PE teachers prepare to apply certain teaching styles and instructional strategies, they must first think about whether each style and strategy is congruent with their program objectives, course content, and the developmental levels of their students. They also need to think about which ways are available for them to modify their instruction to enable matching each of their lessons to their teaching styles. While every teaching style produces unique results, no single instructional style has been proven to improve learning for all students. Therefore, PE teachers can make sure to meet all student needs by incorporating a variety of teaching styles. Their primary goal should be to enable every student to experience **success** in the environment of movement learning. Student achievement defines educational success. If students learned, met lesson objectives, and learned what was intended by the end of a lesson, then the lesson succeeded.

Vocabulary Hot Potato

One activity **combining PE and ELA** is "**Vocabulary Hot Potato**." This meets learning standards to:

- perform fundamental motor and manipulative skills, becoming competent in various physical activities and proficient in a few complex motor and sport activities;
- recognize safety hazards and respond effectively; and
- correctly spell words studied earlier.

It develops eye-hand coordination and manipulation skills for accurate tossing and catching. Materials needed are vocabulary or spelling lists and a small Nerf, foam, yarn, or wadded paper ball. Teacher assessment is via observation and immediate verbal feedback. Teachers first review correct underhand and overhand throwing techniques previously taught in PE classes with students, including foot opposition and follow-through. Teachers announce one word and toss the ball to a student, who gives the word's first letter and tosses the ball to another student, who supplies the next letter, continuing until the word's correct spelling is complete. The students who spelled the word select a whole-class exercise (e.g., jumping jacks, etc.), with as many repetitions as letters in the spelled word. Repeat with other words. Variations include one student spelling the whole word, another identifying its number of syllables, another using it in a sentence, etc.

Adverbs on the Move

"**Adverbs on the Move**" (Clancy, 2006) combines looking up word meanings in a dictionary and finding synonyms and antonyms in a thesaurus with practicing locomotor movements like walking, jogging or jogging in place, skipping, running, hopping, galloping, jumping, etc. Teachers provide the dictionary, a thesaurus, a list of recently learned adverbs, three-inch-by-five-inch cards, and pencils. Assessment is via observation and student verbal responses. Teachers give students cards, each with an adverb they have recently learned at the top. Each student looks up a synonym and antonym for his or her adverb and writes them below it on his or her card. Students move, carrying their cards softly, quickly, heavily, etc., according to the adverb they received. They stop on a teacher signal, each passing their card to the student next to them. On the teacher's "go" signal, they repeat the movement according to their new adverb. Then the teacher changes the movement and repeats the exercise. Teachers can vary adverbs for non-locomotor movements, e.g., angry, stormy, red, etc., or announce a sentence, have students identify the adverb in it, and then make movements the adverb describes.

Aquatics Without a Pool

Typically, state learning standards include **aquatics** as one content area in PE. However, not every school in a state may have a swimming pool in its building. Some solutions for PE departments and teachers include exploring opportunities in the community, such as at YMCAs or YWCAs, community recreation centers, county public swimming pools, or even pools at apartment complexes or private homes whose owners want to help, especially if students in the class live there. Another option is for the school to buy a portable pool if funds are available. If none of these alternatives is available, PE teachers can still teach swim strokes: they write or print task cards on the breathing pattern, kick, arm stroke, and complete combination for each stroke. They assign students to pairs, each with a bench, and give each pair a set of task cards. One student lies on the bench, while the other observes and gives feedback with corrections and reinforcement; then they switch. Each student masters each stroke component, then the complete stroke. An important caution is never to assume that mastering a stroke this way will enable the student to swim in the water safely.

Individual and Dual Activities

A PE teacher can use **individual and dual activities** to help high school students attend to the feedback they get both from their own proprioception—i.e., their sense of their body's location, orientation, positioning, and movements—and from other students, and to analyze this feedback and apply it to improve their performance of complex movements. For example, the teacher can assign students to pairs. One student executes a golf swing and his or her partner supplies feedback about the correctness of the swinger's form and technique. The first student analyzes both the partner's feedback and his or her own proprioceptive feedback. Together, the partners figure out what the first student must do to improve his or her performance. The performer writes down his or her analysis. To help students achieve and demonstrate independent learning of movement skills, the teacher offers students a choice of movement skills. The teacher instructs students to research their chosen skill's correct technique, and develop learning cues for practicing it. Students must then decide which kind of practice is best for the skill, and then write and implement their own plans for practice.

Safety in Extreme Environments

PE teachers can begin by designing lessons and instructing high school students about **extreme environments** and some of the **physical safety hazards** associated with them. For example, the environment of the ocean differs from the swimming environment of a swimming pool or lake because there are waves, undertows, and riptides. Students unfamiliar with these can be thrown by waves or pulled under by currents, and must learn how to address these situations. In the middle of a wave, one cannot see anything and cannot orient to directions like up or down, and even strong swimmers cannot counteract the force of some currents. In the mountains, high altitudes supply less oxygen, making negative impacts on one's breathing ability during physical exertion. Also, at higher altitudes the sun can be very hot during the day and temperatures can plummet to freezing at night. In deserts, high daytime temperatures and lack of water are hazards. In addition to preparing students for activity in extreme environments, teachers can meet learning standards by assigning students to select and research conditions and risks of specific environments, and write research reports about how these would affect physical activity and how to prepare.

NASPE Learning Standards

A volleyball activity for serving and defending can meet **NASPE standards** #1.2: setting, spiking, forearm passing, defensive strategies, and officiating; #3.4: aerobic capacity; and #5.6: cooperating and accepting challenges. Once a team's server hits the ball, team defense requires each player to know their base position, defend that space, and respond timely to offensive attacks by the opposing team. A team's first defensive hit should be a pass to enable effective defense-to-offense transition. PE teachers can give these **tactical cues**:

- Start in rotational position. This means one setter in front, one in the back row, with no overlapping.
- Serve the ball. Students should serve using the assigned method, aim at open spaces, and be prepared to move quickly.
- Transition to base defense. This means upon the serve, players should move from their rotational positions to their base positions.
- Defend against attack. This means players should watch the ball, call it, and start the sequence passing.

After play, teachers can ask students: Did they transition to base defense after the server hit the ball? Why or why not? And did their team defend against attack successfully? If so, how?

Explaining and Demonstrating

According to the **SPARK** website, PE teachers and coaches have **roles during practice** of giving students instruction and feedback; monitoring individual student and team performance; giving students motivation, support, and encouragement; assuring student safety; and managing space, time, and equipment involved. To be effective, teachers and coaches should be responsible in character, patient, good listeners, trustworthy, encouraging, and inspiring to students. To optimize student learning, teachers and coaches using designed practice plans should always follow them in the sequence they are written, and consult these plans and any associated content cards or notes regularly for pertinent information (unless or until they are so experienced they know these by heart). To support timely player setup, teachers and coaches should read aloud each task or component of a practice session. Teachers and coaches should "show and tell," i.e., demonstrate movements or actions physically to communicate them. To give players a mental advantage, give them "think-abouts." The 80/20 Rule means although 100 percent of students will learn or understand by doing or practicing a skill, 80 percent grasp the concept through teacher or coach instruction or demonstration, while the other 20 percent will understand through doing. Teachers and coaches also teach fair play, etiquette, and rules in sports.

High School Doubles Badminton

Badminton can be taught using **doubles teams**. In front-to-back formation, one player is responsible for front court, one for mid-court and back court. This formation enables drop and smash shots, making it offensive. Players recover and communicate centrally to their sides to prevent faults and optimize success. Teachers demonstrate while explaining game format. For rally scoring, players must stay in front-to-back formation, finish a 10-hit rally before scoring points, and rotate front and back positions after every point. Rotate the team with more points up after every game. Cues include: "Determine team strategy": students decide if their team is better at offense or defense; "Communicate": call court positions and shots to prevent faults; "Adjust as partner moves": change court positions as partners move to strike; and "Attack/Defend": attack via front-to-back, and defend via side-to-side team formations. Target and trajectory cues include: (Front) A drop shot has low trajectory and front-court target (both near the net); (Back) A smash shot has steep trajectory and mid-court sideline target. Think-abouts: When playing against a team in front-to-back formation, where should your shots land? What is one advantage of front-to-back formation?

Badminton Practice Plan

In a **high school badminton practice plan**, racquet types should be selected for maximal student success. The first two practice games can be doubles play, both teams in front-to-back formation:

- One player serves, starting a rally; players call "Mine" before hitting or returning any shot. Alternate front and back positions with each rally, completing 10 rallies.
- After serving, play a 10-hit rally; then attempt to score: only a smash or drop shot earns points. Players call as in (1). Play up to 5 points. Switch positions after each point.
- One team is in front-to-back formation, the other in side-to-side formation; both teams maintain formation throughout the game. Serve, complete a 10-hit rally, and then attempt to score. As in (1) and (2), players call before hitting. Play up to 5 points, rotating player positions following every point. Play four games, rotating team formations after every game.
- Teams make up, practice, and play their own games, developing rules by varying clear/drive/drop/smash shot types, short/long serve types, front-to-back/side-to-side formation types, space, and scoring methods.

Think-abouts include: Which shot was most effective against each doubles formation? Which doubles formation did you like better? Why?

High School Basketball Practice Plan

PE teachers and coaches **demonstrate** while explaining game format, e.g., five one-minute periods. Play starts or restarts with a pass from the baseline or sideline. Offense only throws after pick and roll, scoring 1 point per basket. Each foul gives the opposing team 1 point. For the first four periods, stay on offense; rotate offense to defense every period. In period five, offense and defense switch every time ball possession changes. Rotate after each game. Offense cues: "Pick": Set a pick or screen on an opponent defending a teammate; the teammate moves past. "Roll": Roll off the screen to the basket, look at the ball-handler, prepare to pass. "Shoot and follow": If open, throw; follow the shot to the basket. If not open, reset. Defense cues: "Match-up": Defend a player similar in size, fitness, and skill level. "Shadow": Stay close to the offensive player you defend no matter where on the court he or she goes. "Box-out-let": On a throw, face the basket, keeping the opponent behind you; rebound and pass. "Communicate": Talk so your teammates always know what is happening. Think-abouts: Did you roll to the basket after every pick? Why or why not? Did you take shots only when open? Why or why not? Which passes worked best with a pick and roll? Why?

Safety Considerations for Movement

Teachers should instruct students in **moving safely** within general and personal spaces. They must teach skills in the correct order, e.g., stepping into hoops on floors before having to run in and out of them. Games must include skills already taught. Teachers should give activities needing no equipment at the beginning of the school year, and then introduce smaller equipment (hoops, bean bags, etc.) before mobile equipment like utility balls. Teachers should instruct students in floor activities, like balancing when walking on floor lines, before using equipment, like balancing when walking on benches. They should define procedures and rules and give students practice in them, like stop and start signals, looking in the direction they are moving, and safe equipment use, inside the gym before going outside. They must be informed about students with medical conditions, like orthopedic devices or casts, asthma, allergies or anaphylaxis, epilepsy, diabetes, cardiac conditions, etc., that could affect their participation. Pylons, lines, or other markers must be designated away from walls: stages and walls cannot be used as end zones or turning points. Students must always be supervised and never left alone in equipment rooms.

Warm-Up and Cool Down

Teachers and coaches must teach students correct, age-appropriate procedures for **warming up** before movement activities and **cooling down** afterward. PE teachers have been sued for negligence for neglecting proper warm-ups. For **risk management**, teachers and coaches must select activities appropriate to students' levels of cognitive development, behavioral patterns, and mental and physical abilities. Teachers and coaches must possess the skills and knowledge for safely teaching and supervising activities according to risk management guidelines. Generally, if an activity is not included in the physical education curriculum or official safety guidelines, teachers and coaches should first determine whether its educational value matches or supersedes its entertainment value, and then submit a proposal to the school board for approval. If approved, officials, teachers, and coaches must identify and minimize inherent risks in the activity. Coaches and teachers must instruct all students in body contact techniques and skills, concussion safety lessons, and head-injury prevention principles (and document the instruction). They must also require helmets and protective equipment as applicable, and ensure that equipment is inspected before activities, practices, and games. For outdoor activities, they must assure parents know **safety precautions** for extreme weather, temperatures, humidity, smog/air quality, UV rays, frostbite, dehydration, and insects; develop safety protocols and precautions for lightning; and communicate these to students and staff.

Heimlich Maneuver and CPR

For **choking**, quick response is necessary to prevent unconsciousness, even death. For adults and children (procedures for infants differ), perform the **Heimlich maneuver**. First, remember that panicky victims may unintentionally strike out, and protect yourself. Do NOT perform the Heimlich on someone who is speaking, coughing, or breathing—someone who can do these things is not choking. Stand behind the victim. Wrap your arms around him or her as if hugging. Make a fist with your right hand and put it above the victim's navel. Grasp your right fist with your left hand; thrust in and up forcibly. Repeat thrusting until the victim can breathe. If the victim loses consciousness, begin **child CPR** for children aged one to eight years, or **adult CPR** above eight years. Practice universal precautions and use protective equipment if available to avoid contagious and infectious diseases. "Shake and shout," trying to wake the victim. If he or she does not awaken, call 911. If nobody is available, do CPR for two minutes, and then call 911. On children, do two chest compressions per second 30 times and repeat. On adults, do chest compressions at least 100 times a minute, or 30 times in 18 seconds, and repeat.

Naturalistic Observations vs Structured Observations

Naturalistic observations entail unobtrusively observing student performance as it typically occurs in students' usual daily setting, e.g., practice during regular PE classes. While this method has the advantage of seeing realistic instances of typical student behaviors, it has been criticized for allowing the teacher's judgments to be overly subjective. **Structured observations** provide an alternative solution by applying specific criteria, of which teacher and students are both informed, to evaluate observed performance. This criterion reference has the advantage of shifting observational assessment from more subjective to more objective. Teachers may use a rubric to provide the criteria against which they measure student performance. Structured observations are particularly useful for assessing student motor skills, movement skills, and social skills. Two methods of structured observation are station approach and embedded assessment. In station approach, teachers set up a circuit with several stations, assigning students to individual stations. Some stations involve mini-games, some motor skill practice, some exercising, one the testing station where teachers assess student skills. In embedded assessment, teachers instruct and assess simultaneously, evaluating students' learning while they practice skills—through periodic progress monitoring or end-of-unit summative assessment.

PE Checklists

Because so many PE activities must be performed physically to demonstrate learning rather than answering questions on written tests, it is natural for teachers to use **observation** to assess student skill acquisition. When they observe student performance, PE teachers and coaches are typically looking for them to demonstrate skills or skill areas. **Checklists** lend themselves to observational assessment because they list these skill areas in advance; the teacher or coach needs only check a box reflecting the level of the student's mastery, e.g., yes/no; skilled/talented/athletically gifted; etc. For example, a student checklist for PE class might list student demonstration of: strength and endurance; balance and flexibility; skill in moving through space; interest in a sport or activity the student can pursue on a lifelong basis; ability to follow oral directions in games and sports; age-appropriate, ability-appropriate gross and fine motor skills; and participation in noncompetitive group activities and games. The checklist might also include a space at the bottom for the teacher to write district PE objectives.

Sport Checklist

A good **sport checklist** has lines for student name, team, teacher or coach name, and assessment period. Some typical **skills** to assess via checking Yes or No, with a column at the right for comments, include practice punctuality and participation; positive attitude with teacher/coach and teammates; skills in sport-specific techniques, with lines for the teacher or coach to list these; healthy competitive and aggressive levels for sport participation; and equipment use skills, with lines to write specific pieces of equipment. The checklist can include an additional column for notes or comments. A cheerleading performance checklist can include mastery levels, e.g., Skilled, Talented, or Athletically Gifted, to check for skills like these: energy and enthusiasm; voice inflection and projection; memorization and rhythm of routines; jumping height and technique; tumbling and gymnastics; punctuality, attendance, professional attitude, and cooperation; creativity, e.g., changing or developing cheers, routines, and dances; use of pom-poms, flags, and other show props; choreography and dance skills; and additional sections for recommendations and notes.

Psychomotor, Cognitive, and Affective Domains

The psychomotor, cognitive, and affective domains are **interrelated** in PE, which makes physical movement meaningful. The **psychomotor domain** is the performance component whereby students acquire physical skills through environmental exploration. The **cognitive domain** is the knowledge component whereby students think and relate their experiences to learning. The **affective domain** is the personal, emotional, and social component whereby students interact with other people, developing a sense of self and others. When students understand why their bodies function as they do through the cognitive domain, they begin to acquire skill competencies through the psychomotor domain, and learn to associate physical activity with positive feelings through the affective domain. In the psychomotor domain, developing competence in motor skill abilities is the essence of PE. In the cognitive domain, students are enabled to become more efficient at moving and at learning through moving, through understanding the principles and concepts of movement. In the affective domain, students develop acceptable personal and social behaviors in physical activity contexts, behaving responsibly as individuals and group members to afford productive learning environments.

Psychomotor, Cognitive, and Affective Domain Assessment

When a PE teacher assesses a student in the **psychomotor domain**, he or she measures student development of **health-related fitness and motor skills**. For example, when a teacher assesses elementary school student skipping skill, students demonstrate the step-hop pattern; when the teacher assesses older students, they might administer the FITNESSGRAM test battery. When a PE teacher assesses students in the cognitive domain, he or she measures student knowledge about movement concepts, principles, strategies, and tactics. For example, middle school students might be asked to explain verbally a strategy for defending their territory in a sport activity, or to verbalize a "Ready, swing back, step, and follow through" movement skill pattern to use in performing an underhand throw. When a PE teacher assesses students in the affective domain, he or she measures the level to which each student has developed acceptable personal and social behaviors in physical activity settings. As an example, the teacher might have high school students complete written self-reflections about their own performance, write peer performance evaluations of classmates or teammates, or identify, observe, and create (as appropriate) safety rules or guidelines for physical activity participation.

Formal and Informal Assessments

While assessment in PE often uses **observation of student skill performance**, it is not considered assessment unless some written record is made of the observations. When team games are played as part of PE, the game play statistics teachers and coaches record are examples of using **event-recording techniques** to collect student team performance data. Game statistics, wins and losses, fitness scores, skill assessments, and other daily "snapshots" or performance records are **formal**. Checklists identifying specific behaviors/skills/performance characteristics according to established criteria are **informal**, enabling quick evaluations with minimal writing. Rating scales are also informal and brief, identifying the degree or extent to which students perform skills. Rubrics are formal, establishing multidimensional criteria for rating complex skills and behaviors. Student surveys, questionnaires, and interviews are informal, collecting information about how students feel and think about PE. Student logs are formal records of student participation or other characteristics and behaviors over time. Student journals are informal, reflective self-recording tools of student perceptions, attitudes, and feelings about PE experiences. Student projects are formal learning and assessment experiences wherein students investigate, design, construct, and present work. Written tests and worksheets are common formal assessments.

The President's Challenge and FITNESSGRAM

The **President's Challenge** assesses and gives students feedback about their levels of fitness. It tests students using exercises including right-angled pushups, pull-ups, curl-ups, endurance running and walking, the V-sit and reach, and shuttle runs. **FITNESSGRAM** tests student levels of muscular strength, aerobic capacity, flexibility, endurance, and body composition. The President's Challenge is part of the Presidential President's Council on Fitness, Sports, and Nutrition. It replaces the former Physical Fitness Test established in the 1960s under President Kennedy's initial enactment of the President's Council on Physical Fitness. It includes an Adult Fitness Test; the Presidential Active Lifestyle Award (PALA) Challenge for integrating physical activity and healthy eating into everyday life; the Presidential Champions Challenge for individuals with more ambitious activity goals; and the Presidential Youth Fitness Program to teach students lifelong fitness and health. Also part of the Presidential Youth Fitness Program, FITNESSGRAM provides educators with choices of varied test items to assess students using Healthy Fitness Zone standards; separate summary, achievement, data sheet, tracking, statistics,

- 124 -

information, and summary report forms; and Activity Log and ACTIVITYGRAM modules to report test scores to students and parents. FITNESSGRAM and ACTIVITYGRAM reports are also used in educating students, research studies, and teacher education and preparation.

FITNESSGRAM

FITNESSGRAM was designed as a part of the U.S. Presidential Youth Fitness Program for lifelong health and fitness. State departments of education frequently designate the FITNESSGRAM as the test for their school district PE departments to use to assess student physical performance. Three main **components of fitness** evaluated by FITNESSGRAM are

- aerobic capacity
- body composition
- muscle strength, endurance, and flexibility

evaluated through assessment of six corresponding key areas of fitness as subdivisions of these three main components.

Student performance on each test for each fitness area is rated as needing improvement, or in a **Healthy Fitness Zone (HFZ)**, which is the desired performance standard. The HFZ is set by the developers of the test to reflect reasonable physical fitness levels that most students are capable of achieving. Individual HFZs vary according to student gender and age. As an example, one state education code defines passing this physical performance test for ninth graders as satisfactorily performing within the HFZ on at least five of the test's six standards.

Administering the FITNESSGRAM

As a national standardized test battery that education departments administer throughout their states, the **FITNESSGRAM** must be administered with personnel carefully adhering to its prescribed **protocols and regulations** to preserve its validity. School district administrators are responsible to know about current regulations and statutes, and assuring all district personnel comply with these. They are also responsible to make sure that all school district staff members are trained correctly in test administration, and are given needed assistance and resources. Specialized training is necessary for administering the FITNESSGRAM test battery, because teachers have to use their judgment to evaluate how students perform physical skills, e.g., push-ups, etc. Educators also have to plan carefully to establish an environment for testing that maintains safety and dignity for every student. State education department officials in states using FITNESSGRAM advise their school district administrators to create fitness testing plans consistent with its test manual and compliant with current regulatory and statutory requirements for administration and results reporting. The FITNESSGRAM test administration manual and PE Resource Guide can be downloaded from websites including the Presidential Youth Fitness Program, Human Kinetics, Cooper Institute, and state education departments using it.

Standardized vs. Authentic Assessments

A **standardized assessment** can provide a comparison of the learning a student demonstrates to a national or state average. Standardized tests do this by providing norms, i.e., average scores of samples of students that represent an average of the national or state student population. They can show in what position a student ranks among other students in the country or state. In addition to achievement tests, standardized IQ tests can also show student ability compared to average, high-end, and low-end scores. **Subscales** on intelligence testing instruments additionally show relative student strengths and weaknesses in various areas, e.g., immediate memory, reading comprehension, vocabulary, manipulating numbers, manipulating shapes, fluid and flexible thinking processes, and crystallized and retained knowledge and information, etc. **Authentic assessments** can be individualized, whereas standardized assessments cannot. They indicate more about what a student knows and can do in conditions and situations more akin to real life. They can focus more on how a student applies ability and knowledge. They can also reveal more about an individual student's unique qualities than standardized tests of either achievement or IQ can.

Characteristics of a Rubric

A **rubric** specifies certain learning objectives a student should be able to demonstrate, and in what ways. Teachers should first review the rubric with students to inform them of what they are expected to learn. Then they have students use the rubric to guide their learning experiences and work. Finally, they use the rubric to assess whether students have met the learning objective(s). A **norm-referenced test** compares the student's scores to a previously established norm. For example, standardized tests commonly obtain samples of scores from students they have identified as representative of a given national or state population. They then calculate the average or mean score of these students. Whenever other students take these standardized tests, their scores are then compared to these averages. The test authors or publishers provide statistical computations and tables whereby educators can determine how many standard deviations from the norm a student's score falls, and in what percentile of the population the student's score ranks. **Criterion-referenced tests** do not compare student scores to a norm, but instead against predetermined criteria of what learning they should demonstrate, determined by test authors, publishers, school districts, individual teachers, etc. They do not determine student rank, but whether or to what degree the student meets lesson, unit, class, course, or subject requirements.

Validity and Assessment Instruments

Statistical validity means an instrument measures what it claims and is intended to measure. Some types of validity include external validity, internal validity, content validity, construct validity, face validity, and criterion validity. **External validity** includes population validity and ecological validity. **Population validity** is whether a sample population accurately represents the whole population, and whether acceptable sampling methodology is used (e.g., random selection, not convenience sampling). **Ecological validity** is whether the testing environment or process affects behavior. **Internal validity** is how strong a causal relationship between variables can be established, as opposed to only correlation. **Content validity** is how well a measure represents all aspects of the construct measured. **Construct validity** includes convergent and divergent validity. **Convergent validity** shows constructs expected to be related are related; **divergent validity** shows constructs expected to be unrelated are unrelated. A study or instrument with both has high construct validity. **Face (representation) validity** is general, common-sense, non-objective, non-quantified evaluation based on experience and judgment. **Criterion validity** is whether an instrument reflects a specific group of abilities. It includes concurrent and predictive validity. **Concurrent validity** compares an instrument to an established measure; predictive validity tests it over time.

Reliability and Assessment Instruments

Reliability means an instrument gets the same or similar results across repeated administrations. Some types of reliability include test-retest reliability, interrater reliability, internal consistency reliability, and instrument reliability. **Test-retest reliability** shows test stability when administered repeatedly to the same subjects. Surveys and IQ tests are good test-retest choices because individuals rarely have sudden, pronounced changes in their opinions or IQs within a few months. Educational tests are less applicable, as students learn more over time and will score higher on the second administration. **Interrater reliability** or interobserver reliability quantifies the amount of agreement between two, or among several, observers or test administrators. This is important in any research requiring different individuals to make qualitative ratings. For example, Olympics judges must be consistent with one another in their scoring systems. University and school examiners must also adhere to common standards. **Internal consistency reliability** is whether different items measuring the same construct within a test give the same results or scores. **Instrument reliability** in physical sciences is whether equipment is calibrated to yield the same measurements every time (within acceptable error margins), and in social sciences, whether an instrument is statistically stable over time.

High-Quality, Appropriate Assessments

Appropriate assessments of high quality should be informed by local, state, and national guidelines or standards so that their results can be used for establishing instructional objectives that are equally appropriate for teachers and students. In addition all educators, including PE teachers, should choose and apply assessment measures that are suitable for ascertaining what kind of progress their students are making toward fulfilling the instructional objectives that they have designated. This applies to both formative and summative assessments, and includes both informal and formal assessment instruments and tools. And therefore, because assessments help PE and other faculty to determine whether and to what to degree they and their students are achieving the instructional objectives they have assigned for their teaching units, PE teachers should also develop evaluation schemes or plans that reflect whether and to what extent those instructional objectives have been accomplished. Although it is true that assessment results do contribute to the grades that teachers give to their students, grades should not be the only results of their evaluation schemes: assessing whether learning goals and objectives have been satisfied is equally important.

Assessment

Purposes:

- To gauge student learning;
- To evaluate and improve instruction;
- To communicate with students, parents, and administrators and identify curriculum gaps;
- To evaluate and modify programs;
- To validate and support programs through consistently providing objective data; and
- To motivate students to learn through documenting their growth and improvement.

Requirements:

- Validity, by measuring the quantities—skills, behaviors, or performance—it is designed and purports to measure;
- Reliability, by yielding the same results from measuring the same students over multiple administration at different times;
- Objectivity, by yielding very similar results regardless of who administers it;
- Feasibility, by being straightforward, inexpensive to obtain, not taking excessive instructional time, being easy to set up and administer, having instructions who are easy to follow and make reasonable demands on students and administrators, and able to be scored without influencing its objectivity, e.g., if multiple administrators are needed; and
- Usefulness, by having results that can be applied for progress reporting, program planning, self-assessment, and other valid educational uses.

Traditional vs. Alternative Approaches

Traditional assessment approaches involve teacher-generated written tests and worksheets, including

- Selected-response formats, with questions or items giving alternatives from which students select responses, e.g., multiple choice, true/false, and matching tests/worksheets;
- Limited open-ended formats wherein questions or items require brief written constructed responses, e.g., open response, short answer, diagram labeling, and fill in the blank.

Alternative approaches involve student products, including

- Audiovisual, made to display or exhibit, e.g., artwork, concept maps, posters, banners, photo exhibits, PowerPoints, videos, iMovies, audio recordings, and sculptures or models of athletes;
- Written, e.g., research papers, essays, stories, poems, anecdotes, journals, logs, personal fitness plans, checklists, rating scales, brochures, advertisements; teacher, peer, or self-rubrics; performance records, newspapers, constructed magazines, projects, pre-assessment inventories; student surveys, questionnaires, or interviews; editorials, reflection; and
- Performance tasks, i.e., physical or cognitive behaviors, e.g., officiating a game, playing a game, conducting fitness assessments, giving oral reports, teaching lessons; showcases, debates, skits, role plays, interviews, locomotor, gymnastics, or dance movement sequences; and warmup routines.

Physical Activity Descriptor

According to the National Association for Sport and Physical Education (NASPE)'s Instructional Framework for Fitness Education in Physical Education (IFFEPE), which parallels NASPE's National Standards for PE, a **physical activity descriptor** for students is to "Self-monitor physical activity and create an individualized physical activity plan." **Benchmarks** are, for pre-K/K, setting weekly goals to be active during recess; for grades 1-2, using weekly or monthly activity calendars or planning physical activity participation with family outside school; for grades 3-5, using available technology to set personal fitness goals and self-monitor physical activity, including using logs, journals, stopwatches, pedometers or other assessment tools; for grades 6-8, using online tracking, heart-rate monitors, pedometers, and other available technology to self-monitor physical activity and create physical activity plans incorporating self-management skills, environment, social interaction, and personal preferences; for grades 9-12, using available technology to self-monitor and develop personalized physical activity plans to remediate physical activity level deficits; and for higher education, using available technology to self-monitor and develop short- and long-term personalized personal activity plans to correct physical activity level deficits.

Using Self-Assessment

Students can **record their own progress** by writing in a journal, keeping notes in a notebook, or recording information on index cards and submitting these to the PE teacher throughout teaching and learning. **Self-assessment** is a practical, quick method for PE teachers to gather information on student progress; relieves teachers of much extra work; engages students in their own evaluation processes; and allows students to communicate what they want to about their progress from their own perspectives. PE teachers can give K-2 students a student log form to complete for self-assessing regular physical fitness activities: The left-hand column lists fitness categories with easy-to-understand self-statements – Cardiovascular endurance, "I have a strong heart"; Muscular strength, "I have strong muscles"; Muscular endurance, "I can do movements over and over again"; and Flexibility, "I can stretch." The right-hand column is blank; students make drawings or cut out and paste in pictures illustrating which activities they do for each category (e.g., running, dancing, lifting things, etc.). This is fun and creative for young students, helps them categorize fitness activities, and gives teachers assessment information.

Peer Assessment

PE teachers must give students clear instructions about **peer assessments** before letting students conduct them. Students can use rubrics, rating scales, or checklists to obtain the criteria to judge their classmates' or teammates' progress in PE. Students must focus on these criteria to assess peers. This attention to requirements develops their **observational skills**. PE teachers must teach the observational process for students to make effective peer assessments. For grades 6-8, partners can complete basketball assessment checklists: pairs take turns telling partners what they are looking for in each dribble, pass, or shot, making a check mark or X next to every correctly executed technique and leaving incorrectly done ones blank. Skills can include set shots, balancing the ball, eyes on target, knees bent, limb extension when shooting, follow through, lay-up technique (step with each foot, hop, knee up, aim for backboard), chest and bounce passing technique (fingers spread, step forward, elbows out, push ball, snap, backs of hands facing one another, thumbs down) against a wall, and dribbling technique (head up, use finger pads, dribble below waist, switch hands). One checklist can have two columns on either side of these skills, one for each partner.

Assessment in Special and Adapted Education

According to PE Central®, the first step in developing an IEP for a student with disabilities is **assessment**. Assessment is the interpretation of measures attained via testing, and is focused on identifying the student's individual activity needs. Assessment is also utilized for making placement and program planning decisions. The instruction provided for a student with disabilities, which enables him or her to participate with safety and success in PE classes, depends on a foundation of assessment. Federal IDEA regulations for conducting evaluations require local education agencies (LEAs) to use **multiple, varied assessment strategies and tools** to collect pertinent information about the student developmentally, functionally, and academically, including information from parents. This information can help to determine whether the student has a disability, and what should be contained in the student's IEP, including supports needed for general education program success. Educators should never use just one assessment or measure as a criterion to determine student disability or educational placement. They should use not only multiple assessment instruments, but moreover technically sound, valid, and reliable instruments. Assessments should include the relative contributions of cognitive and behavioral as well as physiological and developmental factors.

Assessing Students with Disabilities

Schools must choose and administer assessments without racial or cultural **discrimination**, and supply and administer assessments in the language and form most likely to give accurate information about the student's developmental, functional, and academic knowledge and abilities. Assessments must be used only for the same purposes for which they have been found valid and reliable. Personnel with adequate knowledge and training must administer each assessment. Administration must adhere to any instructions included by the assessment's producer or publisher. Students should be assessed in all areas where **disabilities** are suspected. Assessment strategies and tools utilized should supply pertinent information that directly aids educators in defining student educational needs. Results from norm-referenced or criterion-referenced tests should be combined with observational assessments made within the performance environment. Rather than only measure disability, assessments should also measure ability and describe student strengths and needs. Tests measuring physical fitness or motor skill performance should not discriminate based on student disability. Students with verbal learning disabilities need visual demonstrations and cues added to verbal instructions to perform at their ability

- 129 -

levels. Formal standardized tests that do not permit students to demonstrate strengths and needs may be inappropriate.

Determining Support

Some best practices are to use assessment data to determine if a student requires **support** for PE, and the amount of support needed for the student to succeed in general PE. Support can include curricular or instructional accommodations. For example, students may be provided with adaptive equipment, adaptive physical education (APE) consultation, direct APE teacher services, peer "buddy" support, and other forms of support. To determine the least restrictive, most appropriate PE placement, educators should consider the following: the results of an ecologically based, comprehensive motor and physical assessment made by a PE teacher qualified in APE and certified by the school's state department of education or other designated accrediting organization; the student's individual psychomotor, cognitive, and affective characteristics that would influence student capability for safely, successfully participating in general PE; and the student's capacity for benefiting from an APE program, which includes such factors as the student's ability to comprehend cause-and-effect relationships, capacity for voluntary movement, ability to interact with other people, and demonstration of the emotional behaviors for benefiting from one-on-one instruction.

Referral for Adaptive Physical Education Services

Individual school district policies for **referral** vary. In general, a school must first explore alternative programs and procedures within the general education PE program. If a student has difficulty with regular PE, teachers, parents, and others can refer the student for **APE services** through the student's teacher or other school personnel at an IEP committee meeting, planning and placement team meeting, or child study conference. General education PE teachers and parents who think a student with a disability would benefit from APE can request referral from the Special Education Director or school principal. Upon written parental consent, qualified personnel conduct formal assessments of the student's motor, fitness, and behavioral skills. A meeting is scheduled to discuss assessment results and determine levels of PE support required. The designated team determines student eligibility for special education services. PE staff can identify, assess, and recommend APE for a student not identified as eligible for special education based on APE guidelines entrance criteria. Students eligible for special education with gross or fine motor skills deficits are referred for PT or OT evaluations, which PE teachers use to develop IEP goals and objectives.

Disability Identification and Eligibility

Once a teacher, other school personnel, parent, or professional or agency personnel refers a student for evaluation for **disability identification and eligibility determination for special education services**, the school district convenes a **PPT or IEP team**. The members of this team typically include the student whenever appropriate; the student's parents; at least one regular education teacher, if the student may be or is placed in regular education; at least one special educator; a person(s) able to interpret evaluations, e.g., a psychometrist, school psychologist, educational specialist, or adapted physical education (APE) teacher; a school district representative who knows the general education curriculum and can allocate resources; and any others with expertise or knowledge pertinent to the student. Student evaluation can include standardized test results; information from parents, teachers, and service providers; formal and informal observations; reviews of school work; Birth to Three System records, etc. The team may design individualized evaluations according to referral concerns. Parents are given written notice of consent for evaluation. Federal regulations require IEPs to be developed for students determined eligible within 60 calendar days after written referrals; state regulations may require them to be developed sooner.

- 130 -

Eligibility for Adaptive Physical Education

A student may be identified for determining **APE eligibility** under special education services through testing by a physical therapist (PT) or occupational therapist (OT), or be recommended for evaluation by a student intervention team, teacher, parent, etc. Additional **indications** include these: the student does not perform at his or her ability level in group settings; the student scores below average in two or more parts of the school district's state physical fitness test; the student exhibits social behaviors impeding his or her own or others' learning for more than one-third of class time; or the student scores 1.5 standard deviations (SD) or more below the norm in two or more parts of a designated norm-referenced test. The student should be given a **test of gross motor development (TGMD)**, and if the results are not within normal limits, this is indication for determining eligibility for APE. School personnel should furnish to school PE staff the names of students recommended or identified for APE for the coming school year, plus a copy of each student's TGMD, by the end of the current school year. PE staff should have access to electronic databases for writing IEP goals and objectives for APE.

Collaboration, Reflection, and Technology

Educational Collaboration

When educators use **collaborative approaches**, students benefit from the shared ownership of responsibility for student learning and vision of all educational team members. Members share increased awareness and knowledge of each student's needs, and of current intervention methods and teaching strategies. They also have greater opportunities for mutual contact to monitor and modify student programs, and for ongoing open communication lines. Through a systemic approach, all educators aim for common goals, and all students are instructed in the same core competencies irrespective of their individual teachers. Even the most hardworking and competent teachers working alone would lose such consistency and coordination across classrooms and grades, which for many students would make the educational system ineffective. School placements should benefit each student through individualized educational services. All stakeholders can achieve the same educational goals when they collaborate purposefully. Today educators, administrators, support staff, students, and parents are expected to collaborate to ensure that all students receive meaningful educations. Grade-level achievement is expected of all students at all developmental and ability levels. Teachers must promote all students' growth, most often in general education settings. These expectations make school personnel's collaboration more necessary than ever.

Collaboration Among Educational Professionals

All teachers and other members of school teams contribute various strengths to learning environments and classrooms for **collaborative problem solving**. When teachers collaborate with other education professionals, this assists them in learning new methods for supporting their students and in making informed educational decisions. Despite the challenges in making time for it, experts in education maintain the importance of school administrators ensuring that teachers have the time to work together with other professionals to make decisions regarding their students. This is necessary for all students, and even more crucial for students with disabilities, particularly for meeting these students' needs in general PE classes. Students mainstreamed in PE classes can exhibit a wide variety of ability levels and types. Meeting all of their needs in the general PE class is difficult for a teacher to do alone. To provide opportunities that enable each student to succeed, professionals must work as a team. Regular PE teachers, adapted physical education (APE) teachers, physical therapists, occupational therapists, special education teachers, classroom teachers, teachers of all individual subjects, curriculum and program developers, administrators, parents, school board members, colleges and universities, and their professors and instructors all need to collaborate to ensure student success in PE.

APE Collaborations

Educators from different disciplines can meet on common ground to share their respective areas of expertise in designing and implementing **educational interventions** for students with **developmental disabilities**. This sharing informs, expands, and enriches what all of the collaborating educators can know and do together to benefit their students with special needs. For example, in early childhood education, experts recommend that both APEs and classroom teachers apply instructional strategies they learn from the discipline of occupational therapy (OT) to help preschool children with developmental delays to learn fine motor and manipulative skills. Teamwork enables all collaborators to share ownership, responsibility, and vision for every student's development, growth, and learning. It moreover informs team members better about each child's needs and what intervention methods and strategies are currently being used. Ongoing monitoring and implementation of recommended instructional

- 132 -

modifications are also better supported through the continuing contact and communication afforded by interdisciplinary collaboration.

The Collaborative Team

In representing teams that collaborate to serve the needs of a student who receives regular and special education services, some educators use the graphic of a "**collaboration wheel**." The student is at the center of this circle. Surrounding the student are members of the collaborative team. These include the student's parents and family, who provide the best knowledge about the student's developmental history, medical history, personality, daily living skills, habits, behaviors, interests, and preferences. Family members also contribute personalized strategies they have discovered or evolved to be effective with the individual student, and insights about ineffective methods and interactions. Academic subject and PE teachers are team members who provide the student with curriculum, instruction, and assessment, including needed accommodations, modifications, and adaptations. School administrators supervise faculty and staff; help develop school curriculum, programs and initiatives; manage school facilities; plan and manage school budgets; and much more. Nurses and doctors provide health services. School or private psychologists conduct psychological evaluations, IQ testing, and mental status examinations, and provide therapy, counseling, and behavior management programs, training, and implementation. Paraprofessionals and food service workers are examples of additional direct services. Physical therapists, occupational therapists, and transportation workers are examples of indirect services.

Physical Fitness and Academic Achievement

In a Texas fitness study (Welk et al., 2010) of 6,365 schools in 1,263 districts, equivalent to 83 percent of grade 3-12 students in the state, Spearman correlations showed strong positive connections between student cardiovascular fitness achievement, body mass index, and achievement on the Texas Assessment of Knowledge and Skills (TAKS) at all age and grade levels included. Another study of how **physical fitness affected cognitive task performance** (Hillman, Castelli and Buck, 2005) found children with high physical fitness levels had both quicker reaction times and higher percentages of accurate responses than children with low fitness. Other research also demonstrates cognitive function improving following intense exercise. A study of emerging adults (Hwang et al., 2013) found participants performed better on cognitive measures like the Stroop test (reading aloud color names vs. ink colors of words printed in contradictory colors, e.g., the word "green" printed in blue ink, "blue" printed in red ink, etc.) following exercise. A study (Centeio et al, 2011) comparing teacher-led fitness activities to active gaming found students took nearly twice the steps and burned more calories per minute in the former than the latter.

Experimental Research Study

Physical Activity Across the Curriculum (PAAC, Donnelly et al., 2009) was an intervention to curtail weight gain, overweight, and obesity and promote physical activity in elementary school children. Investigators used cluster randomized selection of students to treatment and control groups in a three-year longitudinal study of second and third graders, whom they followed to fourth and fifth grades. The intervention involved 90 minutes weekly of physically active academic lessons with moderate to vigorous intensity, given by classroom teachers. The experimenters found that receiving 75 minutes or more of PAAC caused significantly less increase in children's body mass indexes compared with schools receiving less than 75 minutes weekly of PAAC. Additional results included that the schools with the 90-minute intervention had significant improvements in their amounts of daily physical activity and their scores on tests of academic achievement. The researchers concluded that the PAAC approach could promote children's daily physical activity and academic achievement while preventing excessive weight gain.

Biomechanics

In **biomechanics**, the subdivision of **kinematics** is the description of motion. This description includes such physics concepts as mass, center of gravity, displacement, inertia, linear and angular motion, linear and angular velocity, vectors, acceleration, etc. Another subdivision of biomechanics is **forces**. These are also physics concepts. In fact, the SI unit used to estimate force is the Newton, named after Sir Isaac Newton, who discovered and articulated the laws of motion that are the bases of physics. Forces include such movement concepts as rotation, couples, resultant force, equilibrium, levers, mechanical advantage, weight, friction, fulcrums, muscular forces, resisting forces, joint forces, joint reaction forces, ground reaction forces, inertial forces, gravitational forces, center of pressure, and force line. Another subdivision of biomechanics is **kinetics**, the study of the forces causing motion. This is where Newton's laws of motion become central, primarily the first law of inertia, the second law of momentum, and the third law of reaction. Kinetics concepts include impulse, linear and angular momentum, work, power, energy, kinetic and potential energy, the work-energy principle, and energy level. Understanding these physics concepts enables corresponding understanding of body movements.

Algebra, Geometry, and Calculus in Biomechanics

In **biomechanics**, one subdivision is devoted to the computational methods used to calculate and manipulate the **quantities** involved. For example, knowledge of geometric shapes like parallelograms informs the parallelogram method for resolving vectors in various directions. Knowledge of algebra informs vector algebra, which is a set of definitions, rules, and operations for computing the manipulation of vector quantities that are coplanar, i.e., they move in the same plane, and concurrent, i.e., they have the same application point. Combining vectors through the use of vector algebra is known as composition of vectors. Its opposite is resolution of vectors. Knowledge of calculus informs the biomechanical technique of finding a quantity's rate of change, a calculus technique called differentiation. Differentiation of a given function or curve obtains quantities called derivatives, e.g., of displacement, including velocity, acceleration, and jerk. Another calculus technique is integration, which determines the area contained between an x-axis and a curve. Integration obtains quantities called integrals, e.g., with respect to time, including velocity as an integral of acceleration, displacement as an integral of velocity, and work as an integral of power.

French and Spanish in Dance

In **ballet**, a foundation for all other dance forms, the terminology is **French**: although it originated in Italy, ballet was largely developed and advanced in France, notably popularized by King Louis XIV. The word ballet itself is French. *Sur les pointes* is dancing on toes in pointe shoes. Only certain terms, e.g., first through fifth positions, are translated into English among English-speaking ballet teachers and dancers. Otherwise, French predominates. Ballet class uses a *barre* for practice. Steps are named in French: *port de bras* is carriage of the arms, *pas de chat* is "step of the cat;" *tendu* means "stretched," *plié* "bent," *ballon* is jumping elevation or height, *grand jeté* is large jump, and *grand battement* is large kick. Turns include *tours, pirouettes, fouettés,* and *chainé* turns. *Pas de deux*, a standard performance element of classical ballets, is a duet. Due to its origins in Spain and Spanish-speaking Latin American countries, **Latin ballroom dance** forms include **Spanish** terminology. For example, the *paso doble* ("double step") is a Latin ballroom style based on the bullfight: the male dancer represents the bullfighter, the female the cape with swirling skirts and movements. *Samba* is Brazil's official dance. Additional Latin dances include *cha cha, rumba, bachata, merengue, salsa, tango*, and Argentine tango.

Arithmetic and Sports

Weight trainers must count the numbers of **repetitions** ("reps") and **sets** they complete, and know the numbers of pounds they can lift or press. Runners must know **distances** in hundreds of yards or miles, and their **times** in minutes completing races, or hours and minutes for marathons. High jumpers and pole vaulters must know the feet and inches of **heights** to clear. Long jumpers must know **distances** they can jump. Shot-putters, javelin throwers, and discus throwers also need to know the **distances** they throw their projectiles. All of these apply not only to measurements, but also previously set records that athletes seek to break or match. In competitive team sports, **scores** are kept using arithmetic. Runs, errors, averages, and innings are counted in baseball; points and fouls in basketball; first downs and touchdowns earn points in football, numbers of yards gained are marked and measured by yard lines, and time and overtime are counted. Strokes are counted in golf, points in tennis, etc. Thus arithmetic is integral to most sports.

Biochemistry and Weight Training

Understanding how muscles are built up through weight training includes some understanding of how **mitochondria** (cellular organelles) in muscle fiber cells produce **adenosine triphosphate (ATP)**, which supplies energy to muscles; the carbohydrate glycogen in muscle cells stores energy; and muscle contraction releases adenosine diphosphate (ADP), expending energy, depleting ATP, and prompting the sarcoplasm (muscle cytoplasm) to replenish the muscle cells' ATP supply. Numerous repetitions of lifting moderately heavy weights trigger muscle fiber cells to increase their numbers of mitochondria, concentrations of cellular respiration enzymes, and ATP stores, all of which make muscles grow larger. This is called **sarcoplasmic hypertrophy**. Another type of muscle growth, which increases muscle density and strength, is **sarcomere hypertrophy**. Understanding this process is informed by knowing when fewer repetitions of lifting heavy weights rupture muscle cells' plasma membranes (sarcolemma), calcium leaks out between the cells, activating enzymes (calpains) and immune system cells (monocytes, neutrophils, and macrophages) to remove and break down damaged tissue, and stimulating nearby muscle cells to make and release growth factors.

Anatomy and Physiology in PE Learning

Knowing how the heart pumps blood to the lungs, how the lungs oxygenate the blood, and how the heart then sends this blood throughout the body to deliver oxygen to its tissues informs an understanding of how the heart, blood vessels, and lungs interact as the **cardiopulmonary system** during exercise to enable sufficient respiration (breathing) to take in enough oxygen and expel enough carbon dioxide (pulmonary ventilation). Knowing the difference between inhalation and exhalation measures oxygen consumption informs understanding **respiration** during exercise. Knowing the maximum oxygen one can consume, VO_2max, equals maximum aerobic capacity, which usually defines cardiorespiratory fitness, informs understanding how the functioning and condition of one's heart, blood vessels, and lungs, i.e., cardiorespiratory fitness, contribute to one's ability to engage in **oxygen-using exercise**, i.e., aerobic fitness, and to continue such exercise for longer durations, i.e., cardiorespiratory/aerobic endurance. Knowing how skeletal muscles, joints, and bones connect and articulate, which muscles control which body movements, and understanding muscle mechanics inform understanding how different **body movements** are accomplished, which muscles and bones need strengthening, degrees of soft tissue flexibility that need increasing/decreasing, etc..

Nutritional Biochemistry and Supplementation

Certain **nutrients** are found naturally in our bodies. For example, **creatine** occurs naturally, consisting of the amino acids arginine, glycine, and methionine. Most of the creatine in our bodies is bound to phosphate groups, i.e., phosphorylated. When we work out, our muscular contractions release molecules of adenosine diphosphate (ADP), depleting the muscle's supplies of adenosine triphosphate (ATP), which they need for energy. To replace our muscles' ATP stores, phosphorylated creatine—phosphocreatine—donates phosphate groups to the ADP. Normally, this natural process needs no supplementation. However, bodybuilders and other athletes may take creatine supplements to speed up and expand muscle growth. Another naturally occurring nutrient is **glutamine**, the body's most plentiful amino acid. Glutamine also occurs naturally in dairy products we consume. It prevents muscle breakdown, making workouts more effective over time. Normally we need no more glutamine, though the body can break down muscle tissue to access amino acids for building protein if protein deficiency exists. Hence bodybuilders and other athletes often supplement with glutamine to ensure plentiful protein supplies. Knowing this information can prevent unnecessary supplementation or inform supplementing only under medical supervision.

Above and Beyond the Blanket

In "**Above and Beyond the Blanket**" (Todorovich), teachers can create lesson plans for fourth and fifth graders to practice with correct meanings and uses of English prepositions and prepositional phrases in sentences, while improving their physical reaction times through immediate body movements responding to teacher cues. The only materials needed are blankets or large towels. The teacher can group the students according to class size, with each student taking turns. An alternate variation if there is enough space is for all students to respond with movements at the same time, using one gigantic blanket or bed sheet. This alternative can add to the fun. The teacher states a sentence, for example, "Susan hid *under* a bush," and the students respond by moving under the blanket as quickly as they can. If the teacher then says, "Thomas sat *beside* the river," then the students sit beside the blanket as quickly as possible. If the teacher says, "Chris lay *on top of* the bed," students would immediately sit on top of the blanket. This activity gives students practice with reacting quickly to verbal cues with physical movements, and understanding the meanings of prepositions and prepositional phrases.

Alphabet Hopscotch

For grades K-3, teachers can provide a lesson, "**Alphabet Hopscotch**," that improves student balance and coordination and also gives students practice with the English-language alphabet at the same time Prerequisites are that students must have learned the game of hopscotch and be familiar with the sequence of the alphabet. An advantage of this game is that it can be played indoors or outdoors. Indoors, desks, other objects, and debris should not be near the board to prevent injury in case someone falls. The teacher draws a hopscotch board on the floor or pavement using chalk or paint. Some teachers might want to create a board or boards on a piece of fabric, paper, cardboard, or plastic for repeated use and portability. (Having multiple boards enables the teacher to vary letter placement.) The hopscotch board must contain all letters of the alphabet, scattered in random order among the squares. Each student takes a turn at hopping through the ABCs, alternating left and right feet. Variations include adding capital and cursive letters, and associating letters and colors to left and right feet.

Developing Productive Relationships

According to the National Board of Professional Teaching Standards (NBPTS), effective PE teachers realize their critical roles in **extended learning communities**, and hence that their responsibilities transcend classrooms to encompass schools and local communities as well as students. They work with their colleagues from different disciplines, generating more profound insights of the learning goals and objectives in each subject area to make instructional programs stronger. They moreover collaborate closely with school administrators, students' families, and members of the community. Good PE teachers actively initiate and support cooperative interactions and relationships with colleagues within PE departments and across the curriculum in their schools and school districts, reciprocally contributing and appreciating the benefits they receive. They work collaboratively to enhance their own and others' teaching practices, and help to design curricula that significantly connect higher-order cognitive skills required in all school subjects. They support learning objectives not only in PE, but in other subjects. They mentor other teachers and learn from them, both inviting and offering mutual observation and feedback.

Mutual Support and PE Teachers

Effective PE teachers are committed to engaging **colleagues** in discussing professional issues and enhancing instruction. They form partnerships of **mutual support**, integrating PE with other fields. For example, a PE teacher might collaborate with a family and consumer sciences teacher, developing a joint nutrition and fitness unit. Students would benefit from assignments to design comprehensive wellness plans, including nutritional goals for which they prepare suitable foods, giving them hands-on experience. With an English language arts teacher, a PE teacher could plan a literature and sport unit wherein students read *A River Runs Through It*; watch the movie adaptation as a supplement, analyze the psychology of its characters, and study the discipline and skills of the fly fishing sport the main characters enjoy. Such interdisciplinary units give students more interconnected, integrated, enriching, and motivating learning experiences. PE teachers might discuss how their students lack focus, extending their conversation into a project collaborating with their school principal on a 15-minute student walking or running schedule every morning, establishing a more productive learning environment. Thus PE teachers enlist and provide colleague and administrator support in inventing innovative strategies for improving student motivation and learning.

PE Teachers Collaborating with Parents

PE teachers can generate **enthusiasm for active, healthy lifestyles** by offering opportunities to families to get involved in their PE programs. They can organize and hold events and discussions with parents and families, contributing to public relations for their programs through effective communication of PE's benefits. Good PE teachers enlist **families as partners** to help with their children's physical educations. For example, they can initiate honest conversations, inviting parents to provide their input about instructional processes and regularly evaluate PE program effectiveness. They take advantage of the insights and experience of parents for enriching educational quality for students. As an example, a PE teacher could invite a parent who works as a cardiologist to visit the school or class to talk about how health is enhanced through exercise, weight management, and nutritional choices, and to show students specimens or models of diseased and healthy hearts to illustrate the impact of different lifestyle and wellness choices. Such collaboration not only supplements student education with enriched information and experience, but also acknowledges and respects family knowledge, gives teachers insights into parental aspirations and expectations for their children, and enables teachers to learn more about students' interests and motivations from parents.

PE Teachers and the Community

Effective PE teachers reach out to members of their **local communities** and work together with them to demonstrate not only the value of good school PE programs and their benefits, but also the significance of its role. PE teachers can engage local residents and their resources in PE programs, not only benefiting the PE program, school, and students but moreover enabling them to assure the PE program represents interests and needs shared by the school and community. For example, PE teachers might ask staff members from their county or city parks and recreation department to visit the school and give a presentation on using community resources properly. A PE teacher could arrange a field trip for a student site visit, giving them hands-on experiences with local trail maintenance. PE teachers can acquire program support by contacting local businesses, universities, government agencies, and private funding agencies; solicit funds from local wellness and health agencies for purchasing sports equipment for students; request refreshments, medals, and ribbons from local trophy companies for student athletic events; and enlist volunteers from a local college for an Olympics-themed event.

Physical Education vs. Physical Activity

Physical education consists of instructional programs provided in safe, supportive environments that teach sequential, developmentally appropriate knowledge, skills, and the confidence necessary for students to establish and maintain active lifestyles. PE teachers instruct students in skills, give students feedback to improve their skills, and evaluate their knowledge, motor skills and social skills. Physical education should be provided daily in schools whenever possible. **Physical activity** is any kind of body movement, which can include sports, fitness, and recreational activities, as well as daily life activities, such as walking to and from school and other places. Students should engage in physical activity several times during each day. Research shows increasing evidence that physical activity is supportive of learning. In addition to providing physical education programs and classes, schools can provide other activities to incorporate physical movement throughout every school day and to serve as transitions between actual physical education classes and activities and academic classroom activities.

Incorporating Physical Activity into School Day

Classroom teachers can integrate **physical movement** into subject areas across the curriculum. They can obtain physical activity guides for including physical activity into language arts, math, science, and social studies at such websites as Brain Breaks (http://www.livebinders.com/play/play?id=188021) Energizers (www.ncpe4me.com/energizers.html), or Take 10 (www.take10.net). Also, while not actual physical movement itself, reading literature and writing assignments about physical activity topics can also be useful for directing students' attention to and educating them about physical activity. For example, when teaching about diverse cultures, teachers can include each culture's games, sports, and dances as study topics. Teachers can also assign book reports about sports, the Olympics, and Olympic and other sports champions. Teachers can reward students with physical activity, e.g., extra recess; lunchtime walks with teachers; dancing in classrooms to favorite music; five-minute dance activities like the hokey-pokey or Macarena; extra physical activity periods on Friday for good behaviors Monday through Thursday; sport or activity challenges between homerooms; and marching in place or jumping jacks during classroom study breaks. School or classroom parties can be dances, relay races, or classroom-modified games.

Individual, Group, and Club Physical Activities

Bicycling promotes physical fitness and can be done individually or in groups or clubs. Various bicycling opportunities and supplies are available at www.biking.com. Another good site to find out about traveling by bicycle for fun, sightseeing, learning, and adventure is www.adventurecycling.org. Students can participate in school bowling programs and clubs during, before, and after school. Numerous websites offer teacher lesson plans for in-school **bowling programs** and for starting school programs in the community. For schools that do not include cheerleaders for their sports teams, teachers can help interested students organize competitive **cheer teams**. **Canoeing** is an excellent outdoor physical activity, combining physical fitness with adventure, safety, and wilderness survival skills, and interacting with nature. Another challenging outdoor activity is **orienteering**. Some teens have developed amazing proficiency at the art of speed-stacking cups, which provides physical activity. The many existing **dance** forms combine physical activity with art forms, self-expression, technical skills, music, competition, and fun. Many school PE programs do not teach **gymnastics**; when they do, experts advise only teaching the basics for safety. Gymnastics provides high conditioning and discipline outside school. **Inline skating** is a recreational activity involving movement and skill.

Physical Activities Outside of School

Running promotes cardiovascular fitness and endurance. For students who do not experience joint problems or impact injuries, it can also dissipate excess energy, enhance self-confidence, improve mood and sleep, and promote healthier eating habits. The Runner's World website includes "Kids Running" resources and articles (http://www.runnersworld.com/tag/kids-running). Athletic apparel manufacturer Nike also provides resources for youth and adults on its site, www.nikerunning.com. A popular activity among many students is **skateboarding**. Nike offers a skateboarding site with products, and an Apple device application, the Nike SB App, for learning tricks, playing games, participating in challenges with professionals and friends globally, and charting personal skate history and progress. For students living in or able to travel to applicable locations, skiing is both fun and challenging as an outdoor physical activity. Another sport popular with many students is **soccer**. A resource for playing outside school is the American Youth Soccer Organization (AYSO); see www.ayso.org for information. **Swimming** is enjoyable and provides overall conditioning with no joint stress. Some schools lack swimming pools, or some students want to swim in addition to school swim teams or PE classes. **Walking** should never be overlooked as a physical activity. Moreover, some students may be interested in **hiking**.

After-School Intramural Sports Programs

Intramurals are indoor sports. Historically, they were confined to teams and individuals from specific schools or institutions; however, recent efforts to expand participation have widened their definition to encompass dance, clubs, open gym days, and other physical activity programs. **After-school intramural physical activity programs** are characterized by the following main criteria. Student activities are voluntary. Regardless of physical activity, all students have equal opportunities for participation. Students are given opportunities to participate in planning, organizing, and administering age-appropriate programs, with qualified adult guidance and supervision. Intramural activities are adjusted to be appropriate to student skill levels and ages. Adults and students who plan, organize, and administer intramural activity events should always establish specific rules and regulations to ensure safety, fair play, and equal opportunities for all participants. Intramural physical activities may be non-competitive or competitive. Sports participation improves or maintains physical fitness, develops social skills, and enables students to extend their PE experience. Community resources include Boys and Girls Clubs, school community education departments, local county and city government parks and recreation departments, local YMCAs and YWCAs, and community, college, university, YMCA, and commercial (e.g., Nike) youth sports camps.

Family Contributions to Student Physical Activity

Research studies show when **parents and siblings** are physically active, teenagers are more likely to follow suit. When children and adolescents have convenient access to play spaces, transportation to and from recreational and sports programs, access to sports equipment, and their parents support their participation, they are more likely to engage regularly in physical activity. Parents can help by encouraging children to be active regularly; serving as role models for their children by being physically active themselves; establishing and consistently enforcing limits on the time their children play computer and video games and watch TV; planning family activities, with parent participation, that incorporate physical activities like riding bicycles or walking instead of driving to destinations; vacuuming and doing active household chores indoors in bad weather; and mowing the lawn, gardening, and playing outdoors in good weather. They can plan vacations, picnics, birthday parties, and other family events that include physical activities. To encourage children and add fun, they can use the buddy system and be children's activity buddies. They can help children participate in school and community sports and physical activity programs, and advocate for quality physical activity programs in their schools and communities.

National Dance Day

Nigel Lythgoe, co-creator, executive producer, and judge of TV's *So You Think You Can Dance* (SYTYCD), started **National Dance Day**, a grassroots campaign to celebrate dance, encouraging Americans to support good health and combat obesity by enjoying dancing. Hosted by charitable organization Dizzy Feet Foundation and co-founded by Lythgoe and choreographer, producer, and movie director Adam Shankman, National Dance Day was created to increase American dance education access and award scholarships to deserving dance students. Congresswoman Eleanor Holmes Norton (D-D.C.) recognized Lythgoe's project nationally with a 2010 congressional resolution officially making the last Saturday in July the annual National Dance Day. The Los Angeles Music Center and Dizzy Feet Foundation hold a NDD celebration in LA's Grand Park, Rep. Holmes hosts NDD events at the Kennedy Center in Washington, D.C., and Lincoln Center's Out of Doors program holds NDD activity in New York City. NDD encourages Americans to create events in their own communities, e.g., fundraising for youth dance access, organizing Flash Mobs, charitable dance events, dance-a-thons, and other creative ideas. NDD instructional videos to music include Lythgoe and Shankman demonstrating an official beginner dance routine choreographed by Lythgoe; Lythgoe demonstrating an adapted, seated version he choreographed for non-ambulatory participants; and an advanced routine by SYTYCD choreographer Chris Scott.

Reflection

PE teachers who engage in **self-reflection** realize their own perspectives and biases relative to their students. They employ rigorous introspective practices to consider these matters, as well as the environmental, physical, cognitive, emotional, and social variables that influence the performance of their students. Effective PE teachers are skilled not only at self-reflection, but also at observing the personalities, dispositions, and behaviors of their students. They are able to gain insights into student motivations and needs, and they apply these understandings to enhance how students learn. For example, a PE teacher can help a student who is capable yet timid to develop more self-confidence by asking the student to model a complex skill for the class, endowing the student with a leadership role. Another benefit of reflection is that it enables PE teachers to comprehend such important information as school demographics, class dynamics, and student abilities and needs, and to consider these data in context. Successful PE teachers **assess** each aspect of every class, which enables them to prepare lessons that are culturally sensitive, relevant and meaningful to students, and deliberately connected to outcomes for students.

Reflective Methods

To improve their instruction, PE teachers can **reflect** on what they know in their field and the experiences they have had while teaching. They use this knowledge to ascertain what their students most importantly need to know and be able to do, and they then base their design and selection of student learning activities on these priorities. PE teachers who are best at their jobs are **creative**, finding ways to combine the promotion of classrooms that assure safe environments and equitable student treatment with the planning of lessons characterized by diversity. In addition, they extend their reflective experience and expertise to students by giving them opportunities for developing **reflective methods** of their own. For example, a PE teacher could give students the challenge of considering what environmental impacts could be incurred by hiking, and of making a commitment to principles of zero impact for their next outdoor activity. By encouraging such personal evaluation, PE teachers help students enhance their attitudes, ethical behaviors, and performance. Effective PE teachers are aware that reflection is an integral thought process, which teachers and students can both apply to their learning environment for its enrichment.

Reflective Practice for Monitoring Instruction

While teaching, PE teachers using **reflection** effectively **monitor** their students' learning experiences and **modify** them accordingly. To assess student comprehension, learning, and progress, they apply a variety of techniques to evaluate critically how every student progresses through each lesson. If students are not attaining one of their learning objectives, or anything is impeding their learning, a good PE teacher will immediately adjust the lesson. As an example, the teacher might include an objective for student heart rates to reach a targeted range during game play, e.g., in soccer. If the teacher discovers most of the students in class did not achieve that targeted range, the teacher might change the speed of play, the rules of the game, or other aspects of how it is played to augment active participation by all students. PE teachers reflect not only on their teaching methods, but also on how they organize learning environments as they evaluate student response to their teaching. Teachers committed to promoting student achievement and growth analyze their design and implementation of learning experiences, evaluate results of their instruction, and determine how to alter it for optimal student outcomes.

Reflection and Assessment of Instructional Effectiveness

Successful PE teachers use **assessment** not only to evaluate student performance, but also to **reflect** on how productive their teaching practices are. They monitor student progress and adjust their lessons and assessments as they find necessary to meet all of their students' needs. Good PE teachers apply the information they obtain through their assessments to create opportunities for optimal comprehension and knowledge that will further students' learning. As an example, after a PE teacher has assigned students to write essays about different aspects of health-related fitness, the teacher can extend this activity in order to develop greater student comprehension by assigning them to make visual graphics displays, create drawings or paintings, or produce short films on the subject. Any time that a PE teacher discovers that the students are unable to perform a given skill with correct form, or that they are not grasping a given concept fully, the teacher examines the instructional process to find out which sequences or cues will help the students to succeed in execution or comprehension. Hence, reflective teacher practices contribute to raising instructional effectiveness levels.

Evaluation of Instructional Practices

To be most effective, PE teachers **compare** the kinds of instruction their students require to the teachers' expertise and knowledge, and determine if there are gaps between the two. To increase their potential for working most successfully with their students, they pursue professional development experiences according to whichever needs they have identified through comparing student needs with their own preparation. PE teachers realize that reflection is instrumental in their achieving lifelong professional and personal growth. They examine all aspects of their teaching practices by utilizing various methods. For instance, a teacher can play back a video recording of a class to pinpoint needs for improvement in the teaching approach, or a teacher might ask a colleague to observe a class session and solicit the colleague's feedback about practices used and possible improvements. PE teachers' ensuring their own accountability to rigorous professional standards is supported by introspection. To support student success, PE teachers continually improve their instructional practices through intentional reflection.

Nature and Applications of Reflection

Effective PE teachers depend on **reflection** as a continual process that they engage in every day for the purpose of improving all dimensions of their instruction. This includes creating curricula and modifying them to promote optimal student learning. In order to satisfy national, state, and local standards and district, school, departmental, class, and individual student learning objectives, PE teachers engage in reflection to help them plan curricula and adapt and adjust them. During reflection, PE teachers think about such subjects as interdisciplinary opportunities, educational resources, and their merits; the interests and needs of their students, as individuals and as classes and teams; their own strengths and weaknesses as teachers and individuals; their own teaching-related passions and interests; and the ways in which they can contribute to and enhance their curricula on the basis of their own individual characteristics. As one example, if an experienced dance teacher realizes that the dance curriculum covers isolated movements adequately but is missing components to provide a foundation for sequential movement, he or she could incorporate more complex techniques in the learning objectives to enhance student learning in this area. Reflection enables the synergy of personal expertise and professional inspiration.

Professional and Personal Growth

The practices of good PE teachers are very **reflective**. They show their dedication to their profession by perfecting their own expertise and behaviors to maximize their support of education for all their students. The impacts that PE teachers have on students and schools and how they think about their instructional strategies, techniques, and overall teaching are changed by their professional growth. Good PE teachers' pursuit of **professional development opportunities** is informed by their own goals for results based on solid research evidence, introspective analysis and discovery, and interaction. PE teachers realize that to continue improving their instruction to be more effective, they must continually refine their pedagogical techniques, skills, and knowledge. They use their professional needs and personal ambitions as the basis of visions for growth. To realize these visions, they expand district and school expectations. To further their growth, good PE teachers are committed to developing well-defined, challenging professional development plans. Realizing the ongoing nature of the growth process, they are proactive by often initiating opportunities for professional development.

Professional Development

Effective PE teachers construct purposeful **personal action plans**. Included within these plans are professional development opportunities, which good PE teachers regard as valuable learning resources. They also engage in continuing reflection in order to ascertain their own goals, strengths, and weaknesses. Based on the insights they attain through such reflection, they determine what kinds of experience and information they need to meet their students' varied needs. Good PE teachers utilize different methods of obtaining **professional development**. These include completing advanced certificates and degrees in PE and in related disciplines, and pursuing enrichment opportunities in education. For example, if a PE teacher finds that a number of students are interested in rock climbing, that teacher might take a course in outdoor adventure expeditions to learn the necessary information and skills, and to obtain certification for rock climbing instruction. This enhances not only the teacher's expertise and the experiences available to students, but the school's curriculum as well. Another professional developmental method is active engagement in educational committees and professional organizations. As examples, PE teachers can serve on national, state, or local committees, share expertise with various media, and present papers at workshops or conferences.

Pursuit of Professional Development

PE teachers who maximize their effectiveness by continually seeking **professional development opportunities** play the roles of leaders, collaborators, and learners in their discipline. In order to meet their students' needs more competently and immediately, they analyze their own development as educators critically, and cultivate their own growth as lifelong learners. As they gain experience and knowledge through professional development, they demonstrate leadership by applying their learning in work with students, schools, professional networks, and communities. They also apply the learning they gain in implementing staff development for their colleagues and themselves. They participate actively in cross-curricular teams and subject-matter study groups. As an example, a PE teacher could attend an in-service in technology and how to utilize social media to augment the relationships among scientific theories, motor skills development, and physical fitness activities. PE teachers fulfill the role of intellectual leaders in their field by disseminating pertinent information school-wide or district-wide to optimize students' learning. For instance, a PE teacher can share research data showing how physical activity enhances academic performance with colleagues, and collaborate with them to plan activities that improve student achievement across the curriculum.

Benefits of Professional Development

As an example of applying **professional and personal growth** to provide students with relevant learning experiences, a PE teacher who has researched and choreographed a dance piece might perform this work in a formal venue, as well as teach the choreography to students capable of learning it in classes. Successful PE teachers acquire new knowledge through professional development and then implement what they have learned in their instruction; in addition to improving what and how they teach and what and how their students learn, they also use their increased knowledge to promote their PE discipline. They moreover make use of their professional growth by developing professional networks, through which they share their experience, knowledge, and skills. They also utilize these networks to establish new connections with educators in a variety of settings, such as professors at local and state colleges and universities, institutions in other states, and international universities; graduate students at local teaching colleges preparing to teach PE; and exercise science specialists and others. To benefit their students, effective PE teachers productively enrich the skills and knowledge in their communities by applying their own political and social judgment and insight.

Improving Teaching Practices

PE teachers use what they learn from professional development experiences for **constructive communication** with colleagues to establish reflective learning communities and productive professional networks, and to collaborate with them for improving the teaching practices they use in their schools. They work together to analyze their teaching practices in individual classrooms and school-wide, which can also be extended to district-wide initiatives. The best professional development simultaneously improves the teachers' personal knowledge, abilities, and skills and those of their colleagues. This reciprocal support that professional development affords within flourishing learning environments is a quality that exemplary PE teachers appreciate. To refine elements of their instructional practices, they solicit mentorship. For example, a PE teacher could request a demonstration from a colleague for better communication with students learning English as a second language. PE teachers also serve as mentors for colleagues. For example, a teacher might observe another teacher's lesson and give advice on how to refine specific feedback prompts. Such learning experiences enable PE teachers to acquire fresh insights and extend the development of current practices.

Professional Growth

Professional growth involves a process that consists of a cycle of reflecting, deliberating, and acting. PE teachers **reflect** on their instructional practices, analyzing what do, how they do it, and what they are not including. They consider what students need to learn and what they need for learning in optimal ways. They compare their students' needs with what they have been doing, identifying gaps between these. They deliberate to determine which approaches, elements, and strategies they need to add in their instruction to meet students' educational needs most completely. By participating in **professional and educational groups and interactions**, PE teachers can stay up to date and informed of the newest scholarship and research results. They can also acquire new, additional, and more in-depth information and skills through such participation. They can exchange ideas with colleagues, collaborate with them, and enhance the quality of their learning communities. By forming **partnerships** with others, they both inspire others' senses of initiative and develop their own self-confidence. By functioning as **role models and advocates**, PE teachers demonstrate achievement and professional integrity, both within their discipline and throughout their wider educational communities.

Substance Abuse and Classroom Performance

Poor academic performance is far likelier in students using **alcohol and other drugs**, according to the U.S. Substance Abuse and Mental Health Services Administration (SAMHSA). For example, students abusing alcohol can have lapses in memory, while students abusing marijuana can have impaired short-term memory and impairment in saving information to long-term memory. When students study the day before an in-class test or assignment and then abuse substances that night before class, they often forget what they studied, having a negative impact on their grades. When students develop addictions to addictive substances, obtaining and using them takes precedence over school performance. This can lead to neglecting homework, skipping classes, and falling behind in school. When these patterns are repeated chronically, school suspension and/or expulsion can be the outcome. In addition, some drugs can trigger violent behavior, also leading to suspension or expulsion. For example, while Ritalin is prescribed as a treatment for attention deficit hyperactivity disorder (ADHD), some teenagers abusing it for its euphoric side effects can experience psychotic episodes and violent behavior. Abusing alcohol, PCP, cocaine, and many other substances can cause physical violence against peers and rebellion against teachers.

Substance Abuse and Physical Performance

Students who **abuse substances** demonstrate higher probabilities of **impaired physical performance** during PE classes. For example, students who abuse marijuana or alcohol have a higher likelihood of impaired physical coordination. They are also more likely to be low on energy, giving them both less motivation and less ability to engage in athletic or physical activity, less ability to continue even if they do begin physical activity, and a greater likelihood of tiring more quickly and giving up on or dropping out of the physical activity. Marijuana use just before a PE class can impair depth perception, interfering with a student's judgment of distances and hence impairing performance during team sports, track and field activities, etc. Alcohol use before PE classes impairs student judgment as well as coordination and energy, increasing accident and injury risk as well as poor performance. While students may excel in the short term at activities requiring strength, speed, etc., from using anabolic steroids, continued use of such performance-enhancing substances has many side effects like high blood pressure, aggressive and violent behavior, acne, liver disorders, and cancer.

Substance Abuse and Overall Health

Substance abuse by teenagers can affect their health in a myriad of catastrophic ways, including injuries from auto accidents caused by driving under the influence. Alcohol abuse and intoxication are particularly implicated in driving fatalities among adolescents. Many teens die from drug overdoses, and others survive but suffer permanent health damage, including loss of teeth, skin damage, damage to the liver, lungs, heart, and kidneys, and destruction of the blood supply (avascular necrosis) to the joints from long-term abuse of alcohol or certain drugs (e.g., steroids). Substance abuse incurs a higher risk of dying from other accidents in addition to auto accidents, as well as from drug-induced illnesses, homicides, and suicides. HIV/AIDS transmission through sharing needles for drug injections is another health impact. Moreover, adolescents abusing substances suffer impaired impulse control and judgment, so they more often engage in risky behaviors exposing them to unprotected sex, leading to contracting HIV/AIDS from infected partners and transmission of the virus to infants from drug-abusing teenage mothers during pregnancy or birth.

Substance Abuse and General Behavior

Some aspects of the effects of **abusing substances** on student behavior include changes from their typical behavior to the **opposite**. For example, students who have usually been introverted, not socializing much with their peers, and shy, socially inhibited, or awkward, can use drugs that cause them to behave more sociably, as well as more impulsively. Alcohol, cocaine, the prescription antidepressant and anti-anxiety drug Prozac, and other substances can lower the user's inhibitions temporarily. This can cause the behavior of typically introverted students to change suddenly to extroverted behavior. Adolescents who do not acknowledge introversion as a personality trait, but view it as a hindrance to social acceptance and popularity, may see such drugs as a solution and repeat their use as self-medication, which can lead to addiction. On the other hand, some students who have typically displayed extroverted and sociable behavior and begin abusing substances can develop introverted behaviors because of their substance abuse. A common symptom of many addictions is **social withdrawal**: teens lose interest in their usual activities, avoid interacting with their friends, and isolate themselves.

Substance Abuse and Interpersonal Relationships

Interpersonal relationships may initially be contributing factors to student substance use. For example, adolescent students may begin using alcohol or other substances in response to **peer pressure**: in social situations, peers using alcohol or other drugs may urge teens to join them, and they do so to fit in with the majority or to gain their acceptance, approval, or admiration. Students may also join friends in using substances as a way of celebrating and partying together, or of easing their social or intimate interactions. Teens using substances socially as part of exploration and experimentation in forming personal identities may find shared substance use a common interest with others. When one student abuses substances and the other does not, they may find no other way to relate or basis for interaction or friendship. When a student with a pre-existing friendship or personal relationship abuses substances, he or she may withdraw from the relationship as procuring and using the substance takes precedence. Another effect of substance abuse is increasing **conflict** within personal relationships. Disagreements and fights become more common, both over one member's substance abuse and due to dysfunctional behaviors that the substance causes.

Legal Aspects of Organization

Because class sizes are generally increasing and PE classes are often large, supervision is harder, accidents likelier, and PE lawsuits are increasing. Teachers risk **liability** because they are recognized as certified professionals with high-responsibility, high-profile roles. Their training should meet national standards. Teachers and coaches are liable for **acts of omission**, e.g., not supervising PE activities, and **acts of commission**, e.g., endangering or threatening students with harm. In lawsuits, **levels of negligence** are decided according to the roles teachers or coaches played in preventing injurious conditions in adequately or inadequately providing post-injury care, and by professional standards compliance or noncompliance. To be judged negligent, four parts are required: duty, breach of duty, cause, and damage. Common areas of negligence in PE include supervision, instruction, classroom environments, first aid emergencies, and transportation. Guidelines to prevent negligence claims include using common sense, being informed of colleagues' best-practice guidelines, and following practices and procedures given in texts and in national organizations' guidelines. PE teachers should continually, actively supervise throughout activities, ascertain whether students are safely and properly executing them, and encourage peer supervision in addition to teacher supervision.

Safety and Teacher Liability

Insufficient or improper advance instruction directly informs **teacher liability**. Also, teachers should not let students lacking judgment of their personal capability perform movements. **Safety instructions** should be stated simply. Instruction in procedures and protocols for equipment setup, use, and takedown is a must. In classroom environments, teachers must watch out for potential dangers. Environmental conditions can vary day to day. Teachers should space students to mitigate problems. PE equipment should only be used as designed to be used. Regarding emergencies, students risk injury more when moving than still. PE teachers are expected to give injured students appropriate help, e.g., first aid treatment before medical access. They should be trained and currently certified in first aid. First aid procedures should be included in class objectives, permanently displayed school-wide, and developed among school personnel. Teachers should know of pre-existing student conditions. They should write detailed reports of any incidents, including prevention measures. Transportation outside school risks liability: teachers should get written parental consent, and always follow school policies, practices, and procedures.

Coach Liability vs. Teacher Liability

In classrooms, student movement is limited; however, in PE classes, **movement** is the primary activity. Additionally, PE teachers and coaches contend with movement by many students simultaneously. Baseballs, softballs, footballs, tennis balls, discus, shot puts, javelins, and other projectiles can injure students, and baseball bats, tennis racquets, golf clubs, and other implements propel projectiles at high speeds, further increasing injury risks. Also, PE facilities are bigger than classrooms, and include both indoor and outdoor spaces, so PE teachers must cover and supervise greater physical areas—with different characteristics—than classroom teachers. Another factor is that PE includes swimming. This introduces water, in swimming pools and showers, presenting additional danger and injury risk in the forms of drowning in pools and slipping and falling in showers. PE teachers should never allow students and athletes to be alone without faculty supervision in these facilities. Teachers and coaches should be first in and last out of pools. Another injury and liability source is personal vehicles owned by teachers or coaches that are used for transport to activities outside school. In some states, statutes cap teacher liability limits within public school duties; however, coaching AAU programs/midget football/Little League, etc., outside school are unprotected by these caps.

Basic Safety Rules

Experts advise **supervising** students between classes, **intervening** in student altercations or fights, **monitoring** and supervising the athletic and PE complexes' multiple entrances and exits, and **collaboratively developing plans** with co-workers for the latter. PE teachers and coaches should lock gyms and pools between classes (particularly when gym equipment is set up), not give students keys, and always check gyms and pools for athletes and students before locking doors. Equipment where students and athletes could fall should always have sufficient mats under it—the more dangerous, the thicker the matting. Legal experts with PE coaching and teaching experience opine only the basic vaulting and tumbling skills of gymnastics should be taught in PE class, and with individual spotters in these. Falls are more likely since most average students lack the strength to support their bodies or hang using their arms. Falls from inverted positions risk spinal damage, paralysis, and even death. Experts warn teachers and coaches never to use trampolines in PE class, and if they are used in gymnastics, cheerleading, or other extracurricular events, to ensure their insurance covers trampolines and trampoline accidents—it often does not, or charges prohibitive premiums for coverage.

Limiting Student Injuries

Experts with both PE and legal experience caution PE teachers and coaches to remember that if **basic rules** are not followed in sports like softball, these seemingly innocent activities can become dangerous. For example, teachers must instruct students to call for fly balls; students who do not should back away from those who do. With 30+ students on a fielding team instead of 9 in a regulation or non-class game, collisions are far more likely. Serious injuries are more probable from head-to-head/smaller-to-bigger student collisions. All sports have safety rules to observe. PE teachers and coaches must check slip-resistant surfaces for wear or inadequacy, particularly in water's presence; inspect facilities monthly, and report any repair or maintenance issues to school administrations and maintenance departments; procure and use eye protection when reasonable; use applicable safety equipment for each sport or activity; prevent non-participating students from getting in harm's way; follow physician instructions in any students' doctor excuses; review safety rules with students before every new activity and sport; never punish or discipline students with strenuous exercise; confer with school nurses regarding any student medical conditions causing strenuous activity intolerance; and avoid student physical contact, except for safety reasons.

Technological Advances

For student success in the "Information Age," educators recognize the need to incorporate **technological advances**. Two examples are:

- U.S. state departments of education now prepare educators and educational administrators with knowledge for using technological learning processes, techniques, and tools; and
- state education departments and local education agencies now incorporate technological knowledge and skills in academic standards, benchmarks, and assessments.

The more educational accountability for outcomes increases, the more technology can help instruction and assessment. PE benefits from technology equally with other school subjects, and in some ways is especially amenable to technological methods and tools. Among the resources available are the website www.pesoftware.com/Technews/news.html, which offers the "Using Technology in K-12 Physical Education Newsletter," with information and tips about how to integrate technology in PE programs; podcasts and vodcasts; research information; standards-based PE curriculum; links to other websites; online courses; professional development presentations and consultations; instructional software; trial software; an online store; a link to order the book *Using Technology in Physical Education,* 8th Edition, by Bonnie Mohnsen, Ph.D.; and more.

Media Related to Technology in PE

ShapeAmerica.org is the Society of Health and Physical Educators (SHAPE), a nonprofit and the largest professional organization devoted to PE, sports, school health, dance, physical activity, and healthy active lifestyles. Its mission is to offer coordinated, comprehensive programs, resources, and support to improve teacher and practitioner skills to further professional practice and research. SHAPE America's most frequently published, comprehensive, and largest periodical is the *Journal of Physical Education, Recreation & Dance (JOPERD)*. *JOPERD* articles cover a broad range of topics, including the use of technology in PE. Recent articles have included, for example, one on apps (applications) that enable efficient, easy digital movement analysis in PE. The article includes explanations of how to use these apps for giving students instant feedback, recording performance, constructing better online and written tests, and assisting students with self-analysis and peer analysis. **PELINKS4U** is a weekly online newsletter that focuses on the use of technology in PE, and can be found at www.pelinks4u.org/sections/technology/technology.htm.

Digital Devices

A family of digital devices gaining popularity today is **Fitbit**. Fitbit devices synchronize (sync) wirelessly with mobile devices like smartphones and tablets, enabling people to monitor and record their activities and progress in numerous fitness areas, and access online tools like charts, graphs, and badges to track their improvement and gain additional insights. Fitbit products include the Zip, a wireless activity tracker that resembles a pedometer; the One, a wireless activity and sleep tracker; the Flex and the Force, both wireless activity and sleep wristbands; Tory Burch for Fitbit Accessories, jewelry by the fashion designer including a brass bracelet, silicone printed bracelets, and a metal pendant necklace making the Flex more attractive and fashionable; and the Aria, a Wi-Fi-enabled "smart scale" that indicates weight, body fat percentage, and body mass index (BMI) and wirelessly syncs with online mobile and graphing tools. PE teachers can encourage students having access to these devices to use them to increase and maintain their motivation and monitor their own progress by tracking active minutes, steps taken, distance covered, calories burned, and stairs climbed; setting fitness goals; challenging friends; and monitoring weight control and sleep quality.

Fitness App

Technology advances today have enabled innovations in many areas of life and education, including physical fitness and PE. A useful app to download free of charge to smartphones and computers is **myfitnesspal**. It helps users track their exercise and diet. Users can create personal diet profiles; the app includes an extensive food database, which facilitates entering meal content. Users can also track how many calories they burn through exercise. Moreover, myfitnesspal offers forums where users can discuss their progress, share information and tips, give each other support and motivation, and collaborate with others. Users can review at the end of a day how many calories they burned and consumed, how much water they drank, and even what percentages of the foods they ate were from protein, fat, and carbohydrates. Additional features include a diary, a newsletter, articles, and social networking to add friends with whom to diet and exercise. In addition, myfitnesspal syncs with Fitbit digital fitness devices, the Endomondo Sports Tracker app, numerous heart-rate monitors, and a great many other apps and devices.

Endomondo Sports Tracker

The **Endomondo Sports Tracker's** manufacturer calls it "The Personal Trainer in Your Pocket." It works with smartphones and GPS watches, enabling users to view statistics for walking, running, and bicycling, including distance, remaining distance, speed, summaries, history, full training logs, and graphs; to set goals and targets; to get "Audio Coach" feedback; to analyze their performance; and to engage in social networking, including news feeds, pep talks, challenges, routes, a global fitness community, and sharing on Facebook, Twitter, and Google+ for positive reinforcement to boost their motivation. This app is available in both free and paid premium versions. The premium version, which is inexpensive, offers advanced statistics, interval training with #tags, heart-rate zones, weather information, personal best history, workout comparison, peer benchmarks, custom settings, an ad-free version, interactive graphs, personalized training plans, and VIP email support. The free version enables users to monitor their duration, distance, speed, calories burned, etc., in outdoor distance sport workouts, and to manually monitor indoor workouts, and includes pictures, tagging, multiple sport tracking, music, and customization. This app is also compatible with the myfitnesspal app, heart-rate monitors, and the Fitbit One device.

AppsGoneFree

PE teachers can download a free app named **AppsGoneFree** to aid them in finding additional free apps they can use to assist their instruction. This app, compatible with iPhones, iPads and other Apple devices, lists applications that originally were sold for prices, but have become free of charge. The apps listed have all been reviewed by experts; AppsGoneFree includes details about why the experts chose each one. It is available at Apple's App Store; the PE Central website also offers a link. AppsGoneFree delivers a daily list of typically 5-10 apps that are free for one day or one week. Another free app for iPhone, iPad, iPad Mini, iPod Touch, and Android devices is Class Dojo. PE teachers can introduce gaming concepts, making PE classes more appealing to many students who love gaming. Teachers can monitor and track student behaviors during PE class; preset criteria whereby students gain or lose points and collaborate toward shared point goals; enable student self-monitoring and tracking via real-time updates by connecting their devices to TVs or projectors; and email weekly behavior updates to parents. PE Central provides links for downloading both Apple and Android versions.

Using Today's Technologies

Today, PE teachers can use **email** or **text message** parents with brief student progress reports, commendations for outstanding performance, notes about behavior, and notifications and reminders of upcoming meetings, conferences, sports events, etc. These methods better ensure that parents receive messages, whereas sending written or printed notes home via students may not. Parents also receive them more timely information; teachers save time composing and sending them. Teachers can text or email students to remind them of scheduled practice sessions, training meetings, athletic meets, and assignment deadlines. Student athletes can text PE teachers coaching them to request instructions, technical corrections, advice, and support outside school hours and locations (without abusing this!); teachers and coaches can respond to motivate, reassure, and encourage student athletes, increasing their confidence and the feeling that their coach is there for them. PE teachers can use weekly or monthly emails to inform parents of class and team progress, news, and accomplishments, and send PE class newsletters. Teachers can join and participate in professional organizations using Internet technology, and network with other PE teachers, experts, and mentors to share information about exercise science, instructional techniques, teaching strategies, motivational tools, programs and systems, etc. Students can network to share sports interests, information, statistics, accomplishments, and support.

Instruction and Assessment Via Technology

PE teachers can use applications (apps) like Apple's **GradeBookPro** for assessment, attendance, and classroom management. They can call roll, monitor day-to-day student behavior during PE, enter specific notes about individual students and classes, assign student grades, and track multiple classes, terms, quarters, and semesters. The device's storage capacity is the only limit to the information this app can accommodate. It offers standard and weighted grading systems, lets teachers email students their current attendance and grade status, and easily produces student and class reports. Teachers can copy assignments and students between and among classes, photograph individual students with their device cameras at the beginning of the year or class, add photos to student files, and learn student names in a timelier way. GradeBookPro also greatly speeds up taking attendance: teachers use one button to mark all students present, and simply tap absent students' names. Teachers report calling roll for a 40-student class in 30 seconds. Generating new assignments and entering grades are equally quick and easy. Tapping a student's name displays single-page data on absence dates, individual assignments, and course percentage, reducing end-of-course grade disputes. Teachers say this app enables them to use most of their time for teaching.

Video Analysis App

Today teachers can download **applications** to teach students sports skills, analyze their use of skills, and enable students to analyze their own sports skills performance. iPhone apps like Coach's Eye, iCoachview, and others enable teachers to teach lessons on their phones, and then use Dropbox to give students feedback on a laptop or desktop computer's larger screen at the end of the lesson. PE teachers report these technologies afford important teaching tools, also helping them plan future lessons. Some teachers use apps to record videos of games, showing these to students while providing constructive feedback, praising exemplary execution, and identifying areas needing improvement. Students enjoy watching their performance in locker rooms post-game. Teachers find it easy to incorporate apps in lessons, even enlisting students to record, review, and comment on peers' performance. Sharing reviewed footage gives students immediate feedback. Teachers find that after a brief demonstration, students easily use apps to record each other, review footage, and give feedback. Teachers also share footage using Twitter or email. By watching footage of themselves, students can identify the most effective strategies and tactics. Students are enthusiastic, enabling teachers to establish positive learning environments where students appreciate constructive criticism and are motivated to improve performance.

Records Tracking Technology

Today PE teachers can use computer programs or tablet and smartphone applications to take **attendance**. Instead of making check marks in roll books, they can record absences, tardiness, and disciplinary actions with just a touch, saving time and ensuring greater accuracy, legibility, organization, security, efficiency, and quick personal access. The same applies to entering, computing, and averaging student grades. Other departments—such as school nursing with medical records, classroom teachers with academic grades, progress reports, disciplinary reports, student commendations, etc., and individuals, practices, and agencies outside of the school like parents, physicians, psychologists, counselors, health and human services, juvenile corrections, extracurricular sports program personnel, and others—can email or fax information and materials to PE teachers electronically, which they can then open, read, forward, and save electronically (always observing the same confidentiality regulations as with paper documents). Sophisticated technology programs and applications can compute **statistical analyses** of teacher-student ratios, student enrollment and attendance, parent involvement, athletic performance, competitive team statistics and community standing, progress toward accountability measures, and comparisons to past years. Thus, these tools produce as well as keep records.

Locating and Presenting Information

Computer, tablet, and smartphone technologies offer great advantages to PE teachers for both **finding** and **presenting information**. For example, teachers wanting to know more about the most cutting-edge innovations in any area of their field—new teaching methods to optimize student learning and behavior management, new techniques in specific sports to optimize athletic performance, new research in exercise science, etc.—can look on the websites of professional organizations for articles, blogs, and actual resources they can contact or obtain. They can search regularly updated databases for new research studies published, and even simply type search terms into search engines. School and district intranets and the Internet's World Wide Web can both offer teachers ways to connect students, families, colleagues, staff, and administrators with community resources for health and human services, private tutoring, counseling, support, funding, and recreational, dance, athletic, and sport-specific extracurricular programs and activities. Teachers can find research sources to write materials for advancing their education and credentials, and furthering knowledge in their field. They can use programs like Microsoft PowerPoint, Word, Excel, Publisher, etc., to present what they write to student classes, faculty meetings, PTA meetings, and professional conferences and conventions.

Enhance Professional Development

Technology has greatly expanded opportunities for PE teachers to pursue **professional development**. For example, through Internet searches, PE teachers can find professional organizations appropriate to their degrees, certifications, areas of expertise and interest, and desired avenues of advanced education and certification, and join quickly and easily online. Through websites, they can also find local chapters in their communities, with schedules of meetings and events to attend. PE teachers can study specific subjects online for advanced knowledge, degrees, and certificates without having to leave work to physically attend classes, seminars, workshops, or conferences, saving in-person attendance for non-work times. They can network online with fellow professionals and mentors nationwide and worldwide to share ideas, information, and support. Technology offers automated test scoring, freeing up time for human activities like interpreting test scores to inform instruction, planning lessons, and teaching. Teachers can use videos of their own instruction to analyze and improve their teaching techniques. Numerous tablet and smartphone applications facilitate and simplify such recording, playback, and analysis.

Praxis Practice Test

1. Which of the following is the smallest of the four muscles in the buttocks?
    a. Gracilis
    b. Gastrocnemius
    c. Gluteus minimus
    d. Tensor fasciae latae

2. What is a definition of body mass index (BMI)?
    a. The ratio of weight to height squared
    b. The ratio of abdominal fat to total fat
    c. The ratio of body fat to muscle cubed
    d. The ratio of total fat to overall weight

3. In the history of research into motor development, which of the following represents the trend from earlier to later findings?
    a. From experience by itself to maturation by itself
    b. From maturation by itself to experience by itself
    c. From maturation to maturation plus experience
    d. From experience to maturation plus experience

4. Related to summation of forces, which is accurate about how body parts move?
    a. The largest body parts are the slowest and move last.
    b. The smallest body parts are the fastest and move first.
    c. The largest body parts are the slowest and move first.
    d. Regardless of speed, all parts move at the same times.

5. Which of the following is true about center of gravity (COG)?
    a. COG is in the same location for each human body.
    b. COG varies according to the body parts' positions.
    c. COG varies among bodies but is constant for each.
    d. COG is the same as center of mass or of pressure.

6. If one skater has longer arms and another has shorter arms, and someone applies equal force to each skater's extended arm, which of these is true about torque?
    a. The skater with longer arms will rotate faster.
    b. The skater with shorter arms will rotate faster.
    c. With equal force, they will turn at equal speed.
    d. Torque involves an axis, not the perpendicular.

7. Relative to spatial awareness, which movement concept involves vertical, horizontal, and circular paths of movement?
    a. Locations and levels
    b. Personal space
    c. Directions
    d. Planes

8. In quality of movement, _____ is bound/interrupted or free/sustained.
    a. flow
    b. effort
    c. speed
    d. rhythm

9. In the movement concept of relationship, which relationship can involve only one body without another body/bodies or object(s)?
    a. The relationship of near and far
    b. The relationship of on or off
    c. Together or with opposition
    d. Symmetrical and asymmetrical

10. When someone bench presses weights to strengthen the arms and upper body, this is an example of which exercise science principle?
    a. Overload
    b. Specificity
    c. Adaptation
    d. Progression

11. Which of the following is an example of the short-term effects of exercise on health?
    a. Exercising releases endorphins, generating euphoria.
    b. Exercising regularly prevents and relieves depression.
    c. Exercising lowers the risk of heart attacks and strokes.
    d. Exercising can reduce one's blood pressure and pulse.

12. Of the following, which most accurately represents an aspect of the relationship between nutrition and fitness?
    a. Exercising regularly and energetically enables you to eat anything you want.
    b. Eating a diet rich in calcium prevents bone density loss, but exercise cannot.
    c. Eating right provides energy for exercise, while exercise can control appetite.
    d. Exercising prevents high blood pressure and cholesterol more than diet does.

13. A part of which body system controls fluid loss, protects deep tissues, and synthesizes vitamin D?
    a. The skeletal system
    b. The muscular system
    c. The lymphatic system
    d. The integumentary system

14. The respiratory system _____ oxygen and _____ carbon dioxide.
    a. inhales; exhales
    b. delivers; expels
    c. creates; absorbs
    d. exhales; inhales

15. In the central nervous system's hierarchy of motor control, which level(s) of the brain produce(s) a motor program?
    a. The highest level
    b. The middle level
    c. The lowest level
    d. All three levels

16. Which of the following is historically accurate about motor development?
    a. It was thoroughly catalogued from the 1930s to the 1940s, progressing less from the 1950s to the1980s.
    b. Due to maturational theory, its description was limited in the 1940s, exploding in the 1950s.
    c. It was described through steady, continuous research from the 1940s through the 1980s.
    d. Researchers lacked the technology to explain it until pioneering work in the 1960s and 1970s.

17. Which statement best characterizes the role of posture in theories of motor development?
    a. As evidence of growing cerebral control, posture was more important to classical theories.
    b. As the biomechanical basis of action, posture is more important to contemporary theories.
    c. For different reasons, posture has been equally important to both earlier and later theories.
    d. In both classical and contemporary theories, posture is a minor part of motor development.

18. Among concepts of movement quality, which one has static and dynamic types?
    a. Flow
    b. Time
    c. Force
    d. Balance

19. Compared to regular baseball, softball has a _____ ball, a _____ infield, _____ innings, and _____ pitch.
    a. smaller; bigger; more; the same
    b. bigger; smaller; fewer; a different
    c. bigger; bigger; fewer; a different
    d. smaller; smaller; more; the same

20. Which of the following is true of soccer as played today?
    a. Each soccer team is composed of nine players.
    b. No player can touch the ball with arms or hands.
    c. All players can use heads or torsos on the ball.
    d. The Fédération Internationale de Football Association (FIFA) World Cup is an annual soccer event.

21. The frog kick is used in which swimming stroke(s)?
    a. The breaststroke
    b. The butterfly
    c. The crawl
    d. All these

22. Among the following common areas of negligence in physical education, in addition to first aid emergencies, which one can teachers and coaches MOST mitigate by enlisting the help of students?

    a. Instruction
    b. Supervision
    c. Transportation
    d. Class environments

23. Regarding physical education teacher and coach liability compared to classroom teacher liability, which is true?

    a. The sizes of classes are similar in both cases.
    b. Other classes are just as likely to be outdoors.
    c. Other classes travel just as often on field trips, and so on.
    d. Projectiles and water increase liability in physical education classes.

24. Which statement about physical education (PE) class safety and teacher liability is a valid one?

    a. PE classes can include advanced gymnastics safely by having group spotters.
    b. PE classes as well as extracurricular activities can include trampolines safely.
    c. PE teachers must instruct students in calling for and backing away from fly balls.
    d. PE teachers commonly and safely discipline students with strenuous exercise.

25. Which of the following effects on performance is more likely to be caused by student marijuana abuse than student alcohol abuse before physical education classes?

    a. Impaired and low energy
    b. Impaired depth perception
    c. Impaired judgment in general
    d. Impaired physical coordination

26. Of the following effects on student health caused by substance abuse, which one results from the largest number of different substance abuse-related causes?

    a. Death
    b. Organ damage
    c. Avascular necrosis
    d. Human immunodeficiency (HIV) and acquired immune deficiency syndrome (AIDS) transmission

27. Which of these is a typical effect of substance abuse on student behavior?

    a. A shy student becomes more sociable.
    b. An outgoing student becomes withdrawn.
    c. An inhibited student becomes more impulsive.
    d. These are all typical effects of substance abuse.

28. Which kinds of physical education activities are both appropriate for boys and girls to participate in together and are less dependent on team assignment by student skill levels?

    a. Activities that involve participant body contact
    b. Activities that require more upper-body strength
    c. Activities that require agility and lower-body strength
    d. Activities of all these types

- 155 -

29. Regarding individual differences that affect physical education activity performance, which of these sports is most appropriate for the ectomorphic somatotype (body type)?

    a. Wrestling
    b. Gymnastics
    c. Shot-putting
    d. High jump

30. Which of the following reflects a physical education teaching technique that promotes cognitive learning?

    a. Keeping times shorter during instruction and demonstrations
    b. Comparing new movement skills to those previously learned
    c. Using universal language in communicating with all students
    d. Giving all students equal responsibility for their own learning

31. Regarding perceptual-motor abilities, which is a performance skill that would be MOST affected by individual differences in control precision?

    a. Playing quarterback in football
    b. Handling a hockey puck
    c. Dribbling a basketball
    d. Driving a race car

32. Among physical proficiencies that affect individual performance, which type of strength is most involved in the activity of kayaking?

    a. Static strength
    b. Trunk strength
    c. Dynamic strength
    d. Explosive strength

33. In one instructional method to promote psychomotor learning, a physical education teacher clearly explains learning goals and skills to be learned to the students; demonstrates the skills for the students; and provides the students with practice time, frequently and regularly monitoring their progress during practice. This describes which of the following methods?

    a. The contingency or contract method
    b. The command or direct method
    c. The task or reciprocal method
    d. None of these methods

34. Research finds that motor skills training, endurance training, and strength training all share which neuroplasticity effects in common?

    a. New blood vessel formation
    b. Motor map reorganization
    c. Spinal reflex modification
    d. New synapse generation

35. Which development in human manual skills emerges the earliest?

    a. Successfully reaching for objects
    b. Coordinated arm–hand movements
    c. Arm flapping and jerky arm extensions
    d. Changing hand shapes before touching objects

36. Which of the following is a typical characteristic in babies' earliest gait development?

    a. Pointing their toes outward
    b. Walking bending the knees
    c. Keeping arms by their sides
    d. Rolling from the heel to toe

37. One teaching method for managing kindergarten through Grade 12 physical education classes uses three steps to address student noncompliance with class rules. In which of the following sequences should these steps be applied?

    a. An oral warning; a brief time-out; a time-out with written response
    b. A brief time-out; a time-out with written response; an oral warning
    c. A time-out with written response; an oral warning; a brief time-out
    d. A brief time-out; an oral warning; a time-out with written response

38. Which of the following is NOT a common theme many kindergarten through Grade 12 physical education teachers across the United States use to manage their classrooms?

    a. Respect
    b. Cooperation
    c. Doing your best
    d. Speaking out freely

39. Among these class rules that many American kindergarten through Grade 12 physical education (PE) teachers commonly define, which are all applicable to other subjects and classrooms, which one is also more important to PE classes?

    a. Kindness and caring
    b. Following directions
    c. Keeping hands to self
    d. Good sportsmanship

40. Of four factors that affect learning in physical education settings, which one is best exemplified by the physiological and psychological variables that influence individual ability and interest for learning?

    a. Readiness
    b. Motivation
    c. Reinforcement
    d. Individual differences

41. In three stages of motor learning, which of these is characteristic of the associative stage?

    a. Understanding an activity's goal and nature
    b. Making attempts that include major errors
    c. Making fewer and more consistent errors
    d. Effortless automaticity in performance

42. For cooperative learning activities to be more productive than competitive or individual learning activities, one of five necessary elements is positive interdependence among the members of a student group, including student awareness of it. What is accurate about the other four required elements?

    a. The students occasionally engage in productive, face-to-face interactions.
    b. The students are accountable for group goals collectively, not individually.
    c. The students use task-relevant interpersonal and group skills frequently.
    d. The students process group functioning to sustain current effectiveness.

- 157 -

43. Which of the following external variables that affect physical education activity is more likely to help than hurt performance by its presence?

    a. Strong outdoor winds
    b. Advancing technology
    c. Equipment conditions
    d. The other participants

44. Concerning the impacts of various resources on student physical education (PE) outcomes, what has research found?

    a. Class size and student–teacher ratio correlate inversely with activity levels, time, safety, and learning.
    b. Students receive a higher quantity and quality of PE from teachers who also teach different subjects.
    c. Student physical activity is the same whether PE curriculum is based on educational standards or not.
    d. PE facilities and equipment are valuable resources but do not change the amount of student activity.

45. Compared to the amount of time in moderate to vigorous physical activity (MVPA) the Institute of Medicine recommends for children to spend daily, how much do research studies find they actually spend in school physical education classes?

    a. About one-sixth of what is recommended
    b. About one-third of what is recommended
    c. About one-half of what is recommended
    d. About the same as is recommended

46. Among strategies for increasing internal student motivation for physical activity, which of these is the best example of giving students freedom of choice?

    a. Providing flexibility for students to adapt activities to their interests
    b. Changing activity rules, space, and equipment to enable student success
    c. Matching the specific kinds of activities with the individual students
    d. Involving students in decision-making processes whenever possible

47. Which of these is an effective strategy for physical education teachers to enhance students' perceived physical competence?

    a. Specify the number of trials to complete during a certain time period.
    b. Specify the length of time for practicing but not the number of trials.
    c. Specify the technical errors students make in instructional feedback.
    d. Specify a certain activity without varying it to keep students on task.

48. Within the TARGET model, which physical education teaching strategy is an example of the R in the acronym?

    a. Varying the difficulty levels among several different activities
    b. Giving students some responsibility for the choice of activities
    c. Acknowledging process and improvement rather than product
    d. Avoiding peer comparison through rapid and variable grouping

49. Findings of research into physical activity and peer interactions are best reflected by which of these?

    a. Health behavior primarily influences students' peer relationships.
    b. Health behavior and peer relationships have reciprocal influences.
    c. Health behavior is mainly influenced by student peer relationships.
    d. Health behaviors and peer relations have no significant interaction.

50. Regarding appropriate physical education (PE) teaching practices, which statement is MOST valid?

    a. PE teachers must use extrinsic motivations to teach student responsibility for learning.
    b. PE teachers should ignore certain inappropriate student behaviors to extinguish them.
    c. PE teachers do not necessarily need to obtain or renew certification in cardiopulmonary resuscitation (CPR) or automated external defibrillator (AED) use.
    d. PE teachers must regularly and consistently inspect facilities and equipment for safety.

51. Which of these is the MOST appropriate physical education teacher practice to establish productive learning environments for students and promote their responsibility and social skills?

    a. Deliberately designing activities and situations that teach and develop needed skills
    b. Using teachable moments and allowing incidental learning to develop needed skills
    c. Teaching all U.S. team sports to culturally diverse students to develop uniform skills
    d. Allowing highly skilled students to dominate as examples for students of lower skills

52. Which of the following is a recommended strategy for physical education teachers to plan effective class behavior management?

    a. Announce at least ten expectations to the students in oral format.
    b. Enforce expectations occasionally for intermittent reinforcement.
    c. Define expectations in terms of what they want students not to do.
    d. Define expectations in terms of what they want the students to do.

53. Regarding effective ways for physical education (PE) teachers to give instructions to students for the smoothest class operation and best behavior management, which of these is accurate?

    a. PE teachers should tell students only what to do as they cannot follow more directions.
    b. PE teachers should tell students when to do something before telling them what to do.
    c. PE teachers should use the rule of threes by giving three instructional cues at a time.
    d. PE teachers using the 80/20 rule let 80 percent learn by doing and 20 percent learn from teaching.

54. When student disputes develop during physical education classes, how is settling them by rock, paper, scissors viewed?

    a. It is believed to be unprofessional.
    b. It is inappropriate by being childish.
    c. It is effective because it is objective.
    d. It is unfair because it is subjective.

55. According to experts, what is true about the primary functions of nonverbal communication?

    a. Nonverbal communication serves a function of performing social rituals.
    b. Nonverbal communication shows personalities rather than relationships.
    c. Nonverbal communication is used to replace, not help, verbal interaction.
    d. Nonverbal communication is not used like words for expressing feelings.

56. The definition of verbal communication includes which of these formats?
    a. Texting
    b. Sign language
    c. Conversations
    d. All these formats

57. Regarding communication with athletes, which statement is recommended by experts for coaches to consider?
    a. Coaches must not only get athlete attention but also explain, so athletes understand easily.
    b. Coaches must determine if athletes understood them but not whether they believed them.
    c. Coaches must get athletes to understand and believe, not necessarily accept, what they say.
    d. Coaches must disregard athletes' individual and group nonverbal cues for controlling them.

58. Regarding feedback that physical education teachers and coaches give students and athletes, which of the following is an example of prescriptive feedback rather than descriptive feedback?
    a. "You can do this!"
    b. "Follow through!"
    c. "That was great!"
    d. "Way to play ball!"

59. When does physical education instruction necessarily require giving feedback to students?
    a. When a skill requires specific correction
    b. When a skill gets environmental feedback
    c. When a student has experience with a skill
    d. When a teacher can comprehensively demonstrate a skill

60. Which of the following is an example of the sandwich approach to giving students and athletes feedback?
    a. Specific skill, general reinforcement, and a different specific skill
    b. General reinforcement, specific skill, and general reinforcement
    c. Positive reinforcement, correction, and positive reinforcement
    d. One correction, positive reinforcement, and another correction

61. When is music useful as a communication medium in physical education?
    a. Dance activities only
    b. Dance and aerobic exercise only
    c. Dance, aerobics, and dribbling basketballs
    d. Dance, aerobics, and many other physical education activities

62. What is MOST accurate about how physical education teachers can use bulletin boards to communicate instructional information to students?
    a. Schools must provide real bulletin boards for physical education teachers to utilize them.
    b. A time-lapse bulletin board accesses student participation and creativity.
    c. A time-lapse bulletin board is a project only the physical education teacher can complete.
    d. Physical education teachers must communicate orally, as students ignore bulletin boards.

63. Relative to video recordings and instructional communication by physical education teachers with students, which statement is correct?

a. Videos can preserve and repeat ideal demonstrations by teachers and students.
b. Videos are not as good for teaching body movements as verbal descriptions are.
c. Videos used by substitute or student teachers are boring in contrast to live action.
d. Videos lack the variation, making live demonstrations different and thus interesting.

64. According to national physical education (PE) standards, to show respect, which of the following should PE teachers do to address a student's behavior problem?

a. The teacher describes the student's behavior, why it was disruptive, and solutions for the problem.
b. The teacher has a classmate describe the behavior, why it was disruptive, and solutions for the problem.
c. The teacher has the student describe the behavior, why it was disruptive, and solutions for the problem.
d. The teacher avoids discussing it but provides concrete consequences and solutions for the problem.

65. A physical education teacher writes an entry task on the board before class. How does this relate to teacher communication toward student understanding and ownership of high expectations for themselves?

a. This is not recommended because the teacher will not be supervising the students for this activity.
b. This supports high classroom expectations because students can begin the activity independently.
c. This supports student independence for activities but not student comprehension of expectations.
d. This is not recommended because the teacher did not structure the learning activity for students.

66. Regarding physical education teacher communication with parents, what is MOST effective related to posting and communicating class rules to students at the beginning of the school year?

a. Giving rules to students, but not parents, so students feel they can trust teachers
b. Giving copies of rules to students with instructions to take them home to parents
c. Sending the rules by postal mail with a cover letter asking parents to review them
d. E-mailing the rules to the parents with a cover letter asking them to review them

67. Among fundamental movement skills (FMS), which two are both part of the same main category?

a. Locomotor and manipulative
b. Manipulative and rotation
c. Rotation and balance
d. Balance and stability

68. Which of these locomotor activities is most appropriate for children younger than five years old?

a. Blob tag
b. Musical hoops
c. Follow the leader
d. Any of these equally

69. In learning how to land during movement activities, which of these is NOT identified as a phase of learning?

a. Mastery
b. Discovery
c. Consolidation
d. Development

- 161 -

70. When students learn to fall sideways and land using their hands, which of the following should be the last activity they do in a sequence of increasing difficulty?

  a. Falling sideways from kneeling
  b. Rolling sideways down a wedge
  c. Falling, rolling, and standing up
  d. Running, falling, rolling, and standing

71. Which of the following is MOST accurate about giving feedback to students and athletes in physical education or coaching?

  a. External feedback should duplicate internal feedback.
  b. Students request feedback most with advanced skills.
  c. Experts recommend more instead of less feedback.
  d. External feedback should stimulate internal feedback.

72. What has research revealed about feedback in teaching physical education?

  a. Feedback quality is more important than quantity.
  b. Skill development needs more frequent feedback.
  c. Feedback quantity is more important than quality.
  d. Beginners need feedback that is the most precise.

73. Of the following statements, which is true about aerobics?

  a. Aerobics originally focused on the flexibility of the body.
  b. Aerobics originally focused on the strength of the muscles.
  c. Aerobics originally focused on cardiorespiratory endurance.
  d. Aerobics originally focused on one thing as it still does today.

74. Among Japanese martial arts, which one uses a weapon?

  a. Judo
  b. Kendo
  c. Karate
  d. Jujitsu

75. In the debate over standardized physical education tests, which of these is NOT a common argument?

  a. To enjoy physical activity as adults, people must enjoy it during youth.
  b. Standardized testing supports motivation for lifelong physical activity.
  c. Standardized testing allows students to gauge their relative progress.
  d. Standardized testing gives physical education equal importance to all school subjects.

76. Among the most prevalent challenges to kindergarten through Grade 12 physical education, which has recently become even more challenging than the others?

  a. Inadequate resources and parental support
  b. Overly large class sizes and teacher burnout
  c. Violence, student drug abuse, and discipline
  d. Reductions in school curriculum times for physical education

77. A physical education teacher addresses a wide range of skill levels in one class by setting up several learning stations to teach a lesson in throwing. Which station activity represents the highest student skill level?

    a. Throwing lead passes
    b. Throwing at a stationary target
    c. Throwing to teammates while defended
    d. Throwing all these ways equally

78. If a student has the condition of atlantoaxial instability, which of the following activities would be safe for a physical education teacher to assign to the student?

    a. A log roll would be safest for this student.
    b. A forward roll would be better for this student.
    c. No kind of roll should be assigned to this student.
    d. It is irrelevant because atlantoaxial instability is so rare.

79. What amount of quality physical education time most reflects the National Association for Sport and Physical Education (NASPE) recommendation for elementary school students?

    a. A minimum of 15 minutes per day
    b. A maximum of 30 minutes per day
    c. A minimum of 30 minutes per day
    d. A maximum of 60 minutes a week

80. When physical education teachers plan lessons and choose teaching methods, which of the following should these reflect?

    a. Lessons and programs should reflect not only national and state but also local standards.
    b. Lessons and programs should reflect individual child physical maturation more than age.
    c. Lessons and programs should reflect individual child fitness levels more than skill levels.
    d. Lessons and programs should reflect best practices more from research than experience.

81. In light of rapidly increasing diversity in U.S. student populations, which of the following is the best indicator that physical education (PE) is effective?

    a. The PE teacher sticks to a single proven instructional style.
    b. Some students have success in the PE learning experience.
    c. Students learn and meet objectives by the end of a lesson.
    d. The PE teacher's practices are consistent despite changes.

82. Of the following, which elementary school activity best integrates physical education skills with English language arts (ELA) skills within the same lesson?

    a. Students perform movements and then look up adverbs and write synonyms and antonyms.
    b. Students look up and write adverbs, synonyms, and antonyms and then perform movements.
    c. Students identify adverbs in teacher-read sentences and describe movements using adverbs.
    d. Students perform movements in ways described by recently learned adverbs on given cards.

83. How can physical education teachers give aquatics instruction in high schools with no swimming pools?

    a. They can use public or private pools in the community with permission from owners.
    b. They can explore (A), but if these are not available, they can teach swimming with (C).
    c. They can use task cards, teach swim strokes, and have students practice on benches.
    d. They can find no way of teaching swimming if their schools have no swimming pools.

84. A physical education teacher designs a student volleyball activity to meet National Association for Sport and Physical Education (NASPE) standards for setting, spiking, forearm passing, defensive strategies, officiating; aerobic capacity; and cooperating and accepting challenges. Which of the following represents the correct sequence of steps in this activity?

a. Rotational positions; serve; base positions; defend against attack
b. Base positions; rotational positions; defend against attack; serve
c. Serve; base positions; defend against attack; rotational positions
d. Defend against attack; serve; rotational positions; base positions

85. Of the following, which is a valid principle of physical education (PE) coaching for teaching movement and sport skills to students?

a. Asking think-about questions gives an advantage to students.
b. Reading tasks or steps aloud only will delay the setup of players.
c. PE teachers should alternate practice plan sequence for variety.
d. PE teachers should either describe or demonstrate but not both.

86. When a physical education teacher gives a defense cue of "Match up" to students during basketball practice, what does this mean?

a. Students always should pair up with another player on the court for defense.
b. Students should stay near to offensive players that they defend on the court.
c. Students should defend players more like them in size than fitness or skill level.
d. Students should defend players similar to them in size, fitness, and skill level.

87. When is performing the Heimlich maneuver on a student indicated?

a. The student says he or she is having trouble breathing.
b. The student is choking and is not able to breathe.
c. The student has trouble breathing and is coughing.
d. The Heimlich should not be done until cardiopulmonary resuscitation (CPR) is tried.

88. Compared to naturalistic observations, structured observations are _____ in physical education assessment.

a. more objective and less subjective
b. more subjective and less objective
c. more to see social than motor skills
d. more realistic regarding behaviors

89. Which of the following methods would be LEAST useful for assessing student performance of physical education skills?

a. Observational checklists
b. Rating scales of skill level
c. Written-response exams
d. Performance data graphs

90. The Presidential Youth Fitness Program's Fitnessgram has three main categories. Which of the following correctly represents one of these categories?

a. Muscular strength, endurance, and flexibility
b. Aerobic capacity, body composition, and strength
c. Body composition, flexibility, and aerobic capacity
d. Endurance, aerobic capacity, and muscle strength

91. Which of these describes a function of formative assessments?

    a. They enable teachers to show accountability for adequate yearly progress and similar requirements.
    b. They enable teachers to compare student achievement to population averages.
    c. They enable teachers to adjust instruction in progress to address student needs.
    d. They enable teachers to see if they helped students meet curriculum standards.

92. When using an assessment instrument meant to measure aerobic endurance, physical education teachers find that maximum student repetitions are limited not by their becoming winded but by specific muscle fatigue. After obtaining the same results over repeated administrations, they conclude that this test measures muscular endurance instead. What have they discovered about this test?

    a. The test is neither a reliable nor valid test.
    b. The test is a valid test, but it is not reliable.
    c. The test is a reliable test, but it is not valid.
    d. The test is valid and reliable, but misused.

93. Of the following assessment approaches, which one is traditional rather than alternative?

    a. Students write down their personal fitness plans.
    b. Students perform a series of dance movements.
    c. Students show learning by playing a sports game.
    d. Students label the team's positions on a diagram.

94. Which of the following describes the most appropriate physical education self-assessment activity for kindergarten through Grade 2 students?

    a. Students write entries in journals describing the fitness activities they are doing.
    b. Students pictorially illustrate their activities in each of several fitness categories.
    c. Students keep notebooks of progress notes and give them to teachers regularly.
    d. Students record their progress on index cards they give to teachers at intervals.

95. What do Individuals with Disabilities Education Act (IDEA) regulations for assessing students with disabilities mandate?

    a. Using one standardized, valid, reliable, technically sound instrument
    b. Using multiple instruments that are similar instead of using just one
    c. Using a variety of instruments, all designed for measuring disabilities
    d. Using multiple, varied, valid, reliable, technically sound instruments

96. Regarding indications that a student should be evaluated to determine eligibility for adapted physical education (APE), which of the following (in addition to referral) correctly states a criterion?

    a. The student performs at his or her ability level in group settings but not on an individual basis.
    b. The student's social behaviors impede his or her or others' learning more than half of class time.
    c. The student has scored below average in at least one part of the state physical fitness test.
    d. The student scored at least one standard deviation low on the norm-referenced test used.

97. How should occupational therapists (OTs) help preschoolers with developmental delays to learn fine motor and manipulative skills in schools?

    a. Only OTs, not adapted physical educators (APEs) or classroom teachers, should apply OT strategies.
    b. Both APEs and classroom teachers should use OT methods they learn.
    c. APEs, but not classroom teachers, should use OT methods they learn.
    d. Classroom teachers, but not APEs, should use OT methods they learn.

98. Among the following members of collaborative teams who facilitate education for special needs students, who provides IQ testing and behavior management training?

    a. Administrators
    b. School nurses
    c. Psychologists
    d. Special education teachers

99. Of the following, which accurately reports research findings related to how physical fitness affects academic achievement?

    a. Cardiovascular fitness and body mass index (BMI) correlate positively with test scores in achievement.
    b. More physically fit children react more quickly but not necessarily more accurately.
    c. Children burn more calories during active gaming than teacher-led fitness activities.
    d. Intense exercise is followed by a significant temporary decline in cognitive function.

100. Among the following divisions of biomechanics that involve physics concepts, which one is MOST closely related to Newton's first three laws of motion?

    a. Coplanar vectors
    b. Kinematics
    c. Kinetics
    d. Forces

101. Which of the following biomechanics subjects are based on calculus?

    a. Vector composition and resolution
    b. Differentiation and integration
    c. The parallelogram method
    d. None of these topics

102. Which non-English language is shared in common by some of the terminology in both ballet and ballroom dancing?

    a. French
    b. Italian
    c. Spanish
    d. Russian

103. Among examples of how physical education (PE) teachers can collaborate with other educators, which one applies most to taking advantage of administrator support to improve student motivation and learning?

    a. Reading *A River Runs Through It* to study fly-fishing and character development and relationships
    b. Watching *Footloose* to study dance movements and themes of freedom, rebellion, and repression
    c. Designing a joint PE and Family and Consumer Sciences unit that combines nutrition and exercise
    d. Developing a morning walk/run project together with the principal to help students focus better

104. Which statement is most reflective of the benefits of engaging parents in student physical education experiences?

    a. Parents can enrich learning with different knowledge and experience than teachers have.
    b. Teachers learn about student interests and motivations from students, not their parents.
    c. Teachers will not learn what parents want and hope for their children by involving them.
    d. Family knowledge is not something teachers can access by collaborating with the parents.

105. What is true about how teachers can engage community members and groups in physical education (PE) programs?

    a. It would be inappropriate to solicit funds from local health agencies to buy sports equipment.
    b. Local trophy companies are in business to make money and will not donate for school events.
    c. Local governments lack departments that could talk to students about community resources.
    d. When PE teachers plan Olympics-themed events, they may find volunteers from local colleges.

106. What is MOST accurate about different physical activities that teachers can encourage students to engage in before and after school?

    a. All schools have cheerleaders established for their athletic teams.
    b. Teachers encouraging students to bicycle will find no help online.
    c. Teachers should avoid advising canoeing because it is dangerous.
    d. Students who like art, self-expression, and music can try dancing.

107. For a student who has joint problems but wants to be physically active, which is the best extracurricular activity?

    a. Skiing
    b. Swimming
    c. Skateboarding
    d. Playing soccer

108. As an event that promotes opportunities for physical activity, which of the following is a characteristic of National Dance Day?

    a. Its events revolve around a single headquarters.
    b. Its activities are limited to certain dance classes.
    c. Its instruction includes nonambulatory persons.
    d. Its dance routines are all for beginning dancers.

109. Which of these characterizes teachers' reflections that best inform their physical education instruction?

    a. They reflect not only on themselves but also on students and class elements.
    b. They reflect on student personalities and behaviors, not school demographics.
    c. They reflect only on emotional and social influences to student performance.
    d. They reflect on each student's abilities and needs rather than class dynamics.

110. A physical education teacher has included an objective for student heart rates to reach a target range when they play a sport. The teacher discovers the majority of students did not reach that target. Which teacher response to this discovery is the best example of using reflection to inform instruction?

    a. The teacher decides students were not playing hard enough and gives them a pep talk.
    b. The teacher experiments with having the students play the next game at faster speeds.
    c. The teacher changes the rules of the game so all students will participate more actively.
    d. The teacher might do either (B) or (C) or even both of these but is less likely to use (A).

111. As employed by effective physical education teachers, what is reflection?

    a. An exercise they engage in periodically to review their effectiveness
    b. A process they utilize to support their curriculum planning and design
    c. A tool that they depend upon for adjusting curriculum and instruction
    d. A process they rely on continually to improve all elements of teaching

112. Among professional development activities a physical education teacher can pursue, which of these would MOST directly enrich the students' learning experiences?

    a. Obtaining an advanced certification in physical education or some related discipline
    b. Obtaining certification for an activity that many students want to do
    c. Obtaining a position on a national, state, or local physical education committee
    d. Obtaining invitations to present papers at workshops and conferences

113. Professional development at its best accomplishes which of these?

    a. Improves primarily the teacher's own knowledge and skills
    b. Improves both a teacher's and his or her colleagues' expertise
    c. Improves primarily the expertise of the teacher's colleagues
    d. Improves teaching practices primarily at the classroom level

114. What do professional growth and educational interactions enable physical education teachers to do?

    a. To learn more, stay current, partner, and improve learning communities
    b. To develop their own self-confidence rather than inspire others' initiative
    c. To perform the functions of role modeling more than those of advocating
    d. To demonstrate achievement taking priority before professional integrity

115. What advantages does Fitbit technology include for physical education teachers and students?

    a. Weight control but not sleep quality
    b. Self-monitoring but not competition
    c. Fashion appeal as well as motivation
    d. Stand-alone fitness progress tracking

116. The MyFitnessPal, Endomondo, and Fitbit digital fitness apps all share what in common?

    a. Sync
    b. Recipes
    c. Audio feedback
    d. Social networking

117. According to experiences reported by physical education teachers, what are some characteristics of technology in applications such as GradeBookPro?

    a. Apps like this enable physical education teachers to use most of their time for teaching.
    b. Apps like this reduce final grade disputes by consolidating student data.
    c. Apps like this can exponentially speed up the task of taking attendance.
    d. Apps like this streamline all these and a great many more teacher tasks.

118. What have physical education teachers found about using apps like Coach's Eye, iCoachview, and so on with their students?

    a. Student enthusiasm helps them appreciate constructive criticism.
    b. Students typically cannot use apps after only brief demonstration.
    c. Students are uncomfortable seeing their performance postgame.
    d. Students experience delayed feedback when teachers play videos.

119. What is true about technology tools that let schools and teachers use electronic records?

  a. They are more efficient but only for maintaining records.
  b. They permit faster, easier access but afford less security.
  c. They not only keep records but also produce new records.
  d. They are not subject to paper confidentiality regulations.

120. Which of the following activities represents a physical education teacher's using technology to enhance his or her professional development?

  a. Spending more time on scoring tests instead of time on interpreting them
  b. Recording, playing back, and analyzing teaching practices for improvement
  c. Searching online for research resources with their field's latest innovations
  d. Using programs to organize and deliver information to students and others

Answers and Explanations

1. D: The gracilis (A) is an inner thigh muscle that runs between the pubic bone and the tibia (shin bone). The gastrocnemius (B) is a muscle in the lower leg. The gluteus minimus (C) is the third of the four buttocks muscles: The gluteus maximus is the largest; the gluteus medius is the second largest; the gluteus minimus the third largest. The tensor fasciae latae (D) is the fourth and smallest.

2. A: Body mass index (BMI) is the ratio of weight to height squared, which shows the relationship between a person's weight and height. It is not the ratio of abdominal to total fat (B), fat to muscle (C), or fat to weight (D). Healthy BMIs are generally between 18.5 and 24.9. Below 18.5 is considered underweight, and 25 to 29.9 is considered overweight (with a few exceptions; e.g., some people with very high muscle mass rather than fat may have higher BMIs). A BMI of 30 or above is considered obese.

3. C: Earlier researchers attributed motor development to genetically determined maturation, not experience alone, (A) and (D). Later research findings show that a combination and interaction of maturation and experience are responsible for motor development. Thus, the trend has not been away from maturation alone toward experience alone (B) but toward growth and development combined with learning and their interactions.

4. C: Summation of forces refers to producing the maximum possible force from any movement using multiple muscles. Adding up the forces generated by each individual muscle yields the total force or summation of forces. Related to this, the order of use is that the largest body parts are slowest, and being stronger and hence the initiators of power, they move first; the smallest body parts are fastest, and being in charge of coordination and refinement, they move last. Thus, the largest, slowest parts do not move last (A), and the smallest, fastest parts do not move first (B). Therefore, (D) is also incorrect.

5. B: Center of gravity (COG) is not in the same location in every human body (A); neither is it always in a certain location of every individual body (C). Rather, it shifts corresponding to changes in the positions of the body parts (B). COG is not precisely the same as center of mass, but their difference is negligible, so for all practical purposes they are considered synonymous; however, center of gravity or mass is not the same as center of pressure (D).

6. A: Torque equals force times its perpendicular distance from the axis of rotation. Thus, (D) is incorrect. The greater the perpendicular distance between the axis and the force, the greater the torque. Thus, the skater with longer arms will rotate faster because that skater's arms have a longer perpendicular distance from the body, that is, axis of rotation. The skater with shorter arms will rotate slower, not faster (B). Hence, with equal force applied, they will not both rotate at equal speeds (C).

7. D: In spatial awareness, locations and levels (A) of the body or body parts can be high, middle, or low. Personal space (B) refers to the space immediately surrounding an individual person, as opposed to general space, which refers to the total space available or playing area. Directions (C) of movement in space include forward, backward, up, down, and sideways. Planes of movement in space include vertical, horizontal, and circular paths (D).

8. A: In quality of movement, the flow of movement can be bound, that is, interrupted, or free, that is, sustained. Effort (B), or the amount of force in a body movement, can be strong, medium, light, or other increments within each of these. Speed (C) of movement can be quick, slow, or any degree in between these. Rhythm (D) of body movement can be constant, accelerating, or decelerating.

9. B: The relationship of on or off means engaged in a movement activity (on) or in suspension of a movement activity (off), which may involve multiple bodies but also can involve only a single body. The

relationship of near or far (A) must involve a body plus another body or an object as it refers to the distance between them. The relationship of moving together or with opposition (C) necessarily involves two or more bodies. The relationship of symmetrical or asymmetrical (D) movement involves a body plus one or more other bodies or objects: If they have corresponding points or proportions, their relationship is symmetrical; if they do not have these, their relationship is asymmetrical.

10. B: In exercise science, the principle of specificity means that, to improve certain body parts, muscles, or sports movements and techniques, one must exercise those specific parts, muscles, or movements and techniques. Exercising the lower body will not strengthen the upper body or vice versa. Specificity also means that one must practice football skills, for example, to improve in football rather than only exercising for general body conditioning: The latter may be required for and benefit playing football but will not improve specific football skills; only practicing those skills specifically will. The principle of overload (A) means extra or unaccustomed stimuli are required to make the body respond beyond its normal levels. If the question had said someone bench presses more weight than usual to make the upper body stronger, this would illustrate overload as well as specificity. The principle of adaptation (C) means the body adjusts to processes and demands, making activities easier over time and eventually requiring variation for continuing progress. The principle of progression (D) means individuals must progress at certain rates natural to them to achieve results and avoid injuries.

11. A: When we exercise, our bodies access their stored glycogen supplies for energy; glycogen depletion triggers the release of endorphins, hormones that generate feelings of euphoria. These feelings of well-being are short-term effects of exercise. The prevention and relief of depression through regular exercise are long-term effects. So are lower risks of heart attacks and strokes (C), which result from consistent aerobic exercise over time. While a short-term effect of exercise is an immediate increase in blood circulation, a reduction of blood pressure and pulse (D) can be a long-term effect of exercising regularly for at least a few months.

12. C: Good nutrition provides the body with more energy, which enables and motivates people to exercise. Reciprocally, getting regular exercise can help to control the appetite and prevent overeating. Exercising does not mean you can eat anything you want (A). Both calcium and other nutrients in the diet and weight-bearing exercise can prevent loss of bone density and osteoporosis (B). A combination of exercise and a nutritious diet, not one or the other, prevents high blood pressure, high cholesterol (D), diabetes, and other diseases that unhealthy lifestyles often contribute to or cause.

13. D: The skin is a part of the integumentary system, along with the hair, nails, nerves, and glands. The skin controls fluid loss, protects deep tissues, and synthesizes vitamin D. The skeletal system (A) gives the body its bony supporting structure, protects vital organs, collaborates with muscles in body movement, stores calcium, and produces red blood cells. The muscular system (B) maintains posture, collaborates with the bones in body movement, uses energy, and generates heat. The lymphatic system (C) retrieves fluids leaked from capillaries and contains white blood cells, and parts of it support parts of the immune system.

14. B: Our respiratory systems inhale air, of which oxygen is one component. From that inhaled air, the respiratory system delivers oxygen to the body. Through gas exchange, it then expels carbon dioxide (CO_2) from the body as we exhale. The respiratory system obtains oxygen from the air we inhale; it does not create it, and it expels CO_2 rather than absorbing it (C). We do not use our respiratory systems to exhale oxygen or inhale CO_2 (D).

15. B: The highest level (A) of the brain contains command neurons that initiate the intention to produce body movement and send the message to the middle level. The mid-level neurons (B) in the sensorimotor cortex of the cerebral cortex, the basal ganglia of the subcortical nuclei, the cerebellum, and the brain

- 171 -

stem produce a motor program by determining necessary postures and movements and coordinating these with information about body posture and surroundings that they receive from eye, vestibular, skin, joint, and muscular receptors. They send this program to the lowest level (C) of the motor neurons and interneurons, which determine muscle tension and joint angles. Therefore, (D) is incorrect.

16. A: Pioneers in the study of motor development, including Arnold Gesell and Myrtle McGraw, achieved extensive, thorough catalogues of the stages and milestones of motor development during the 1930s and 1940s. However, from the 1950s to the 1980s, there was little further progress in the field as scientists assumed everything had been covered. Thus, (B), (C), and (D) are incorrect. During the 1980s, further research was stimulated when new technologies and methods, pioneered by Nicholai Bernstein's dynamic systems concept, Esther Thelen's extension of it, and James and Eleanor Gibson's modern motor skills theory emphasizing perceptual-motor learning, shifted scientific perspectives away from the former emphasis on neuromuscular maturation as the explanation for motor development and toward more complex interactions of perceptual information, adaptive learning of movement control, and peripheral factors with maturation.

17. C: Posture has played an equally significant role in classical and contemporary theories of motor development. In classical theories attributing motor skill development to neuromuscular maturation, increasingly vertical posture was evidence of babies' progress as their cerebral cortices developed more control over their abilities to overcome gravitational pull. In contemporary theories attributing motor development to dynamic systems and relationships between perceptions and actions, posture became the stable biomechanical basis for action and was evidence of learning about new perception–action systems. Hence, posture was not more important to either classical theories (A) or contemporary theories (B). Neither did these theories regard its role in motor development as minor (D).

18. D: Balance includes static balance, that is, the ability to balance while remaining stationary, and dynamic balance, that is, the ability to balance while shifting the weight as in walking, climbing, dancing, and so on. Flow (A) involves combining different movements and movement sequences in a smooth, continuous manner and performing movements within limited times and spaces. Time (B) involves distinguishing among various speeds and being able to increase and decrease movement speeds. Force (C) involves producing the amount of tension or effort required for various movements and modifying these as necessary.

19. B: Compared to regular baseball, softball has a bigger ball, a smaller infield, fewer innings, and a different pitch. Softballs are 11 to 12 inches around, whereas baseballs are 8 to 9 inches around. Softball infields have their bases 60 feet apart, whereas baseball infields have their bases 90 feet apart. Regulation softball games consist of seven innings, whereas regulation baseball games consist of nine innings. Softball requires underhand pitching, whereas baseball typically uses overhand pitching.

20. C: In soccer, all players are allowed to contact the ball with their heads or torsos. Soccer teams consist of 11 players, not 9 (A). Soccer goalies can touch the ball with their arms or hands within their penalty areas, while it is in play (B). The Fédération Internationale de Football Association (FIFA) World Cup is held every four years, not every year (D).

21. A: The breaststroke uses the frog kick. The frog kick is also used in self-contained underwater breathing apparatus (SCUBA) diving and can be used for treading water. The butterfly (B) stroke uses the dolphin kick. The crawl (C) typically uses the flutter kick. Therefore, (D) is incorrect.

22. B: Physical education (PE) instructors can address negligence in instruction (A) by ensuring they teach students the correct procedures and protocols for safety and for equipment setup, use, and takedown and ensuring students understand and practice how to execute sport and movement activities

beforehand. Because PE classes often are large and getting larger, they can address negligence best in supervision (B) by ensuring they continually and actively supervise students throughout all activities and enlisting students to practice peer supervision in addition to supplement teacher supervision. In transportation (C), teachers and coaches are liable outside of school and must obtain written parental consent; follow all school policies, practices, and procedures; and supervise student behavior on buses. In class environments (D), teachers and coaches must be alert for possible dangerous conditions, which can vary daily, and space students to limit hazards.

23. D: Physical education (PE) classes are generally larger than regular classes (A), increasing PE teacher liability. PE classes are also more likely to include outdoor as well as indoor activities than regular classes (B), so PE teachers must not only cover larger areas but also address areas with different physical characteristics. While regular classes may travel for field trips, PE classes travel much more often (C) to away games, meets, and other activities outside of school. Two more liability factors in PE classes are sports equipment: baseballs and bats, footballs, tennis balls and racquets, golf balls and clubs, discus, shot-puts, javelins, and so on can become or propel projectiles at high speeds, risking student injury; and swimming classes include the presence of water, risking slips, falls, and drowning.

24. C: When physical education (PE) classes involve a baseball, for example, injuries are much more likely when fielding teams include 30 or more students instead of only 9 as in regulation games. Teachers must instruct students wanting to field fly balls to call for them and other students to back away from them. Experts with legal and PE experience warn teachers to limit any gymnastics to only basic vaulting and tumbling and these only with individual spotters (A). Most average students cannot support their bodies or hang by their arms, making falls likely; falling from inverted positions risks spinal damage, paralysis, and death. Experts additionally warn PE teachers never to include trampolines in PE classes and also not in extracurricular activities (B) like gymnastics, cheerleading, and so on unless school insurance includes trampoline accidents, which are often not covered or incur excessive premiums. PE teachers should never discipline students using strenuous exercise (D), which is unsafe.

25. B: Abusing marijuana before physical education (PE) classes is more likely to cause impaired depth perception, which interferes with student ability to judge distances accurately in team sports, track and field, and so on. Both alcohol and marijuana abuse before PE classes are likely to impair and lower student energy (A). Alcohol abuse before PE classes is more likely to cause generally impaired judgment (C). Both alcohol and marijuana abuse before PE classes are likely to impair physical coordination (D).

26. A: Student substance abuse can cause death through auto accidents from driving under the influence, drug overdoses, homicide, suicide, drug-induced illnesses, human immunodeficiency (HIV) and acquired immune deficiency syndrome (AIDS), and so on. Organ damage (B) is primarily caused by substance abuse itself. Avascular necrosis (C), that is, loss of blood supply to a joint, is caused by abusing anabolic steroids to enhance performance or by abusing alcohol. HIV/AIDS transmission (D) is caused by sharing needles to inject drugs, by engaging in unprotected sex under the influence of substances, and from mothers to babies by abusing drugs during pregnancy or childbirth.

27. D: Alcohol, cocaine, Prozac, and other substances temporarily can reduce inhibitions so that students who are usually shy or introverted behave more sociably around peers (A). When students see substance use as a solution to being socially awkward and unpopular, they repeat it, which can lead to addiction. Conversely, students who were normally extroverted often withdraw socially when they become addicted to substances (B). Students who normally demonstrate self-control often behave more impulsively under the influence of substances (C).

28. C: Activities that require agility and lower-body strength, which do not involve body contact (A), are most appropriate for coed participation and are less dependent on team assignment by student skill

levels. For activities that require more upper-body strength (B), it is more important for physical education teachers to assign teams according to individual student skill levels to prevent injuries. Therefore, (D) is incorrect.

29. D: Ectomorphs have long, narrow, thin body shapes with little muscle or fat. The high jump (D) and long-distance running are examples of appropriate sports for this somatotype. Wrestling (A) and shot-putting (C) are more suitable for endomorphic body types, which tend to be pear-shaped with more fat on the torso and limbs but small wrists and ankles. Gymnastics (B) is more appropriate for mesomorphs, who tend to have triangular shapes and strong limbs with more muscle and less fat.

30. B: When physical education (PE) teachers help students to identify the similarities between new movement skills and those they learned previously, this promotes cognitive learning by helping students to transfer their existing knowledge. Other things PE teachers can do to promote cognitive learning include allowing slightly longer times for instruction and demonstrations (A) to enable student memorization of new skills and cues; varying their language to communicate appropriately for individual student vocabulary, cognitive level, processing ability, and comprehension (C); and giving students with greater capabilities more responsibility for their own learning (D) to promote their conceptual thinking.

31. B: Handling a hockey puck is an example of a performance skill that would be affected most by individual differences in the perceptual-motor ability of control precision. Football quarterbacking (A) is an example of a performance skill that would be affected most by individual differences in the perceptual-motor abilities of response orientation or choice reaction time. Dribbling a basketball (C) is an example of a performance skill that would be affected most by individual differences in the perceptual-motor ability of manual dexterity. Driving a race car (D) is an example of a performance skill that would be affected most by individual differences in the perceptual-motor ability of rate control.

32. C: Kayaking is an activity that most involves the physical proficiency of dynamic strength. Static strength (A) is most involved in an activity like weight lifting. Trunk strength (B) is most involved in an activity like pole-vaulting. Explosive strength (D) is involved most in an activity like the standing long jump.

33. B: This is a description of the command or direct method, which uses teacher-centered task instruction to promote psychomotor learning. The contingency or contract method (A) is a behavioral approach that uses specified rewards that are contingent on student task completion to reinforce psychomotor behaviors. The task or reciprocal method (C) uses stations whereby student learning of specific psychomotor tasks is integrated into the learning setup. Because (B) is correct, (D) is incorrect.

34. C: Research studies find that motor skills, endurance, and strength training all modify the spinal reflexes according to the specific behaviors each task requires. New blood vessels are formed (A) through endurance training but not motor skills or strength training. Motor maps are reorganized (B) through motor skills training but not endurance or strength training. New synapses are generated (D) through motor skills and strength training but not endurance training.

35. B: Human babies actually display coordinated arm–hand movements in the womb before birth, such as moving their thumbs to their mouths. The amniotic fluid provides buoyancy to make this easier. After birth, gravity makes arm and hand movements harder for newborns, who initially exhibit arm flapping and jerky arm extensions (C) before progressing to successfully reaching for objects (A) around four to five months old. At this age, they only adjust their hand shapes to object shapes after touching them. They develop the ability to use visual information to change their hand shapes before touching objects (D) around the age of eight months.

36. A: In the earliest stages of their gait development, babies typically walk with their legs wide apart, toes pointing outward. They keep their legs straight rather than bending their knees (B). They do not let their arms swing in opposition as adults do, but they do not keep their arms by their sides (C) either. Rather, they tend to bend them upward at the elbows with the palms of their hands facing the ceiling. They do not roll from the heel to toe (D) of the foot as adults do. Instead, they either set each foot down flat all at once, or some babies walk on their toes. From first steps to toddling to adultlike walking, children go through marked yet gradual gait changes until around the age of seven years.

37. A: These steps are sequenced in order of ascending severity: First, the teacher gives the noncompliant student an oral warning that he or she is not following class rules. If the student fails to comply, second, the teacher gives the student a brief time-out from class to refocus his or her attention. If the student is still not complying upon returning, third, the teacher assigns another time-out wherein the student must write a response, for example, identifying the rules he or she broke and what he or she will do now to follow the class rules.

38. D: Among many kindergarten through Grade 12 physical education (PE) teachers across the United States surveyed about their class rules, themes that commonly and frequently recurred included that students should show respect (A) for themselves, others, the PE equipment, and the environment; that they should cooperate (B) with one another and their teachers; that they should try or do their best (C); and that they should be good listeners, not talking when teachers or classmates are talking and knowing when to talk, look, listen, and be quiet. Keeping eyes and ears open and mouth closed, and so on rather than speaking out freely (D) was not mentioned by any of the teachers surveyed.

39. D: While all of these class rules used by many American kindergarten through Grade 12 physical education (PE) teachers apply equally well to other subjects and classrooms, good sportsmanship—though also important in other classrooms in terms of treating others fairly in general, using teamwork in collaborative activities, and being good winners and losers whenever competition is involved—is even more important in PE classes, which more frequently and regularly involve competitive activities and team sports or games. Choices (A) and (B) are equally applicable to any classroom. Keeping one's hands to oneself (C), as well as one's feet and objects, applies more in PE classes due to their more physical nature but also can become an issue in other classrooms. However, sportsmanship is the most important rule for PE classes.

40. A: Physiological and psychological variables that influence individual ability and interest for learning are examples of the factor of readiness for learning. Examples of the factor of motivation (B) are internal conditions of needs and drives that are required for individuals to initiate goal-directed activities. Examples of the factor of reinforcement (C) are positive or negative events and behaviors that make an individual more likely to repeat the same behavior in response to a stimulus. Examples of the factor of individual differences (D) are student abilities, backgrounds, intelligence, personalities, and learning styles.

41. C: In the first, cognitive stage of motor learning, learners understand the activity's goal and nature (A) and make initial attempts to perform it that include major errors (B). In the second, associative stage, learners engage in practice to master the timing of the skill, and they make fewer errors that are more consistent in nature (C). In the third, autonomous stage, learners perform the activity effortlessly and automatically (D), enabling them to redirect their attention to other aspects of the skill.

42. C: In effective cooperative learning activities, the students engage in productive, face-to-face interactions frequently and substantially, not occasionally (A). They are accountable and responsible for their group goals not only collectively but also personally and individually (B). They frequently do apply their interpersonal and small-group skills that pertain to their specific cooperative learning activity (C).

- 175 -

They regularly, frequently conduct group processing of how their group currently functions in order to improve their group's future effectiveness, not simply to sustain its current effectiveness (D).

43. B: More advanced computer and video technology is more likely to help than harm physical education (PE) activity performance by enabling improved feedback and analysis. Strong winds affecting outdoor activities (A) either can help or hurt performance: For example, wind can interfere with tennis performance but improve sailing performance. The condition of equipment (C) can help performance when it is better but hurt performance when it malfunctions or fails. The other participants (D), for example, teammates or opponents, can help individual and team performance when they perform well but harm performance when they perform poorly.

44. A: Researchers have found that smaller class sizes and student–teacher ratios correlate with larger quantities of activity time, activity level, safety, and learning for students, whereas larger class sizes and student–teacher ratios correlate with smaller quantities of student activity times, levels, safety, and learning—that is, an inverse correlation. Studies show that students receive more and better physical education (PE) from teachers who teach only PE rather than dividing their teaching time and attention between PE and other subjects (B). Researchers are coming to increasing consensus that standards-based PE curriculum results in greater student physical activity (C). Well-maintained, safe, appropriate, and aesthetically appealing PE facilities and equipment also are found to increase and improve student activity (D).

45. A: The Institute of Medicine recommendation is for children to spend an hour a day in moderate to vigorous physical activity (MVPA). But studies show that, in actual schools, physical education (PE) classes last about 23 minutes a day, with only 10 of those minutes spent in MVPA. In other words, children get about one-sixth the MVPA that is recommended from school PE classes. Researchers conclude that not only must children be physically active outside of PE classes, but also schools must increase how much children are active during PE class times.

46. D: Involving the students in decision-making processes whenever possible is an example of the motivational strategy of giving students the freedom to choose among physical education (PE) activities. Another example of this strategy is giving students choices among more than one activity. Providing flexibility for students to adapt PE activities to their individual interests (A) and needs is an example of the motivational strategy of modifying activities and skills. Another example of this strategy is changing the rules, space, or equipment in an activity to facilitate student success (B). Matching the specific kinds of activities with individual students (C) is an example of the motivational strategy of giving ideal challenges to every student. Another example of this strategy is letting students select among materials or equipment to use in certain activities.

47. B: To enhance students' perceived physical competence, it is better for physical education (PE) teachers not to specify how many trials to complete during a certain time period (A) but rather to specify the time period for practicing without requiring any specific number of trials (B). This allows students to focus not on how many times they complete the actions but rather on perfecting their technique. Rather than emphasizing technical errors they make (C), it is better to emphasize which things students do well technically, providing positive reinforcement that increases their motivation to practice. Varying assigned activities is more effective to minimize off-task student behavior than not varying them (D).

48. C: TARGET stands for task, authority, recognition, grouping, evaluation, and timing. Varying difficulty levels (A) refers to task. Giving students some responsibility for choice of activities (B) refers to authority. Acknowledging process and improvement rather than product (C) and outcome refers to recognition. Avoiding peer comparison through strategies that get students to form groups quickly and switch groups frequently (D) refers to grouping.

49. B: Research into physical activity and peer interactions consistently finds that health behavior and peer relationships influence one another reciprocally. Health behavior does not primarily influence peer relationships (A); neither do peer relationships mainly influence health behavior (C). Rather, their interactions are mutual. Therefore, it is not true that health behavior and peer relationships in students have no significant interaction (D).

50. D: Physical education (PE) teachers must always conduct regular safety inspections of facilities and equipment on a consistent basis. Rather than using extrinsic motivations (A) like external punishments or rewards, PE teachers are advised to enhance intrinsic student motivations to be responsible for learning. When student behaviors are inappropriate, PE teachers should not ignore them (B) but address them immediately. PE teachers do need to obtain and regularly renew certification in cardiopulmonary resuscitation (CPR) and automated external defibrillator (AED) use (C).

51. A: The most appropriate practice for physical education (PE) teachers to create productive environments and promote student responsibility and social skills is to design activities and situations deliberately for teaching and developing those skills rather than only taking advantage of teachable moments or allowing incidental learning to develop them (B). To support all students equally, PE teachers should include culturally diverse activities rather than only teaching U.S. team sports (C). Rather than letting highly skilled students dominate (D), PE teachers should provide challenges and encouragement equally to students of all developmental levels, ability levels, and disabilities.

52. D: For effective class behavior management plans, physical education (PE) teachers should define their expectations positively in terms of what they want the students to do, not negatively in terms of what they want them not to do (C). They should limit expectations to five at most, as students will be unable to remember more than that, and put them in writing, not orally (A), posted visibly in locker rooms and on classroom bulletin boards. They also should enforce their stated expectations consistently, not just occasionally (B).

53. B: Physical education (PE) teachers should not just tell students what to do (A) because they will stop listening to further instructions to follow the first one. For example, if the teacher says, "Each team pick up a ball," they will immediately do that and stop paying attention. Instead, PE teachers should tell students when before telling them what, for example, "When I say 'go,' each team pick up a ball." This way, students will keep paying attention while they wait for the teacher to give them the prompt before acting. The rule of threes does not mean giving three cues at a time (C); it means using the number three uniformly to help students remember, for example, three passes, three feet, three minutes, three seconds, and so on. The 80/20 rule does not mean 80 percent learn by doing and 20 percent from teaching (D) but the opposite: PE teachers should teach a concept until 80 percent of the class understands it because, during subsequent practice, the other 20 percent will learn by doing to understand it.

54. C: Experts recommend the rock, paper, scissors method for physical (PE) teachers to settle student disputes during classes because it is random and hence objective rather than subjective, which would be unfair (D). These experts do not consider this method to be unprofessional (A), inappropriate, or childish (B). Using a random method ensures they are not treating any student preferentially in their decisions.

55. A: According to social psychologists, nonverbal communication has these primary functions: performing social rituals (A) like greetings, farewells, and so on; revealing personalities as well as interpersonal relationships (B); supporting verbal interactions (C); and expressing feelings (D).

56. D: All these formats are included in the definition of verbal communication: sending and receiving text messages (A); communicating among the Deaf using sign language (B); spoken conversations (C), both in

person and over the phone; writing and reading e-mails; speaking on and listening to radio and TV programs, Skype, online videos and vlogs; and writing and reading on paper.

57. A: Experts advise coaches that they must first determine whether they have athletes' attention before communicating with them successfully, and second, whether they are explaining in a way that athletes can understand easily. Third, coaches must determine whether the athletes have in fact understood what they said, and fourth, whether the athletes believed what they told them (B). Fifth, coaches must determine whether their athletes have accepted what they told them (C) as well as understanding and believing it. To control a team or group of athletes, coaches also must be sensitive to the nonverbal cues they give (D), while the coaches are talking. These cues communicate whether the athletes are puzzled, confused, disbelieving, bored, resentful, disrespectful, and so on toward a coach and what he or she is saying.

58. B: "Follow through!" is an example of prescriptive feedback, which is specific. It specifies an instruction that corrects or improves what the student or athlete is doing or needs to do. In this example, it tells the student or athlete that, when batting, kicking, throwing, and so on, he or she must follow the movement through for it to be effective rather than stopping it abruptly upon contact or release. The other examples are all descriptive feedback, which is general. It gives students or athletes positive social reinforcement by encouraging or praising their performance in general but does not specify exactly what it was that they did well or need to do better or differently.

59. A: While feedback is important in physical education (PE) instruction, knowing when and when not to provide feedback is equally important to effective teaching. PE teachers need to give feedback to give students specific corrections to incorrectly performed techniques, for example. However, when a task furnishes inherent environmental feedback (B),—for example, a student throws a basketball, and it goes through the hoop—additional feedback may be unnecessary. When a student already has enough experience with a skill (C), sometimes PE teachers need not give them feedback. Also, when a teacher's demonstration enables students to see easily how to perform a skill correctly (D), they may need little or no additional feedback.

60. C: The sandwich approach consists of first giving the student or athlete positive reinforcement for something he or she did well, identifying one thing to correct or improve, and then giving positive reinforcement for something else he or she did well. By sandwiching the correction between two pieces of praise, the physical education (PE) teacher or coach makes it feel more acceptable and less critical of the student or athlete. This technique does not sandwich one piece of positive reinforcement between two corrections (D) but vice versa. The congruent feedback technique involves giving general reinforcement followed by specifying the skill being reinforced; for example, "Good job following through." This not only gives the student or athlete praise but specifies what he or she did well. Repeating the general reinforcement after specifying the skill (B) is not necessary. While teachers or coaches might also specify the skill and follow it with praise—for example "You followed through; good job!"—this is not followed by a different specific skill (A).

61. D: Music obviously is used along with choreography and performing dance movements, and it increases student motivation, control, endurance, and enjoyment during aerobic exercise (B). But it also is helpful in a wide range of other physical education (PE) activities. For instance, PE teachers can help students gain control over the speeds, rhythms, and evenness with which they can dribble basketballs (C) by having them practice in time to recorded music. They can play music for students to practice repeated chest passes and bounce passes with basketballs; this enables students to practice for longer times as well as control their speeds and intervals. Teachers can use music with different tempi for warm-up and cool-down exercises. Also, they can assign students to complete as many of a given action as possible while music continues to play.

62. B: A time-lapse bulletin board can begin with the physical education (PE) teacher labeling a board's theme (e.g., balance, strength, speed, teamwork, sportsmanship, a certain sport, etc.) posting about a dozen pictures to provide examples and ideas for students and get them started. The teacher then assigns students to bring in pictures—drawings, photos, diagrams, art, and so on that they have found or made—that apply to the board's identified theme. Over time, student contributions fill the board with pictures, which students can view, discuss, and use as illustrations to help them understand aspects of a learning unit or topic. PE teachers need not even have schools provide (A) or have to buy their own real bulletin boards; they simply can create a board by hanging large pieces of paper, poster board, or fabric on the wall. This project is completed by students, not just teachers (C). Students do not ignore such boards (D), especially when they contain their own and classmates' contributions.

63. A: Video recording technology has many advantages for physical education (PE) teachers in communicating instructional information to students. When a teacher demonstrates a technique or movement with outstanding expertise, this can be captured and preserved on video and repeated for many future demonstrations. This eliminates the possibility that another time the teacher is having a bad day and does not demonstrate as well. Body movements are much better demonstrated visually than described verbally (B): Students can see what to do and how rather than having to imagine it. Videos of the regular PE teacher's demonstration also help substitute and student teachers who cannot demonstrate, or demonstrate very differently, which can confuse students. Videos provide consistency and continuity, not boredom (C). To learn body movements, they must be repeated exactly the same way each time to form muscle memory; thus, variation is not interesting (D) but detracts from learning. Variation can be interesting when a dancer improvises from one performance to another but not for students to learn new movements.

64. C: The National Board for Professional Teaching Standards (NBPTS) include creating an environment of respect and rapport with students. The board provides an example for addressing student problem behaviors of having the misbehaving student describe his or her behavior, state what made it disruptive, and identify solutions for the problem. This standard's example does not advise for the teacher to do these things (A): The student must do them for ownership, responsibility, and understanding of his or her behavior. Neither should the teacher ask a classmate (B) to do them for the same reasons. The standard does not recommend giving concrete consequences and solutions instead of discussing the problem (D).

65. B: When the teacher writes a task on the board that students can begin upon entry to physical education (PE) class, this supports high expectations for students to take responsibility for classroom procedures and routines. While it encourages their independence in starting the activity, this does not mean the teacher will not be supervising them (A) thereafter. This teacher practice not only supports student independence in initiating activities; it also helps them comprehend their learning objectives and expectations (C) by the teacher's structuring the learning activities (D) he or she has provided for them.

66. D: It is not a good idea to keep class rules from parents in a misguided attempt to gain student trust (A). Parents need to be informed of the rules, so they know what is expected of their children and can make sure their children understand the rules. Teachers also protect themselves by informing parents of rules in advance: In the event of student behavior problems, injuries, or disputes, parents cannot subsequently deny knowledge or accuse teachers of not informing them. Giving the students copies of the rules to take home to parents (B) often means the parents never receive them. Postal mail (C) is much slower when today's technology enables almost instant transmission of e-mails (D), eliminating the potential for events to occur before parents receive the information.

67. C: The three main categories of fundamental movement skills (FMS) are locomotor (A), manipulative, (A and, (B), and stability (D). Within the main category of stability are included the subcategories of rotation, (B) and (C), and balance, (C) and (D). Activities like spinning, twirling, rocking, bending, and

- 179 -

turning demonstrate rotation. Balance can involve both stationary and movement activities. Both rotation and balance are components of stability. Locomotor skills involve activities like walking, running, and so on. Manipulative skills include activities like throwing, catching, hitting, batting, kicking, and transporting objects.

68. B: Musical hoops is played like musical chairs, except children must jump into hoops instead of sitting on chairs when the music stops. This is appropriate for younger children. Freeze tag or blob tag (A) is more appropriate for children older than 5 years, up to 12 years old. Children must try to tag others while holding hands with those in their blob. This demands higher levels of coordination than younger children have. Follow the leader (C) is better as a warm-up activity for children age 5 to 12 years, as younger children can have difficulty with leading and following and with the variations in leaders and locomotor skills that teachers can use with older children. Therefore, (D) is incorrect.

69. A: Mastery is not one of the three phases of learning identified in landing skills. The three learning phases are: (1) discovery (B). In this phase, children do not yet demonstrate any stable base of support, land flat-footed with little knee bending, and explore how to land. (2) Development (D): in this phase, children show stable support bases. They learn to appreciate the value of shock absorption, bending their knees after their heels touch ground. They rotate forward upon landing and are more consistent about landing in order from toes to ball of foot to heel. They are able to land from various distances and heights. (3) Consolidation (C): in this phase, children demonstrate wide, stable bases of support; can land during unpredictable or changing circumstances; can land safely with control; use their hips, knees, and ankles to absorb shock; and land with confidence.

70. D: When learning to fall sideways and land on the hands, students should first learn to fall sideways from a kneeling position (A). Then they can practice rolling sideways down a wedge (B) to simulate falling down an incline. Then they learn while moving to fall, roll sideways, stand up (C), and keep moving. They begin this exercise from a walking speed and gradually increase to jogging then running (D). Thereafter, they can practice this activity with dodging. After mastering these activities, students can try in pairs to pull each other off balance and take turns tipping each other sideways from an all-fours position.

71. D: Experts advise physical education (PE) teachers and coaches that external feedback should not duplicate internal feedback (A). Rather, external feedback should replace missing internal feedback, as when a student asks the teacher why he or she keeps repeating the same technical error. Students do not request feedback most with advanced skills (B) but earlier in learning new skills. Experts recommend that lesser feedback is preferable to more feedback, not vice versa (C): As one author at Kinetics.com put it, "When in doubt, be quiet." To support the problem-solving skills necessary in learning, PE teachers and coaches help most by giving external feedback that directs students or athletes to focus on sources of internal feedback, for example, body parts, positions, movements, and relationships to inform their learning processes.

72. A: Research finds that a higher quality of physical education (PE) teaching feedback is more important than a higher quantity (C). Studies show that skill development does not need more frequent feedback (B); in fact, practice can be more effective without feedback than with it. Researchers theorize that learners are forced to do more independent problem solving and attend more to internal feedback when they are not given external feedback. They also find that students and athletes become dependent on external feedback when they receive too much of it, regressing when it is withdrawn. Beginners need less precise feedback (D), while more advanced athletes need more precision to refine their skills.

73. C: When Cooper and Potts developed and named aerobics in the late 1960s, it originally focused on the ability of the heart and lungs to use oxygen in sustained physical activity. Cooper was the first to differentiate aerobic capacity from body flexibility (A) and muscular strength (B) and to notice that some

people who were very flexible or very strong still did not have good endurance for running, biking, or swimming long distances. Although aerobics initially focused on cardiorespiratory endurance exclusively, today's aerobics classes combine all the elements of fitness (D), incorporating stretching for flexibility and strength training for the muscles along with movements that raise heart and breathing rates for cardiovascular fitness in their exercises.

74. B: Judo (A) is a Japanese martial art that uses throwing types of grappling. Kendo (B) is a Japanese martial art that uses a sword. Karate (C) is a Japanese martial art that uses strikes, mainly with the hands, though the legs are secondarily involved. Jujitsu (D) is a Japanese martial art that uses grappling holds. Of these four, Kendo is the only weapon-based martial art; the other three are unarmed.

75. B: Common arguments in the debate over standardized physical education (PE) tests include these: Opponents of standardized PE testing say people must enjoy physical activity in their youth to enjoy it in adulthood (A), and they argue that standardized testing does not support motivation to engage in lifelong physical activity. Proponents of standardized PE testing say that test scores enable students to gauge their progress relative (C) to national standards and student averages. Additionally, they argue that national standards and assessments accord PE the same importance as all other school subjects (D) that it deserves.

76. D: Recently, the issue that has become the greatest challenge to kindergarten to Grade 12 (K–12) school physical education (PE) is that time in school curricula for PE classes and activities has been reduced significantly to make time for other academic classes. Inadequate resources and parental support (A); overly large class sizes and teacher burnout (B); and violence, student drug abuse, and discipline problems (C) are also challenges to K–12 PE, but these are also equal challenges to other school subjects and to education in general.

77. C: Throwing at a stationary target (B) represents a beginner level of throwing skill. Throwing lead passes (A) represents an intermediate level of throwing skill. Throwing to teammates while being defended (C) by another player represents an advanced level of throwing skill. Therefore, these do not all represent similar levels of throwing skill (D).

78. A: Atlantoaxial instability consists of excessive movement at the junction of the atlas, or first cervical vertebra (C1), and axis, or second cervical vertebra (C2), due to bone or ligament abnormality. It includes neurological symptoms when the spinal cord also is involved. This condition would make it unsafe for a student to perform a forward roll (B). However, to meet a learning objective, a physical education teacher could substitute a log roll, which would be safe for a student with this condition (A). Therefore, it is incorrect that no kind of roll should be assigned (C). Atlantoaxial instability is not necessarily that rare (D): It is caused by Down syndrome, a number of metabolic diseases, birth defects, traumatic spinal injuries, upper respiratory infections, rheumatoid arthritis, and surgeries to the head or neck. With so many different etiologies, the chances for a student to have this condition are not so remote.

79. C: National Association for Sport and Physical Education (NASPE) recommends that elementary school students should receive a minimum of 150 minutes per week of quality PE time in schools, meaning that somewhat more than this would not be too much. Thirty minutes per day most reflects the recommendation of 150 minutes per week as school is in session five days per week. A minimum of 15 minutes per day (A) is not enough. A maximum of 30 minutes per day (B) implies that more than this is bad, which does not reflect the NASPE recommendation. A maximum of 60 minutes for an entire week (D) is also far too little: This would break down to only 12 minutes daily, or two 30-minute classes per week, or three 20-minute sessions, four 15-minute sessions, and so on.

80. A: Physical education (PE) teachers should plan their lessons and programs and choose their teaching methods to reflect national, state, and local PE standards; the physical maturation and age of each individual child equally (B); the fitness levels and skill levels of each individual child equally (C); and the best instructional practices identified equally through research studies and teaching experience (D).

81. C: With U.S. populations and hence student populations rapidly becoming increasingly diverse, all teachers, including physical education (PE) teachers, must change their practices to adapt to these changes rather than simply continuing to do the same thing regardless (D). No single teaching style is proven to enhance all students' learning (A), so PE teachers are most likely to meet all student needs by using a variety of styles. The measure of educational effectiveness is the success of all students, not just some (B). If all of the students learn and meet the targeted learning objectives by the end of a lesson (C), this indicates that the PE teacher's educational efforts have succeeded.

82. D: Teachers can give students cards with adverbs they recently learned, have them look up synonyms and antonyms for these, and write them on the cards. The teacher then directs the students to perform movements in ways described by the adverbs on their cards. The teacher then has students pass their cards to classmates and repeat the activity with new words. This lesson integrates physical education (PE) and English language arts (ELA) skills. Performing movements and then working with words separately or vice versa, (A) and (B), do not integrate PE and ELA skills together into the same activity. Describing movements using the adverbs (C) makes a mental connection between words and movement, but the students are not actually performing any body movements; they are only describing them verbally, so this is an ELA activity rather than an integrated PE and ELA activity.

83. B: In high schools that do not have swimming pools, physical education (PE) teachers can look for opportunities such as pools at community recreation centers, county public pools, YMCA or YWCA pools, or privately owned pools, especially by parents and families of their students and ask for permission to use them. Another option at some schools having sufficient funds is to buy portable pools. If none of these is possible, PE teachers can teach swim strokes; make and give students task cards with written directions and diagrams of each stroke, kick, and breathing pattern and combination; and pair students to take turns, with one practicing on a bench and the other watching and giving feedback. Thus, it is not true that there is no way to teach swimming without a pool (D). However, PE teachers also should not assume it is safe for students to swim in water after mastering strokes on benches only; they will need supervised lessons and practice to transfer the skills.

84. A: The first step in the volleyball activity is for students to assume rotational positions, that is, with one setter in front and one in the back row, without overlapping. The second step is for a student to serve the ball. In the third step, following the serve, students move from their rotational positions to their base positions. The fourth step is for players to defend against attack by watching, calling, and passing the ball.

85. A: When physical education (PE) teachers pose think-about questions to students, for example, asking them what the pros and cons are of certain playing formations, positions, or strategies or where they should be aiming their shots, and so on, they give the students a mental advantage by getting them to consider, analyze, and then plan their playing strategies. Thinking about what they just did in one practice session enables them to plan ahead for the next one and improve their game. When PE teachers read aloud the tasks or steps of a practice session, they ensure that player setup is timely rather than delayed (B). They should not alternate the sequence of practice plans (C) but always follow them in the sequence they are written. PE teachers should both verbally describe and physically demonstrate movements or actions, not do only one or the other (D).

86. D: "Match up" as a defense cue in basketball means that students should defend other players who are as similar to them in size, fitness, and skill level as possible—not just in size (C). This cue does not mean

to pair up with another player (A). Staying near to the offensive players they are defending wherever they move on the court (B) is indicated to students with a cue of "Shadow" rather than "Match up."

87. B: The Heimlich maneuver should be performed only on someone who is choking and cannot breathe. This means the person cannot speak, so the Heimlich maneuver should not be performed on a student who says he or she is having trouble breathing (A). Someone who is choking and cannot breathe also cannot cough, so the Heimlich maneuver should not be performed on a student who is coughing (C), which means he or she can breathe. The Heimlich maneuver should be done first if someone is choking; cardiopulmonary resuscitation (CPR) should be started after that if the victim loses consciousness (D).

88. A: Structured observations involve informing both teacher and student of the observation and applying specific criteria for evaluating student performance in physical education (PE) assessment. Naturalistic observations involve not informing students of the observation to capture typical student behavior, such as during their daily practice in regular PE classes. Though naturalistic observations are more realistic regarding behaviors than structured observations, not vice versa (D), they have been criticized for being more subjective, whereas structured observations are more objective, not vice versa (B). Structured observations are equally good for assessing social skills, motor skills (C), and movement skills.

89. C: Tests on which students must write answers are least useful for assessing their performance of physical education skills, which typically must be physically demonstrated. Observational checklists (A) are more useful as teachers can watch students perform the skills to be assessed and mark whether they can do them or not or mark the degree to which they have mastered them. Rating scales of skill level (B) are more useful as teachers can observe student skill performance and then rate the level of mastery or skill they have attained on a scale with degrees between most and least. Graphs of performance data (D) are more useful as teachers can record numbers of successful demonstrations per session, and so on as points and connect these to form a line or curve showing progress over time. Graphs also can include a line indicating a criterion for reference, so performance points can be seen as above, below, and at this line.

90. A: The three main categories assessed by the Fitnessgram are: (1) aerobic capacity; (2) body composition; and (3) muscular strength, endurance, and flexibility. (A) correctly represents the three components of the third category. (B) lists categories (1) and (2) plus one component of category (3). (C) lists category (2), one component of category (3), and category (1) in that order. (D) lists one component of category (3), category (1), and another component of category (3) in that order.

91. C: Formative assessments measure student progress during the instructional process. They enable teachers to use the assessment results to inform ongoing instruction and adjust it to meet their students' particular needs and strengths, for example, making their pace faster or slower according to student learning rates; spending more or less time on different skills or areas according to which students have already mastered or are struggling with more; or replacing teaching methods that are ineffective for some students with different ones. Showing accountability (A), comparing student achievement to state or national population averages (B), and assessing whether instruction has helped students meet curriculum standards (D) are all functions of summative assessments rather than formative assessments.

92. C: According to the description, the test is reliable, meaning that it gives the same results every time it is administered, but it is not valid, meaning that it does not measure what it was intended to measure. Therefore, it is not correct that the test is neither reliable nor valid (A). It is not true that the test is valid but not reliable (B) but, rather, vice versa. The test is not both valid and reliable, and it is not simply misused (D); it is actually not valid because it does not test what it means or claims to test but assesses something else instead.

93. D: Labeling a diagram is an example of a traditional assessment approach. Other traditional approaches include short-answer, constructed-response, and fill-in-the-blank written questions; written matching tests or worksheets; and written multiple-choice or true–false questions. Writing down a personal fitness plan (A) is an example of a written alternative assessment. Additional examples include research papers, essays, stories, poems, anecdotes, journals, logs, checklists, rating scales, brochures, advertisements, rubrics, performance records, newspapers, magazines, projects, pre-assessment inventories, surveys, questionnaires, interviews, editorials, and reflections. Performing dance movements (B) and playing sports games (C) are examples of alternative performance task assessments. Additional examples include locomotor or gymnastics routines, officiating games, making fitness assessments or oral reports, teaching lessons, warm-up routines, showcases, debates, skits, role-plays, or interviews.

94. B: Physical education (PE) teachers can provide kindergarten through Grade 2 (K–) students with log sheets with a prepared left column and an empty right column. The left side uses simple statements like "I have a strong heart," "I have strong muscles," "I can do movements over and over again," and "I can stretch," accompanied by graphic pictures (a heart, a bicep, a figure with arrows indicating repeated movement, and a figure with arrows or lines depicting stretching) to represent cardiovascular endurance, muscular strength, muscular endurance, and flexibility, respectively. In the blank right side, children make drawings or cut and paste pictures illustrating their activities (e.g., running, lifting, dancing, stretches, etc.) in each category. Teachers can guide this activity and collect the products to get assessment information. Writing journal entries (A), notes (C), or cards (D) is inappropriate for students with the limited writing skills of K–2 levels, as is independently turning in records regularly (C) or periodically (D) on a schedule at these ages.

95. D: Individuals with Disabilities Education Act (IDEA) regulations mandate that students with disabilities should be assessed using multiple instruments rather than just one (A). While these instruments should be valid, reliable, and technically sound, they may or may not be standardized: If a formal standardized test does not allow a disabled student to demonstrate individual strengths and needs, it may be inappropriate. While multiple instruments are required, they should be varied rather than all similar (B). The assessment instruments should not only measure disabilities (C) but also abilities.

96. B: In addition to referrals, criteria indicating that a student should be evaluated to determine eligibility for adapted physical education (APE) include that the student performs below his or her ability level in group settings (A); has social behaviors that interfere with his or her or others' learning more than one-third of class time (B); has scored below average in two or more parts of the state physical fitness test used by the school district (C); and scored 1.5 or more standard deviations below the norm on the norm-referenced test used (D) by the school or district.

97. B: As one example of how educators can and should collaborate to meet student needs, both adapted physical educators (APEs) and classroom teachers are advised by experts to use the instructional methods they learn from occupational therapists (OTs) to help preschoolers with developmental delays to learn fine motor and manipulative skills. These strategies are not limited to implementation by OTs only (A), APEs but not classroom teachers (C), or classroom teachers but not APEs (D). All three disciplines should use them to meet these children's needs.

98. C: Psychologists provide IQ testing and behavior management programs, training, and implementation as well as mental status examinations, therapy, and counseling. Administrators (A) do not. They supervise faculty and staff; help with curriculum development, programs, and initiatives; manage school facilities; plan and manage school budgets; and have many other duties. School nurses (B) provide physical health services, not mental health or psychological services. Special education teachers (D) provide specialized instruction in a variety of areas to students with disabilities who require special

education services; write and coordinate implementation of individual education plans (IEPs), and have many other duties, but they do not conduct IQ testing, mental health status examinations, or psychological evaluations used to determine eligibility for special education services; psychologists or behavior specialists do.

99. A: Large-scale state research has found that student cardiovascular fitness achievement and healthy body mass index (BMI) scores correlate positively with student scores on the state academic achievement test of knowledge and skills. Other research has found that children who are more physically fit demonstrate not only quicker reaction times but also more accurate responses (B). Another investigation found that children burn more calories and take nearly twice as many steps during teacher-led fitness activities as during active gaming, not vice versa (C). Other studies show that intense exercise is followed by improvement in cognitive function (D).

100. C: Kinetics is the division of biomechanics that studies the forces causing motion. Newton's First Law of Inertia, Second Law of Momentum, and Third Law of Reaction are most closely related to kinetics. Coplanar vectors (A) belong in the biomechanics division of vector algebra. Kinematics (B) is the biomechanics division that describes motion. Kinematics involves physics concepts including mass, center of gravity, inertia, displacement, linear and angular motion, linear and angular velocity, and acceleration. The biomechanics division of forces (D) involves concepts including center of pressure; force line; resultant force; muscular forces, joint forces, joint reaction forces, ground reaction forces, resisting forces, inertial forces, and gravitational forces; and fulcrums, levers, rotation, couples, equilibrium, weight, friction, and mechanical advantage.

101. B: Differentiation is a calculus technique for finding a quantity's rate of change, used in biomechanics to get derivatives of curves or functions like velocity, acceleration, and jerk, which are derivatives of displacement. Integration is a calculus technique to determine the area between an x-axis and a curve, used in biomechanics to obtain integrals like velocity as an integral of acceleration, displacement as an integral of velocity, and work as an integral of power. Composition and resolution of vectors (A) in biomechanics are ways of combining coplanar and concurrent vector quantities by using vector algebra, not calculus. The parallelogram method (C) is a method for resolving vectors in different directions in biomechanics that is based on geometry, not calculus: The parallelogram is a geometric shape. Because (B) is correct, (D) is incorrect.

102. A: Other than terms that have been translated into English for use by English-speaking people, a great deal of ballet terminology is in French because, historically, the dance form was popularized in France. While ballroom dance uses many Spanish (C) terms, especially related to Latin ballroom styles and techniques, ballroom also incorporates many French terms taken from ballet to describe steps also taken from ballet, for example, the passé step, chainé turns, pirouettes, and so on. Italian (B) is not shared in common by ballet and ballroom dance. Although ballet technique was highly developed in Russia later in its history after its early popularization in France, and Russia remains a stellar center of the ballet discipline today, ballet does not use Russian (D) terms, and neither does ballroom dance.

103. D: Working together with the principal to develop an exercise program that benefits student learning by enhancing the environment is an example of using administrator support and collaboration. (A) is an example of collaborating with an English language arts (ELA) teacher by using a novel to study a sport for the physical education (PE) component and character development and relationships for the ELA component. (B) is also an example of how to collaborate with an ELA teacher by watching a movie, studying its dance movements for the PE component and its themes for the ELA component. (C) is an example of collaborating with a Family and Consumer Sciences teacher by combining nutrition with exercise—a very natural and valuable combination as good nutrition and physical activity interact and mutually support one another in healthy lifestyles.

104. A: Teachers have expertise in the subject areas they teach and often in other areas as well, but parents who work in various occupations can enrich student education further by contributing their knowledge and experience in additional areas when physical education teachers invite them to collaborate. For example, a parent who is a cardiologist can talk to students about how choices in physical activity, nutrition, and weight management affect the heart. While teachers learn about their students' interests and motivations directly from the students through relationships and conversations with them, they also can learn additional information from their parents (B). Moreover, teachers can learn about parental expectations and aspirations for their children by involving them (C). Another benefit of engaging parents in their children's physical education is that teachers not only access family knowledge (D); they also have opportunities to communicate their recognition and respect for it, strengthening their relationships with students, parents, and families.

105. D: When physical education (PE) teachers want to hold events with Olympics themes for students, their local colleges are good places for them to find students willing to volunteer their time and work to help. PE teachers whose schools are short on funds for sports equipment can solicit financial assistance from local health and wellness agencies, which is not inappropriate (A) as these organizations may be able and often want to help. PE teachers also can ask local trophy companies to donate some of their products—and even refreshments as well—to student athletic events; these businesses frequently welcome the good public relations and advertising they can get by helping out schools (B). Local governments do have a department where PE teachers can recruit representatives to present to students about the use of community resources (C): their county and city Parks and Recreation Departments.

106. D: Dancing is a way to engage in physical activity before and after school that incorporates artistry, self-expression, and music. Teachers can encourage students with these interests to try some style of dancing to get enjoyable physical activity. Not all schools have cheerleaders for their athletic sports teams (A). Therefore, in schools that do not, teachers can encourage and help interested students to organize competitive cheer teams as a form of physical activity. Teachers encouraging students to bicycle for physical fitness, learning, sightseeing, adventure, and fun can find plenty of resources on the Internet (B) that offer biking supplies, information, and opportunities. Teachers should not avoid advising able and interested students to try canoeing for fear of danger (C): It provides an outdoor physical activity that combines physical fitness, safety skills, wilderness survival skills, adventure, and interaction with nature. Trained, experienced instructors and guides are available to teach and supervise learners and ensure their safe experiences.

107. B: Of the activities named, swimming is ideal for students with joint problems because it puts no weight or stress on the joints. The buoyancy of the body in water keeps weight and impact off the joints. Students can be active and get exercise without aggravating joint conditions or pain. Skiing (A) requires a lot of knee bending and turning, hip swiveling, and bearing weight on the joints, so it is not compatible with joint problems. Skateboarding (C) also involves much knee bending and turning, as well as jumping and landing, and would be hard on joint problems. Playing soccer (D) requires running and kicking, again putting too much impact on the joints. These other sports also are done on the ground and subject to gravity, whereas swimming relieves the joints of weight.

108. C: National Dance Day (NDD), the brainchild of TV show *So You Think You Can Dance (SYTYCD)* creator, producer, and judge Nigel Lythgoe, is hosted by the Dizzy Feet Foundation charity, which Lythgoe and movie director, producer, choreographer, and *SYTYCD* guest judge Adam Shankman cofounded. This national day was made official by Congresswoman Eleanor Holmes Norton (D–D.C.). Its events are held jointly in Los Angeles, California; Washington, D.C.; and New York, New York; giving it multiple locations (A). Americans also are invited to hold events in their communities nationwide on NDD. NDD encourages creative applications like flash mobs, dance-a-thons, charitable dance events, fund-raising to support access to dance for youth, and whatever ideas people have (B). It incorporates video instruction, including

a video choreographed and demonstrated by Lythgoe, while seated for nonambulatory persons (C). NDD videos also include both beginner and advanced dance routines (D).

109. A: Effective physical education (PE) teachers who are skilled in reflection engage not only in productive self-reflection but also in reflection about their students and about every element of their classes. They reflect about individual student personalities, behaviors, and dispositions as well as about the demographics of their schools (B) and how these affect class composition, student needs and interests, and interpersonal student interactions. In addition to emotional and social factors that influence student performance, reflective PE teachers also reflect about environmental, physical, and cognitive factors that affect their performance (C). They reflect not only on student abilities and needs, but also on classroom dynamics (D), and consider all of these in context. This reflection about every aspect of each class enables PE teachers to plan and deliver culturally sensitive, personally meaningful, and outcome-oriented lessons for their students.

110. D: A teacher using reflection to inform instruction is less likely to use (A) as placing the responsibility for meeting the objective entirely with the students betrays a lack of reflection. Reflective teachers evaluate how students respond to their instruction, analyze their own design and implementation of lessons, evaluate the results, and determine how they can change what they do to promote the best outcomes for their students. Thus, the teacher using reflection might see whether having the students play the next game faster (B) will increase their heart rates to the target range, or change the game rules to enhance more active participation by all students (C), or even both of these.

111. D: Effective physical education teachers do not use reflection periodically (A), or only for planning and designing curriculum (B), or only for adjusting the curriculum and instruction (C) after planning and designing. Rather, they utilize reflection continuously every day to improve all aspects of their teaching (D). They use reflection to incorporate their students' interests and needs and their own interests as well. They use it to consider teaching resources and interdisciplinary opportunities. They also use it to consider their own strengths and weaknesses as teachers and how they can supplement their instructional practices to take advantage of the strengths and compensate for the weaknesses.

112. B: These are all examples of good ways that physical education teachers can pursue professional development. However, if a teacher finds out that many students are interested in a certain activity, then obtains certification to teach that activity, that would most directly enrich their learning experiences. At the same time, this also would expand the teacher's expertise and enrich the school's curriculum.

113. B: The best professional development not only improves a teacher's own expertise (A) and that of the teacher's colleagues (C) but both mutually as well as enabling physical education teachers to promote their own discipline. It enables teachers to improve instruction not only at the classroom level (D) but also at schoolwide and districtwide levels.

114. A: By pursuing and achieving professional growth and participating in professional educational interactions, physical education teachers are able to learn more information and skills; stay up-to-date on current research; collaborate with colleagues and exchange ideas with them; and improve their learning communities' quality. They not only develop their own self-confidence; they also inspire initiative in others (B). They function as both role models and advocates (C). They demonstrate not only achievement but also professional integrity (D), both in their own disciplines and beyond in their wider educational communities.

115. C: Fitbit devices can help physical education teachers to support and increase student motivation and also include a line of designer fashion accessories. They can be used for both controlling weight and monitoring sleep quality (A). Students can self-monitor their own progress using Fitbit devices; they also

can use them to challenge and compete with friends (B). They are not just stand-alone progress trackers (D); they also sync wirelessly with mobile smartphones and tablets and with charts, graphs, and badges available online for documenting improvements and gaining insights about physical fitness.

116. A: MyFitnessPal is an app that features healthy recipes (B) and an extensive food database, whereby users can enter meals to calculate caloric and nutritional content. The Endomondo Sports Tracker features Audio Coach feedback (C) on user exercise performance. Endomondo and Fitbit both include social networking (D) capabilities for sharing fitness motivation, goals, progress, support, and reinforcement with friends. One thing these apps share in common is that they all sync (A) with each other as well as with other apps, devices, and online tools. MyFitnessPal and Endomondo sync with heart-rate monitors as well as with each other and Fitbit.

117. D: Physical education teachers report that apps like Apple's GradeBookPro enable them to spend much more of their class time actually teaching by reducing the time it takes them to perform administrative tasks like taking attendance (C); using standard or weighted grading systems; and displaying assignment, absence, percentage, and other student data all on one page, making disputes at the end of the course or year less likely (B). This app and similar ones enable teachers to create reports and assignments easily; e-mail current attendance and grade status to students; send copies of assignments across classes; quickly take and attach student photos to files, helping them learn students' names sooner; record grades with far greater speed and ease; and overall, streamline and make more efficient all of the tasks that used to be cumbersome, even irrelevant, yet are necessary.

118. A: Physical education (PE) teachers find that their students are enthusiastic about apps that allow them to view their and classmates or teammates' athletic performance. This enthusiasm makes it easier for teachers to create positive learning environments wherein students are more appreciative of constructive criticism and more motivated to improve their performance. PE teachers find that, after only a brief demonstration, students can easily use them (B) for recording one another, viewing the recordings, and giving each other feedback. Teachers find student athletes really enjoy watching their performance postgame (C) in the locker room. They can much more easily identify which strategies and tactics they used were most and least effective through this viewing. Also, when PE teachers use apps to record video and they play it back, students get much more immediate feedback (D).

119. C: Technology tools are more efficient and not just for keeping electronic records (A): They also can produce new records; for example, advanced programs and applications can compute statistical analyses of many kinds of educational data, like student enrollment, attendance, teacher–student ratios, athletic performance, parent involvement, statistics on competitive sports teams, community standing, progress relative to accountability measures, and comparisons of current years to past years. Today's technology tools not only maintain more accurate records and perform calculations to produce new records; they provide more organized and legible documents, enable quicker and easier access, and yet are also more secure (B) than paper records. Electronic records are subject to the same confidentiality regulations as paper records (D).

120. B: When a physical education (PE) teacher records video of his or her own teaching practices, plays it back, and analyzes those practices to improve them, this represents using technology to enhance professional development. Technology enables PE teachers to spend less time on scoring tests and more on interpreting them, not vice versa (A). With automated test scoring, they have more time to interpret test results to inform the lessons they plan and the instruction they give. When a PE teacher searches online for research resources containing the field's latest innovations (C), this represents the teacher's using technology to locate resources. When a PE teacher uses programs (e.g., Microsoft Word, Excel, Power Point, etc.) to organize and deliver information to students and others (D), like other teachers,

parents, and attendees, to professional conferences and conventions, this represents using technology to present information.

Thank You

We at Mometrix would like to extend our heartfelt thanks to you, our friend and patron, for allowing us to play a part in your journey. It is a privilege to serve people from all walks of life who are unified in their commitment to building the best future they can for themselves.

The preparation you devote to these important testing milestones may be the most valuable educational opportunity you have for making a real difference in your life. We encourage you to put your heart into it—that feeling of succeeding, overcoming, and yes, conquering will be well worth the hours you've invested.

We want to hear your story, your struggles and your successes, and if you see any opportunities for us to improve our materials so we can help others even more effectively in the future, please share that with us as well. **The team at Mometrix would be absolutely thrilled to hear from you!** So please, send us an email (support@mometrix.com) and let's stay in touch.

If you'd like some additional help, check out these other resources we offer for your exam:

http://MometrixFlashcards.com/PraxisII